ROBOT JESUS

AND THREE OTHER JESUSES YOU NEVER KNEW

KYLE R. BESHEARS

To my wife, Heather
You help me more in this field of study
than anyone else in every capacity
...
especially when you had to convince
our new pastor's wife we are not Mormon
despite my collection of Mormon action figurines.

I love you.

TABLE *of* CONTENTS

NOTE:

This book examines different viewpoints of Jesus from different worldviews and opinions or interpretations within those worldviews. Not all opinions and interpretations of the examined worldviews are represented in this book, simply the ones deemed most popular or important by the author. Furthermore, those opinions and interpretations used are presented at the discretion of the author and may not reflect accurately what all adherents of those views believe. Please research for yourself what other religions believe about Jesus to be a better–informed Christian and apologist.

Why Robot Jesus?

Many different people have many different opinions about
the person and work of Jesus Christ.

Some people think Jesus was a really nice guy. Others believe he was an influential rabbi. Still others believe Jesus was a liar, a leader of liars, or a victim of Jewish fanaticism blowing him way out of proportion. Some believe Jesus was simply a type of myth, perhaps just another Hercules. Mormons believe Jesus is our spirit brother, along with Satan. Jehovah's Witnesses believe Jesus is actually Michael the Archangel. Muslims believe Jesus was the precursor prophet to Muhammad. Scientologists believe Jesus was a tool for mind corruption and the root of depression for many people in the world.

But what should you believe about Jesus?

The goal of this book is to examine what members of rival worldviews to Christianity believe about Jesus, thus equipping us to engage in fruitful dialogue about him. The more we examine how others view Jesus, the better we can relate the gospel to other worldviews. For example, the Jesus of Mormonism is actually our spiritual big brother. If a Mormon told you we were all spirit siblings of Jesus and Satan, what would you say? Does that really matter? More importantly, could you carry on a conversation about this big brother Jesus with them? Some Scientologists have been taught to believe Jesus is actually a fictional character designed by space aliens to keep our god–like potential to mere monotheistic worship. Could you account for the real Jesus as opposed to this robot Jesus? What about the Archangel Jesus of Jehovah's Witness? Or the Silver Medal Jesus of Islam?

There are many different Jesuses in the world... are
you prepared to give an account of the savior Jesus?

CHAPTER ONE

Apologetics in Dialogue

" I reject all other religions. In that way I find an answer to all objections. It is right that a God so pure should only reveal Himself to those whose hearts are purified."

BLAISE PASCAL (1623–1662)

Dang.

So there you were perusing books on a shelf when you found a cover with 'robot' and 'Jesus' in the same title. "Hey," you thought to yourself, "I like robots *and* Jesus. This book must be awesome!" Well, maybe you didn't think that exactly, but the title at least caught your attention. So you picked it up and flipped to this page, excited to read about a giant 10,000–foot, mechanical Jesus. Undoubtedly, you were shocked to discover the first chapter was not titled *Robot Jesus vs. Son of God–zilla: the Battle for Salvific Supremacy*, but rather something about apologetics or whatever. For one, you should be relieved that this book is not as terribly heretical as you first believed, what with imagining that Son of God–zilla thing. Shame on you. Secondly, you should know that this book is about evangelism to members of rival worldviews to Christianity, specifically concerning the person and work of Jesus.

Outside Christianity there are many opinions and misunderstandings of Jesus. Influential rival worldviews to Christianity in North America, to include Mormonism, Jehovah's Witness, Islam, and Scientology, teach caricatures of Jesus to their members. This leaves them all with one thing in common – the need to learn about the true person and work of Jesus. As representatives of Jesus, we Christians have the honored duty to ensure this occurs through evangelism; however, due to the nature of evangelizing to members of rival worldviews a specific method of evangelism is often required to make the most impact. This specific method is called *apologetics*.

---

[1] Blaise Pascal, *Penseés* Section XII: Proofs of Jesus Christ, 737.

Unfortunately, apologetics is one of those topics many Christians tend to shy away from simply because of the name. Some hear the term *apologetics* and immediately think about apologizing to someone. Others hear it and become instantly bored while their mind wanders far away as if their monotone, Ben Stein–esq, college professor had just begun his lecture on the importance of a random variable to the root–mean–square of a standard deviation and the values from its mean. Those who know what apologetics is and have a certain distain toward it fail to see its importance, citing such slogans as, "Jesus can defend himself." And while this is very true, we are nonetheless called to be the tools in which Jesus takes up his defense. Can Jesus defend himself against those who misrepresent him? Of course he can! He has, however, given us the opportunity to serve him in a way that should blow our minds. We are called to defend the faith by working for Jesus to represent truth in the face of the enemy's influence.

The question deserves to be asked then; is defending Jesus really necessary? Does the very existence of apologetics mean that God is dependent on us to get his message out? An important thing to understand is that having a defense for the gospel, and ultimately Jesus, doesn't mean he can't speak for himself or is dependent on us to shield him from attack, objection, or even rejection. Jesus is by no means some weak, wimpy nerd who paid a jock all his lunch money for bully insurance during after school hours. The Book of Revelation definitely paints a much different picture.[2] Rather, God wants us to be used by him to defend the message of truth given by Jesus. In light of this, the term '*defend*' takes on a different meaning than its normal use.

Sometimes the idea of *defense* is associated with weakness or dependency. We tend to think of defense as a negative thing needed only by those who can't strike first. Yet, without defense, even the strongest of people, organizations, and countries would not be able to exist. For example, think about the United States military defense force. Without it, the United States would most certainly not be viewed as one of the most powerful military forces in history; however, a strong defense force does not imply a weak society. In other words, defense does not mean weakness. Rather, defense means to resist attack or to justify something. Apologetics acts in this capacity

---

[2] Rev. 1:16

by resisting the attack of objections and justifying the truth of Jesus as a response. Besides this, we are actually commanded by scripture to take part in the defense of the gospel through apologetics.[3]

WHAT IS APOLOGETICS?

So what is apologetics? The word *apologetics* comes from the New Testament (Greek) word απολογία (*apologia*), which means 'to defend.' We find *apologia* used eight times throughout the New Testament. Peter uses *apologia* to urge his audience in defending the gospel in 1 Peter 3:15. "But in your hearts set apart Christ as Lord. Always be prepared to give an answer to everyone who asks you to give the reason for the hope that you have. But do this with gentleness and respect." For the concept of '*giving an answer*' in this passage Peter chooses the word *apologia*. And it means just that – to give an answer or to make a defense. The defense we make is for Christianity's place as the only salvation–providing faith, Jesus' place as the only messiah and savior, and why there is only one God.

Have you ever been told by someone that Jesus is not the only means of salvation or that other ways besides Jesus exist to connect with God? What was your response? If you responded by defending Jesus' rightful position as the one and only mediator between God and humanity, you made an apologetic argument. You made a defense. But why did you need to make a defense in the first place? Most likely it was in response to an objection to Christianity similar to the two examples given above. These types of objections may be common in your life as most people generally object to the person and work of Jesus.

Because of this, apologetics should be an active part of our life as Christians. We shouldn't put apologetics off or keep it at a distance. Rather, we should embrace it as something scripture has commanded of us. Likewise, we shouldn't place it on the shelf for the highly educated to ponder and discuss. We should have coffee with those who object and give apologetic arguments to clarify who Jesus is and what he wants from every one of us. When this happens, your friend, neighbor, or family member just might come

---

[3] 1 Pet. 3:15

around to accepting the very same Jesus they may have previously rejected. Therefore, apologetics, when used biblically, can be used as a powerful weapon against the enemy; however, this statement itself is the caveat. We need to use apologetics *biblically*.

LORD OVER THE HEART OF APOLOGETICS

To find out how we use apologetics biblically, let's look back at 1 Peter 3:15. The first thing Peter tells his audience is that we need to set apart Jesus as Lord in our hearts. This is a crucial part of apologetics. Not only does Peter set Jesus as the foundation for apologetics, but he also requires that the apologist be truly Christian. Granted, the prerequisite of being a Christian to defend Christ may sound funny and perhaps even blatantly obvious, but how many times have you seen people claiming to be Christian attack someone with a different worldview?

You know the ones I'm talking about – Christians with an axe to grind but can't grind it on other Christians, so they intentionally seek out non-Christians of different faiths. They're fired up and ready to argue with the ammunition they received from the recent apologetics conference they attended the weekend before, to aggressively parrot everything they've ever heard on their favorite apologetics podcast or blog, even if it makes absolutely zero contribution to any sane conversation. Whatever it takes to mask the pain of their own intellectual insecurities about their faith, they'll gladly mow others down. This is the exact opposite of what Peter had in mind.

Peter tells us that Jesus should be the reason and focus of apologetics, and that Jesus should be Lord in our hearts. If Jesus is not Lord in our hearts, then apologetics turns from evangelism into argumentation. If Jesus is not Lord in our hearts, then we really don't know him well enough to defend him, and if we want to show members of rival worldviews who the real Jesus is, how can we without knowing him intimately? By Peter telling us to have Jesus as Lord in our hearts, he's not stating the obvious observation that the Christian apologist should be a Christian; rather, Peter is reminding Christians why they are evangelizing. It's all for Jesus. Peter is also reminding us of the primary motivation for evangelism and where that motivation should stem from.

Apologetics as evangelism to members of rival worldviews can only stem from one place – the heart. Not the worldly, touchy–feely heart, but the renewed, passionate, and motivated heart. The reason this is so important is because it will dictate the outcome of our apologetic method (which is a fancy term for whether we're being argumentative jerks or loving, compassionate Christians). With Jesus as Lord in our hearts, our apologetic method is more likely to involve treating our dialogue partners with respect, patience, and love regardless of their response, be it positive or negative. Just because the person we are speaking to may be arguing or trying to win a debate doesn't mean we should be playing the same game. Apologetics is much more than just winning a debate.

Someone once said, "We can win the debate, yet lose the soul."[4] We will never truly communicate Christ to others if Jesus is not Lord over our hearts, and we may actually cause harm in the process. Without Jesus reigning over the passion and motivation of our apologetic in dialogue on the gospel, we will inevitably lose the soul every time, barring God's sovereign will to save them regardless of our misrepresentation of his character. With this in mind, we must ask ourselves – if we win the argument and lose the soul, then what's the point of apologetics in dialogue? The soul of that person is exactly what we should be concerning ourselves with, which is the next point Peter makes.

THE THREE A'S OF APOLOGETICS: ALWAYS ANSWER ANYONE

Always answer anyone. In so many words, Peter summarizes the concept of *apologia* as 'always answer anyone.' These are the Three A's of Apologetics; *always* being the time, *answer* being the method, and *anyone* being the target audience. The Three A's of Apologetics precisely summarizes apologetics. It's the second thing Peter tells us concerning the defense of the gospel as he writes, "*Always* [be] prepared to make a defense (*answer*) to *anyone* who asks

---

[4] *Origin Unknown*

you."[5] Let's examine the Three A's of Apologetics by looking at them one word at a time.

Always – There is never a time when it is okay to be unprepared, unwilling, or disinclined to defend the person and work of Jesus. Defending the faith is for all seasons and times. This is why Peter says we should *always* be prepared. The liberation in this is that we do not have to attend Bible college, seminary, or even read books like this to be ready to defend the faith. Although these things are good, they aren't necessary.

Additionally, the idea that a person needs a seminary degree to engage in apologetics is another factor that tends to make Christians shy away. Peter tears down any wall built by the lie that Christians must be highly educated individuals to participate in apologetics. Always means just that – *always*. Regardless of our life, education, intelligence, social standing, or maturity in Christ, we should always be ready to defend the gospel. Now, if we are called to always defend the gospel, how is it we are supposed to go about defending it?

Answer – As Christians defending the faith we are called to always answer questions or objections about Jesus. It is important to realize that when Peter tells us we must answer for the hope that is in us, this implies that people will ask. As Christians, people will inevitably ask about what we believe and why we believe it, which is the hope that is in us. It's not a matter of if, but a matter of when. If our life is bearing spiritual fruit, people are going to ask who the gardener is. Followers of Jesus are like cities on hills in the night.[6] People are going to ask what makes our life different from theirs. That's the opportunity of evangelism we live for. When they ask, we need to be ready. And as Peter suggests, that seems to be always.

Anyone – The door of apologetics is open to anyone. The type of people we defend the Christian faith against do not necessarily need to be anarchist street punks with a copy of a New Atheist's latest dribble about how they didn't like church services as an 8–year–old kid and there were Crusades. They can be everyone and anyone. Perhaps a Christian friend of yours needs encouragement by hearing a good, solid argument for the deity of Christ. But

---

[5] 1 Pet. 3:15
[6] Matt. 5:14

of course, on the opposite side of the table, apologetics might be used to provide information to unbelievers to further convict the conscience and guide the person to Jesus. It can truly be *anyone*.

It is good to remember as well that *anyone* can mean we will be sharing the gospel with people from all different cultures, backgrounds, and presuppositions. This is especially true with members of rival worldviews. Therefore, it's important to accommodate our conversations to their needs, not ours. Listen to what they believe, ask them why they believe it, and then present them with the gospel based on their background. Never make assumptions about what they believe and why they believe it. *Anyone* is just about as wide as a demographic can get, so we must be careful not to lock ourselves into evangelizing based on our own stereotypes.

THE ANTITHESIS: NEVER LOVE ANYONE

So, if *always answer anyone* is the summary of apologetics, the antithesis would have to be *never love anyone*. The reason I use *love* as the antonym of *answer* is because love is truly the greatest apologetic anyone could ever offer in defense of the Christian faith. However, I am getting ahead of myself – we'll get back to that later.

Peter doesn't say to *never* be prepared when he speaks of defending the gospel. God doesn't share the same sense of timing as we do. It is crucial that we understand this. For example, when a debate team forms they are usually given a schedule to follow and ample time to prepare. When God throws us into debates we are usually given two seconds to realize what is happening and absolutely no time to prepare. This is why Peter tells us to always be prepared. When the time comes to make an apologetic argument for the Christian faith we may fall short and misrepresent our king by not reading scripture, not studying how others view Jesus, not listening to those whom God has gifted with wisdom and intelligence, and not seeking after the guidance of the Holy Spirit. And in that time of failure the enemy will do his best to make sure we feel it.

Keep in mind that God isn't being cruel by neglecting to inform us three hours in advanced about the upcoming debate we'll be in. God wants us to use what we've already learned, but he also wants us in a posture of dependency on his spirit to guide the conversation.[7] If we over prepare for a conversation, we may be tempted to rely solely on what we know. But, if we regularly study scripture along with what rival worldviews teach about Jesus, then the moment we find ourselves surprised by a conversation, God will meet us halfway by reminding us what we've learned and giving us things to say.[8]

Aside from not preparing to answer objections to the Christian faith, not answering those objections altogether would be even worse. It is reasonable to assume that if Peter tells us to *always answer anyone*, and we don't give any defense at all, then we've completely missed the point of this verse. Simple enough. Never shy away from a conversation. While it's better not to throw our two cents into a topic we're unfamiliar with, it's not good at all to stay silent on something we are familiar with. Being omissive in evangelism can be just as bad as being argumentative. Be strong and have courage – always remember who guides the conversation.[9]

KNOWLEDGE PUFFS, LOVE BUILDS

What about those who do answer objections to Christianity, yet do it with a spirit of callousness? Remember the Christians with an axe to grind? These armchair theologians could probably list every single theological viewpoint of salvation from every major world religion, but rarely do they actually talk to anyone about Jesus aside from posting on their favorite blog. They have taken nothing but theology and philosophy courses at the local Christian university and petitioned that Lee Strobel's works be placed directly after Revelation. I'm sure the first question Peter would ask them is, "How many people has your mean–spirited 'apologetic method' led to Jesus?" I bet the humbling answer would be none. Always remember that the goal of apologetics is not to win a debate and make yourself look like a super intelligent Christian while converting people at the same time.

---

[7] Matt. 10:20
[8] Luke 21:14–15; John 15:5
[9] Josh. 1:9

It must likewise be said that where we get our knowledge is just as important as how we use it. There are many avenues available to us today for learning about other cultures, beliefs, and religious systems. It is crucial that we be discerning about where we receive our information concerning rival worldviews. News broadcasts, personal blogs, social media, and emails are usually poor sources, spun in a fashion to present a particular bias. Typically, as with the case of chain emails, the information is inflammatory and completely unfounded regardless of whether or not it is believable. Gaining knowledge from poor sources of information is also a telltale sign of being a lazy researcher. It is much easier to regurgitate rhetoric than it is to research and formulate opinions based on raw facts. For these reasons, we should stick with trusted authors, professors, pastors, and friends who are well studied on the worldview we are currently engaging.

Once we have knowledge received from a trustworthy source, we must keep in mind that the main goal of apologetics in dialogue on the gospel is to break down the barriers of doubt or confusion, leaving only the truth of the gospel to be accepted or rejected by the hearer.[10] Many people we dialogue with have a misunderstanding of the person and work of Jesus. Apologetics is intended to help them understand the truth about Jesus by taking apart those barriers of doubt or confusion. Remember, "you can win the debate, yet lose the soul."[11] This could be coupled with another saying; "knowledge puffs up, but love builds up."[12] That second saying was Paul writing to a church about different levels of maturity in Christians.

Again, we are forced to check ourselves, our maturity, and our pride before we enter into an apologetic dialogue with someone. If we are proud of the knowledge we have obtained about God, which is ironic since all knowledge is a gift from him anyway, then we will become puffed up with pride. When we are prideful, we will begin to act as if those around us are somehow lower than us or should be treated without love. If this is the case, those we share the gospel with will never get the opportunity to see the love Jesus wants to show them through us. We miss the entire point of evangelism.

---

[10] 2 Cor. 10:5
[11] Origin unknown
[12] 1 Cor. 8:1

Perhaps an even bigger problem is presented when we turn apologetics into a debate club. Essentially, we are telling Jesus that his love is not good enough to bring lost people to him. We need to throw in our intellectual weight to help the Holy Spirit with communicating Jesus' love for the person we are talking to. What that person really needs is to understand Jesus' love for them despite us or any lofty argument we can devise to convince them of his love. Argumentative apologetics is no more useful a tool of evangelism than a guy writing a twenty–five page thesis on why his girlfriend should marry him as his engagement proposal. Wouldn't it be better for him to just get on one knee and show her that he loves her?

The same principle applies to apologetics – we should simply show people we love them and the Holy Spirit will fill in the blanks during our conversations. If we are not sure whether we are evangelizing lovingly or selfishly, the key question to ask ourselves is simple; "Am I doing this for my glory or for God's glory? Do I meet up with this person every Wednesday for coffee just so I'll feel smarter, or do I really want to see this person come to know Jesus?" If we cannot in good conscience answer these questions immediately, then we should probably stop and reevaluate how we are approaching our apologetics in dialogue.

Keeping our focus directly on showing people the love of Jesus by humbly pointing out the error of their worldview is the only way scripture prescribes apologetics. The details of that 'pointing out' can only be worked through the Holy Spirit and the knowledge God has gifted us with. This leads us to the specific type of apologetics we want to discuss – apologetics to members of rival worldviews. But before we start, it would be wise to begin by defining what a *rival worldview* is.

WHAT IS A 'RIVAL WORLDVIEW' EXACTLY?

A *rival worldview* for the remainder of this book is defined as any religious–based worldview that follows, preaches, worships, and/or teaches a different Jesus than that of classic, orthodox Christianity.[13] It is a term presented as an

---

[13] The term *orthodox Christianity* should be understood as the core beliefs anyone claiming to be a Christian should adhere to, and should not be understood as a denomination (Greek Orthodox,

alternative to *cult*, *religion*, or *faith*. Recently, theologian Dr. R. Albert Mohler used *rival worldview* to describe Mormonism's relationship to Christianity, in that Mormonism was an imitation for Christianity in the lives of Latter–day Saints.[14] I believe Mohler's use of *rival worldview* is a more accurate way of describing the faiths spoken of in this book in lieu of other terms like *cults* or *religions*, which are either too specific or too broad to describe the belief systems of people we are evangelizing. *Worldview* is a much broader term than *faith* or *religion* since, for many faiths and religions, one's beliefs affect more than how they understand God – it affects how they view the world, be it politics, economy, society, etc.

Additionally, all worldviews aside from Christianity are vying for the place of Jesus and Christianity in peoples' lives, and in this way rival the Great Commission. Thus, *rival worldviews*. Although they vary widely in different beliefs, one thing is common between all of them – none believe or teach that the Jesus of scripture is necessary for salvation. At the end of the day, this is what makes them dangerous. Religions that fall under this definition include Buddhism, Mormonism, New Age, Jehovah's Witnesses, Christian Scientists, Islam, Unification Church, Scientology, Baha'i, and Wicca.

Many people view these worldviews as different choices between religions all with the same results. You may have heard someone say, "Well, Buddhism is just right for me," or, "I practice Islam because it fits my life the best." "Besides," they may protest, "all religions lead to the same place." Many people believe they can pick up and put down these religious choices on a shelf, along with Christianity, as if they were books to choose depending on one's interest. But the truth is just the opposite. There are actually only two worldviews and faiths – Christianity and a lie. We either worship Jesus or we do not. We either believe the truth or a lie.[15] None of these rival worldviews are on the same level as Christianity since they are all simply substitutes for Christianity.

Russian Orthodox, etc.) The word *orthodox* simply means "correct belief." From the Greek *orthos* (true) and *doxas* (belief).
[14] Paul Stanley, "Albert Mohler Suggests Mormonism is a 'Rival Worldview.'" *The Christian Post.* http://www.christianpost.com/news/albert-mohler-suggests-mormonism-is-a-rival-worldview-57753/ (accessed January 24, 2012).
[15] Rom. 1:25

Christianity is the only worldview that coheres with reality and, thus, cannot be compared as an equal rival to competing worldviews. Think of it like this – there is only one way to smell a flower, by putting it up to our nose and breathing in. If someone said we might also smell a flower by putting it up to our forehead and holding our breath, would you agree this is an equally valid method? Of course not. The same can be said about rival worldviews. If Jesus is truly the only way to the Father, then all other alternatives are irrational. I realize these are very large claims to make, and we will examine a few rival worldviews in detail later in the book; however, solidifying our definition of *rival worldview* is very important, not only for this book but for our lives.

CONTEXTUALIZATION – BIG WORD, BIGGER IMPLICATIONS

Now that the term *rival worldview* is defined, how do we share the gospel to their members through apologetics in dialogue? A key term to remember is *contextualization*. It's a big word that simply means we must share Jesus by using someone else's terminology, vocabulary, social setting, and culture. This is because, for example, it is very difficult for a Muslim to understand grace after a lifetime of works-based salvation, just as it is difficult for a Jehovah's Witness to understand the Trinity after a lifetime of denying it.

The reason we study rival worldviews is to gain the ability to speak their language, understand their mindset, and aid in sharing Jesus to those lost without him. When we take the time to learn the language, understand the concepts they've learned, and apply our knowledge to create a framework of understanding for them, we contextualize the gospel for those we are engaging. This is very important considering the goal at hand.

Contextualizing the gospel does not mean changing it to fit the needs of others. It means explaining the gospel in terms that someone outside Christianity can understand. Missionaries live and die by contextualization. For example, how successful would you imagine a North American church model to fare in Afghanistan? Not very well, I assume. For this reason, missionaries contextualize the gospel to make it tangible to those they are evangelizing. If someone spends their whole life in a certain worldview, it is very difficult for them to understand anything outside that worldview without a little contextualization.

Think of it this way – how would one go about describing water to a goldfish? The goldfish has spent its entire existence in something that is painfully obvious to the outside observer but as invisible as the air we breathe to the goldfish. Likewise, those who spend their entire lives in rival worldviews will not immediately understand the truth of the gospel if we present it in the same fashion we would speak to our pastor.

REACTIVE APOLOGETICS VS. PROACTIVE APOLOGETICS

To summarize thus far, while evangelizing to members of rival worldviews we should bear the Three A's of Apologetics in mind, keep our pride in check, have Jesus as Lord over our hearts, and contextualize the gospel. However, all this might be for naught if we overlook one important facet of apologetics in dialogue – being *proactive* over being *reactive*. This is because the manner in which we present the gospel is crucial to how the gospel will be received.

Reactive apologetics usually entails a knee–jerk response from challenges by a rival worldview to us, our sphere of influence, or even the public. In this instance, we use apologetics to respond to a challenge, rather than proactively meeting the challenge head–on. Proactive apologetics involves proactively pursuing members of rival worldviews because we want to see them meet Jesus without regard to any ulterior motives. Determining whether or not we are engaging in reactive or proactive apologetics calls for a heart check; why are we motivated to evangelize members of rival worldviews? If our first answer is not to see someone come to a saving understanding of the person and work of Jesus, then we really need to take a step back for a moment and reevaluate why we want to defend the gospel. This was made painfully clear to me a year ago in England.

On a sunny, summer day in Cambridge I was out and about in the city center running some errands. The city sponsors a year–round outdoor market, so this was usually our favorite place to get fresh groceries. On this particular day I saw a booth off to the side with a large sign that read, "SO YOU THINK YOU KNOW YOUR BIBLE?" Other smaller signs indicated that the sponsors of the booth wanted to share the gospel and hand out free Bibles. Naturally I was intrigued, so I went to speak with the man behind the booth. We greeted each other, talked about the denomination he was representing, and why they had set up this booth.

"Well, I had come out here fairly regularly in the late–90s," the man explained. "So what made you start back up?" I asked. His response caught me a little off guard. He lowered his tone, nodded his head towards another booth across the way, and said, "Honestly, I started it back up because of the Muslims. They've been setting up a booth to hand out Qur'āns for the past few weeks, and I just got sick of it." There was a brief moment of awkward silence as I assume he saw the confused look on my face. "So," I slowly responded, "the only reason you're out here is because the Muslims are?" His response was as curt as his apparent animosity towards them. "Yes."

As I ended the conversation and walked away, I remember thinking to myself that his attitude of counter–evangelism would be counter–productive. His heart and attitude were in the wrong place for the mission he set out to accomplish. There was no way he could successfully share the gospel *in spite* of Muslims. If his focus continued to remain on counter–acting Muslims, rather than presenting and defending the gospel to any and all, then I didn't believe he would ever see a fruitful ministry. Funny enough, I saw him over the next few months and never once saw someone stop by his booth.

This is a huge problem, a huge heart problem. It clearly illustrates the difference between reactive apologetics and proactive apologetics. Reactive apologetics occurs when we respond to something we feel is a threat to the gospel, character of Jesus, or Christianity in a negative form because we are afraid of a paradigm shift in our culture, political systems, neighborhoods, or relationships. We use evangelism and apologetics reactively as a tool to frustrate the efforts of other rival worldviews in gaining converts.

Proactive apologetics, however, occurs when we respond to something we feel is a challenge to the gospel, character of Jesus, or Christianity in a positive form because we genuinely want to see people meet Jesus regardless of who they are. We use evangelism and apologetics proactively as a tool to remove stumbling blocks of understanding or to dissolve misunderstanding of the person and work of Jesus so that members of rival worldviews may fully understand the implications of the gospel. And the fact that apologetics can be used in two forms, reactive and proactive, indicates the deeper nature of the struggle we face when engaging challenges to the Christian faith. It is a struggle that goes deeper than social constructs. Our struggle in apologetics is a spiritual one.

APOLOGETICS IS SPIRITUAL

If our struggle is spiritual, then apologetics is spiritual. Paul emphasizes this when he declares; "our struggle is *not* against flesh and blood, but against the rulers, against the authorities, against the powers of this dark world and against the spiritual forces of evil in the heavenly realms."[16] Paul is telling Christians that we do not struggle against people (flesh and blood), but rather ideas people believe (spiritual forces). This should keep one thing at the forefront of our mind; apologetics shouldn't be directed towards the *person* we are sharing the gospel with, it should be directed towards the misconstrued *idea* that the person has about Jesus. If our battle is not against flesh and blood, then we may certainly rule out using apologetics as an art form of debate and fully embrace it as a tool for the Holy Spirit to use our loving dialogue in convincing the lost of the truth that is found in Jesus.

This leads to the fundamental question of how members of rival worldviews came to misunderstand Jesus in the first place. If we understand that we are called to defend God's truth in Jesus, then we must also acknowledge the fact that at some point the truth was twisted or corrupted. At the spiritual level, something went wrong and now people are subject to "spiritual forces." But how and why? Simply put, the enemy has seen his purpose as that of lying and creating confusion to entice people away from the loving communion and community of their creator. The enemy loves to lure people away through lies, deceit, and accusations against God.

It is good to know that in the plainest of terms the word *Satan* means '*the accuser*' in Hebrew. This is exactly what he does; accuses God of lying, being unfair, and incorrect. He then twists God's truth to confuse or persuade people to believe something other than what will reconnect them with the

---

[16] Eph. 6:12, emphasis added.

eternal presence and love of God.[17] This is why apologetics is contending for people in a spiritual struggle rather than a physical one.

We can see examples of God's truth twisted all around us in everyday life. You might know of people who believe that the God of Christianity is a malicious bully or an impotent god. Yet, because they still believe that God exists, they subscribe to one of the many other rival worldviews available, some of which have the appearance of Christianity, but are very different under the surface. Since they've been lied to, and believed a misconstrued idea about Jesus, they "exchange the truth about God for a lie."[18] Reversing that exchange is a part of our gracious responsibility and joyful obligation from God – to represent our king properly. Therefore, to sum it all up, we are called to correct and reprove the damage the enemy has done to those of rival worldviews by *contextualizing* the gospel into terms they understand and *defending* the gospel through proactive apologetics while remembering that this struggle is completely *spiritual* in nature.

ITCHING EARS & EISEGESIS

So, why do rival worldviews have differing opinions of Jesus in the first place? Furthermore, if rival worldviews subscribe to belief in the Bible's authority, why do they have such different views of Jesus? I believe the answer is two–fold: itching ears and eisegesis. First off, itching ears. Scripture tells us that, "the time will come when men will not put up with sound doctrine. Instead, to suit their own desires, they will gather around them a great number of teachers to say what their itching ears want to hear."[19] People will inevitably want to hear someone teach them what they want to hear, when they want to hear it. They will be less concerned with truth and more concerned with how good a lie will make them feel.

Today, this warning has come true. All we need to do to validate this is walk outside of our houses, apartments, dorms, and even churches. The time when man will not put up with sound doctrine has most definitely arrived. By

---

[17] Zech. 3:1; Gen. 1–5
[18] Rom. 1:25
[19] 2 Tim. 4:3

suppressing the truth of God in unrighteousness, men and women have flocked in huge numbers to counterfeit Christianity and bogus religion to hear from, learn about, and worship a god that fits into their lives, their wishes, and their desires.[20]

Considering humanity's itching ears, perhaps another way of defining apologetics could be the act of exposing counterfeit faith that members were taught and subscribe to. On face value, there seems to be a simple solution to the problem: if people have itching ears then perhaps they simply need exposure to the truth found in scripture. Pointing out why their beliefs do not match up with the Bible could bring people back into a true understanding of Jesus, if they believe the Bible is an authoritative source. This may be black-and-white with some people, but with others there may be some grey areas.

For example, a Scientologist rejecting the authority of scripture may be a relatively straightforward conversation as the Bible is not on the table for discussion; however, what about Mormons who accept scripture as part of their own? Mormons will often point to the same scripture we use to argue their position. How do we approach this issue? That's a fairly grey area – they accept scripture, yet hold a skewed interpretation. Moreover, sometimes they may even use scripture against us. How is it that some rival worldviews can be so close to Christianity, yet preach something so completely different? How are pseudo–Christian rival worldviews even possible with scripture in their own hands?

The answer comes back to itching ears. Rival worldview leaders know that truth exists, and that eventually those with itching ears under their leadership will inevitably be exposed to the truth. So, in a preemptive measure of defense, these leaders must use something authoritative in a manner that agrees with their teaching. The Bible is a prime target since, generally speaking, it is a trusted source of knowledge at least in the Western world. Picking up scripture, the leader twists God's word to make the lie seem like the truth. They use Christian scripture against Christianity. This is usually accomplished through an interpretative method called *eisegesis* that allows them to manipulate scripture for their own gain.

---

[20] Rom. 1:18

Eisegesis is the act of reading something into a text that isn't really there and is a very common technique among rival worldview leaders. For example, Muslim leaders and apologists may use the terms 'the Helper' or 'the Comforter' in the Gospel of John to prove that Jesus predicted the coming of Muhammad. A prime example of this eisegesis is something Jesus said in John 16:7; "Nevertheless, I tell you the truth: it is to your advantage that I go away, for if I do not go away, the Helper will not come to you. But if I go, I will send him to you."[21]

Muslim leaders explain to their followers that this verse teaches that Jesus was referring to Muhammad as the next prophet in line when he mentioned *the Helper*. In this interpretation, Jesus needed to leave his disciples so that a greater prophet would come later. That prophet, to Muslims, was Muhammad as predicted by the New Testament. So, how do we combat such an eisegetical error? In this instance, context is everything. Jesus was actually referring to the Holy Spirit when he mentions '*the Helper*' as he had explained earlier in the Gospel of John; "But the Helper, the Holy Spirit, whom the Father will send in my name, he will teach you all things and bring to your remembrance all that I have said to you."[22]

Furthermore, '*the Helper*' could better be translated from the Greek *paraklētos* as 'one who pleads another's case before a judge.' Muhammad is never referred to as an attorney, acting instead as Allah's representative to condemn humanity rather than humanity's representative to plead their case before God. Thus, this is a clear case of eisegesis used by Muslim leaders to read something into the New Testament that isn't there. Nonetheless, in the end, eisegesis works not because leaders are clever, but because people are either too lazy, unwilling, or afraid to question what is being interpreted to them.

ANYONE CAN DO IT, EVEN THE DISCIPLES

Combating eisegesis requires us to find these corrective explanations in scripture. Finding corrective explanations requires patience and diligence with

---

[21] John 16:7
[22] John 14:26

people and with God's Word. "But," you may interject, "the level of knowledge I would need to defend the Christian faith against seasoned members of rival worldviews is well beyond my local church Bible study." This idea is the problem with equating patience and diligence in scriptural studies with professional, academic training. The two aren't mutually exclusive, but they are closely related.

Regrettably, many Christians believe that in order to dialogue with Muslims, Mormons, and Jehovah's Witnesses, they need theological training to hold their own. Instead, they defer the heavy lifting to those with a framed piece of paper hanging on their office wall. Unfortunately, the "professionals" are usually not the ones in the field, at the university campuses, or in the work force. Pastors need us because, for the most part, they are not present when members of rival worldviews open up for dialogue at work or school. It is the "average Joe" Christian God uses – no seminary training required!

Christians must resist the idea that apologetics should only be left to those who attended Bible college or seminary as this is exactly what the enemy would want us to believe. How much easier is his job if Christians believe they are not trained enough to defend the gospel? Paul dispels this myth when he writes; "For it is only right for me to feel this way about you all, because I have you in my heart, since both in my imprisonment and in the defense and confirmation of the gospel, *you all* are partakers of grace with me."[23] Notice that it is *you all* who are defending and confirming the gospel in grace with Paul. This tells us that apologetics in dialogue on the gospel is not an intellectual chess game, it does not require a Ph.D., and it is nothing we should shy away from regardless of our maturity in Christ. In large part apologetics is a matter of faith through grace, not intelligence through seminary degrees.

This is demonstrated in the apostles themselves, as their credentials were far from prestigious. In fact, Jesus only chose one highly educated person in the field of theology to be an apostle. That person was Paul.[24] All the other disciples he chose were mainly blue–collar, illiterate fishermen with a tax collector here or there, none of which had any advanced formal training in theology, religion, or Jewish studies as far as we can tell. In fact, after healing a man, Peter and

---

[23] Phil.1:7, emphasis added.
[24] Acts 9:1–6; Phil. 3:5–6

John preached to some of the most religiously educated men of their day and caused them to rethink what it meant to be educated. "When they saw the courage of Peter and John and realized that they were unschooled, ordinary men, they were astonished and they took note that these men had been with Jesus."[25] The word *unschooled (agramatos)* in this passage literally means that they were 'unlettered' or illiterate. *Agramatos* is not a trait we would expect in two men who astonished the most highly educated men in their culture at that time.

So, if the disciples were mainly *agramatos*, what was it that made them so bold, intelligent, eloquent, and successful at defending and proclaiming the faith? Just that – *faith.* God chooses to use the normal, day-to-day, average Joe's to represent him and bring people to a saving knowledge of the gospel. Sometimes we'll succeed and sometimes we'll fail from our perspective, but at all times God will use us to accomplish his will. A skinny academic resume shouldn't bog us down when bringing up an apologetic argument to members of rival worldviews. If we study up a little and dive into scripture, God will use us in amazing ways.

The fear of looking stupid, or being wrong, or failing at "winning souls" really holds Christians back when Mormon missionaries come knocking on their door, but it shouldn't. Even Peter faulted and failed periodically. Yet, in the end, he faithfully proclaimed the gospel and defended it to the end of his life.

PETER'S EXAMPLE

Remember the verse about the Three A's of Apologetics (always answer anyone)? How did Peter have the insight to give us such great advice? He learned it through experience that came at a steep cost. Peter, perhaps like some of us, really botched things up when it was his time to shine and defend Jesus. He completely misrepresented Jesus as his disciple in the face of danger. But he didn't start out botching things up. In fact, Peter was the first recorded person in history to make the confession that Jesus Christ is the Son of the living God.

---

[25] Acts 4:13

> "Now when Jesus came into the district of Caesarea Philippi,
> he asked his disciples, 'Who do people say that the Son of
> Man is?' And they said, 'Some say John the Baptist, others
> say Elijah, and others Jeremiah or one of the prophets.' He
> said to them, 'But who do you say that I am?' Simon Peter
> replied, 'You are the Christ, the Son of the living God.' And
> Jesus answered him, 'Blessed are you, Simon [Peter]! For
> flesh and blood has not revealed this to you, but my Father
> who is in heaven.'"[26]

While this was Peter's confession, he wasn't really the one who figured this out on his own. He had some help. Notice that Jesus specifically says the Father revealed that knowledge to Peter. Peter, like us, needs the Father's assistance to even understand him, let alone know him. If this weren't the case, we would never succeed.[27] This should take the weight of worry off our shoulders. If Peter didn't figure out that Jesus was the Son of God without the Father's assistance, why should we worry about having enough knowledge to share Jesus with members of rival worldviews?

Doesn't it make sense for God to provide us with the right knowledge and words at the proper time if he uses us to share his gospel? Our insight about what to say to people is not entirely self-gained; rather, God gives it to us in a timely manner. This is not to say that we have full access to an infinite theological Wikipedia in the sky. God will give us the knowledge, wisdom, insight, and words to say at just the right time when we diligently study his word.

Another thing to consider in this passage is the first question Jesus asks Peter, "Who do people say that the Son of Man is?"[28] Think about that question for a second. Reread it. Mull it over for a minute. Let it take root in your mind. Who do people say that Jesus is? This question is one of the most profound questions asked in all of scripture. Who is Jesus? Is that not our underlying question for members of rival worldviews? No question from scripture has more apologetic relevance in our day than maybe Pilot's famous inquiry, "What is truth?"[29] Honestly ask yourself, who do people say Jesus is?

---

[26] Matt. 16:13–17
[27] Rom. 8:8
[28] Matt. 16:13
[29] John 18:38

That's partially what we are attempting to learn through studying rival worldviews – what people believe about Jesus.

Some people think Jesus was a really nice guy. Others believe he was an influential rabbi. Still others believe Jesus was a liar, a leader of liars, or a victim of Jewish fanaticism blowing him way out of proportion. Some atheists believe Jesus was simply a type of myth, perhaps just another Hercules. Agnostics believe Jesus was a nice guy, a moral leader, maybe even anti-establishment. Mormons believe Jesus is our spirit brother, along with Satan. Jehovah's Witnesses believe Jesus is actually Michael the Archangel. Scientologists believe Jesus was a tool for mind corruption and the root of depression for many people in the world. But what should we believe about Jesus?

As Peter so eloquently put it, Jesus is the Son of the living God.[30] This confession was a high point for Peter. Again, this was by nothing he merited or earned on his own outside of simple obedience to God the Father, time spent with Jesus (studying and learning), and a listening ear to the Holy Spirit. No special apologetics classes, no seminary lectures, no Bible college seminars. It was simple obedience to God and time with Jesus.

Sadly, Peter doesn't always stay on top of his game, as we all fail to do from time-to-time. While Peter enjoyed an apologetic victory, he also suffered an apologetic failure.

> Now Peter was sitting outside in the courtyard. And a servant girl came up to him and said, 'You also were with Jesus the Galilean.' But he denied it before them all, saying, 'I do not know what you mean.' And when he went out to the entrance, another servant girl saw him, and she said to the bystanders, 'This man was with Jesus of Nazareth.' And again he denied it with an oath: 'I do not know the man.' After a little while the bystanders came up and said to Peter, 'Certainly you too are one of them, for your accent betrays you.' Then he began to invoke a curse on himself and to swear, 'I do not know the man.' And immediately the rooster crowed. And Peter remembered the saying of Jesus, 'Before the rooster crows, you will deny me three times.' And he went out and wept bitterly.[31]

---

[30] Matt. 16:16
[31] Matt. 26:69–75

Ouch. Not only was Peter scared of a little teenaged girl, but it also seems like he cussed out the bystanders. Peter has just completely blown his witness for Jesus. At a time when the question was being asked, 'Who is Jesus?' and the answers were liar, fraud, rebel, madman, blasphemer, wrong, insane, fiendish, etc., Peter neglected to give a defense. After all the time Peter had spent with Jesus, had grown with Jesus, had eaten as friends with Jesus, had loved Jesus, after all they had been through together, and when Jesus was at the most critical point in his earthly life, Peter denied him because he was afraid to defend him. He wholly misrepresented Jesus.

Later in scripture, James tells us that we will all misrepresent our good and loving king; it's just a matter of *when* not *if.* We live in a fallen world, make mistakes, and need God's grace even after he saves us.[32] Worrying about failing apologetically in front of Jehovah's Witnesses or Muslims is a spirit of timidity placed in our lives by the enemy. He silences our tongues and tells us that the chance we could misrepresent Jesus is so great that we should not even try.

To add insult to injury, once we do fail we feel like throwing in the towel. We tell ourselves that there are far greater evangelists, or better Christians, or more eloquent speakers who will reach the lives of the people we just fell flat on our face in front of. It's time to give up, give in, and like Peter weep bitterly. But Peter's story doesn't end there. The man who denied Jesus, the same guy who refused to give an apologetic defense for Jesus, bounces back from timidity and shame, only by the grace of God.

After Jesus' resurrection, the early church was facing a lot of persecution. The religious leaders of the day knew they would lose influence if the Jesus cult would take off, so they ordered Jesus' disciples to be arrested. On one such occasion, Peter was allowed to explain to the religious leaders why they needed Jesus as well. Peter, the guy who cussed people out and was afraid of a little girl who revealed he was a disciple, stood up in confidence after being challenged by some of the most powerful men in his culture and said;

> Rulers of the people and elders ... let it be known to all of you and to all the people of Israel that by the name of Jesus Christ of Nazareth, whom you crucified, whom God raised from the dead–by him this man is standing before you well.

---

[32] James 3:2

> This Jesus is the stone that was rejected by you, the builders, which has become the cornerstone. And there is salvation in no one else, for there is no other name under heaven given among men by which we must be saved.[33]

I think he overcame his timidity and failure. Not only is this passage an expansion of his original confession that Jesus is the Son of the living God, but Peter publicly criticizes these powerful men for their hand in Jesus' crucifixion.

Peter has given us a great example of bouncing back from our inevitable failures. From prestige, to coward, to evangelist, we can rest assured that God is never done with us, just like Peter, even when we think we've blown it. Like Peter being challenged by the religious leaders of his day, we are challenged by rival worldviews over the person and work of Jesus Christ. And when we are challenged, despite previous failed attempts to declare the truth of Jesus, we need to overcome our timidity and fear with God's grace. Peter regained the boldness he once had before losing it after his denial of Christ. Perhaps part of Peter's regained boldness comes from a promise that Jesus made to all Christians – that when people challenge us over his character we should not be anxious about what we are going to say because he will give us the words.[34]

This is the critical difference between Peter's shameful denial and his bold declaration at Pentecost. During Jesus' trial, Peter was anxious about what to say, yet later he is able to speak in boldness. Why is this? I believe it's because he finally realized that human wisdom or understanding or rhetoric or philosophy is not how we declare Jesus to be Lord. It is done in the power of the Holy Spirit, for the glory of God the Father, and through faith in Jesus Christ that we give apologetic arguments for the person and work of Jesus. There is no other way.

Peter also knew that God's word does not return void. Never be afraid to give an apologetic argument because you are unsure whether or not people will understand, care, or respond. God's word always achieves what it sets out to accomplish.[35] This should take tons of weight off our shoulders. When someone objects to the Jesus of scripture and offers a gospel contrary to the one found in the Bible, we should give an apologetic defense and not worry

---

[33] Acts 4:8–12
[34] Mark 13:11

about whether or not it will affect that person. It's not our job to convert people – that's the Holy Spirit's job.

If God's purpose in that instance is to bring that person to a saving knowledge of Jesus Christ, then it will happen. If God's purpose is just to plant a seed and have them saved later in life, they might react differently than you expect. Never worry about the outcome of your apologetic, just proclaim Jesus' name, teach Jesus, gently correct people when they speak falsely about Jesus, and rest in the knowledge that God has used you in the exact way he wanted to.

What we learn from Peter's successes and failures is that God takes people who are available and willing to be used by him, transforms their minds, and fills them with the Holy Spirit as they are used as vessels for him. Although we fail, God still uses all things for his glory. "And we know that for those who love God all things work together for good, for those who are called according to his purpose."[36] We do apologetics by faith and confidence for the glory of the king's name.

FIRST BANK OF NEGATING FAITH & TRUST

This all may sound good since most Christians will agree that God uses us to bring people to Jesus; however, some might object to apologetics as being the means. In fact, some believe that demanding proof or spending time with apologetics is wrong because it takes away the need to have child–like faith in Jesus. They would argue that apologetics is simply a compromise people use to reach the lost, and that apologetics sends the wrong message that we do not need child–like faith as scripture teaches.[37]

For example, one evening in Cambridge, England I attended a public lecture given by Dr. William Lane Craig over God's existence. During the Q&A session, a Christian woman argued that Christians should not engage in apologetics because we are called to have child–like faith, and that our personal experience is argument enough for faith in God. She was smirked at

---

[35] Isa. 55:11
[36] Rom. 8:28
[37] Mark 10:13–31

by the non-theists in the crowd, and as I looked around, I noticed many Christians became red in the face, embarrassed by the party association of which this "representative" of our faith had dragged us into. The non-theists now believed that Christians argue for baseless, evidential-less faith in God. But is this really a legitimate argument in the first place? Is there a difference between child–like faith and child–like naiveté? Is it okay for Christians to question their faith and come up with arguments as to why Christianity is correct, or should Christians simply take everything at blind "child–like" faith? Was the woman in Cambridge correct?

To answer those questions, we must first explore what *faith* means. Scripture defines faith as, "the assurance of things hoped for, the conviction of things not seen."[38] With that definition we could apply faith to a lot of things. For instance, we have faith that the earth will continue its orbit around the sun. This is both hoped for (since we would all fly off into space if the earth stopped orbiting the sun) and a conviction we have for something we can't plainly see. We don't wake up in the morning and think to ourselves, "Boy, I sure hope the earth continues its orbit around the sun at the same velocity as yesterday."

As foolish as this sounds, many critics of faith want to apply the same scenario to Christians and our faith in God. They want to ascribe a sense of dangerous naiveté to a group of people who believe in myths and fairytales. But this is for critics of faith who do not believe. What about those who do believe in God and demand others around them to blindly follow their leadership without ever inquiring as to why? This is where the child–like faith/child–like naiveté distinction comes into play and why apologetics actually sharpens our child–like faith by rejecting child–like naiveté. Here's an analogy to help us understand the difference.

A guy, we'll call him Bruce, walks into his bank and makes his way to the teller. Bruce's purpose for the visit is to learn how much money he has in his bank account because he has a few bills to pay soon. He reaches the teller's booth, asks to see his account balance to which the teller replies, "You have enough money." Smiling, Bruce thanks her for her time, leaves without knowing how much he has, but believes the teller when she says he has enough.

---

[38] Heb. 11:1

Bruce is, as I'm sure you would agree, an idiot. He does not consider what the teller's opinion of "enough money" actually means or that the teller may be lying. Furthermore, "enough money" is a subjective statement, ambiguous at best, considering the context of the question. Does the teller know the amount of Bruce's upcoming bills? Of course not. So why should Bruce accept the teller's answer? Bruce exhibits child–like naiveté in the teller because he blindly accepts what was told to him as truth. If mommy told little Brucey that he had "enough money" in his allowance then we wouldn't think twice about the logic of that scenario, but not a grown man.

Another guy, we'll call him Timmy, walks into the same bank, speaks with the same teller, and gets the same answer as Bruce. Not being satisfied by the teller's answer, Timmy demands to know the exact amount of money in his account. It's not that he doesn't trust the teller, but he's more comfortable placing faith in a bank that gives him unambiguous, non-subjective answers. The teller informs Timmy of the exact amount he has in his account. Timmy is then satisfied with the answer and he leaves trusting that the teller told him the truth, not demanding to see and count the money for himself. Timmy exhibits child–like faith in the bank in that he knows how much he has in his account, trusts that the bank will not lose his money, and believes the bank will be there tomorrow. His faith in the bank is both hoped for (that it will be there tomorrow) and unseen (that the amount the teller gives him is actual).

Outspoken critics of 'child–like faith' stand on one of two sides of the fence. One party will argue that God is the teller and we should simply trust that he knows our life and what we need. On the other side of the fence are critics of faith in God who would criticize Timmy for leaving the bank, knowing the exact amount in his account but neglecting to demand proof of security for the bank or the ability to physically count the money himself. So who's right?

Scripture tells us two things about Bruce and Timmy. Much like Timmy who demands to know the exact amount in his account, not because he doesn't trust the bank but needs to know for practical purposes, scripture invites us to explore and inquire about the Lord. Psalms declares, "Oh, taste and see that the LORD is good!"[39] The Proverbs state, "Blessed is the one who finds

---

[39] Ps. 34:8

wisdom, and the one who gets understanding."[40] These are not verses that would indicate it is wrong to question God and what he was doing in our lives. In fact, there are many psalms that question God and his will, not out of pride, but holy, reverent fear. If the motive of our heart is pure in seeking wisdom and understanding about God, then there is absolutely nothing wrong with honest and humble inquiry.

THE "SIN" OF INQUIRY

This is fundamental to engaging in apologetics. Many members of rival worldviews have been taught that an inquiring mind is one not far from sin, blasphemy of the Holy Spirit, damnation, excommunication, etc. This teaching, for example, is so engraved into Islam that it is inescapable. The Qur'ān teaches obedient Muslims never to question anything concerning Allah.

> O ye who believe! Ask not questions about things which, if made plain to you, may cause you trouble. But if ye ask about things when the Qur'ān is being revealed, they will be made plain to you, Allah will forgive those: for Allah is Oft-forgiving, Most Forbearing.[41]

This passage states that Muslims are not allowed to question anything about Allah unless they are having it read to them by an Imam (Islamic leader). Even then, Allah must forgive them the sin of asking a question. This would be akin to saying we aren't allowed to question God or the Bible unless we have a pastor present. Afterwards, we aren't allowed to question what the pastor told us, and God would need to forgive us for questioning the Bible in the first place. Praise God that the one, true living God does not put such demeaning and forceful restrictions on us, his creation, whom he loves.

Unlike some rival worldviews, God does not promote ignorance of his being, and doesn't show special merit to those who "require" less faith for belief in him. This is something we should make perfectly clear when sharing Jesus. Christianity invites challenging inquiry, thought provoking dialogue, and the prodding of its more core doctrines. Christianity is as revolutionary

---

[40] Prov. 3:13

and life changing as Jesus himself, the god–man who challenges us to examine his life, his truth claims, and his trustworthiness.

Belief in God requires the type of faith that already acknowledges he is a good, living God and wants only to restore relationship and community between you and him. Our faith in God doesn't begin with blindly believing his existence and trustworthiness of his word; rather, our faith is grounded in historicity, beginning with the assurance of things hoped for and conviction of things unseen.[42]

I have never heard a respectable Christian leader demand blind faith in God from their congregation. Usually that demand is coupled with, "And now, to the ceremonial punch bowl!" or "So, anyway, about your minimum tithe to the ministry..." Leaders who demand blind faith desire blind followers. This is the apex of mind control techniques. They associate questioning their religious system with sin, folly, or rebellion. It is pathetic, inexcusable, and dangerous. Leaders who espouse blind faith in their followers have aggressively selfish motivations for their own gain at the expense of the people they lead. They are men who cannot command their lead but perniciously warp the minds of weaker people to steal them from God, family, and friends.

The question we should ask ourselves is how scripture describes inquiry into itself? Does the Bible condemn our inquiry into its claims, namely of the person and work of Jesus? The answer lies with Jesus himself and one of his more skeptical disciples. If anyone in the Bible received a bad rep for something they did, it was Thomas. Not familiar with Thomas? How about *Doubting* Thomas.

> So the other disciples told him, 'We have seen the Lord.' But he [Thomas] said to them, 'Unless I see in his hands the mark of the nails, and place my finger into the mark of the nails, and place my hand into his side, I will never believe.' Eight days later, his disciples were inside again, and Thomas was with them. Although the doors were locked, Jesus came and stood among them and said, 'Peace be with you.' Then he said to Thomas, 'Put your finger here, and see my hands; and put out your hand, and place it in my side. Do not disbelieve, but believe.' Thomas answered him, 'My Lord

---

[41] Sūra Al-Mā'idah 5:101, *Yusuf Ali*
[42] Heb. 11:1

and my God!' Jesus said to him, 'Have you believed because
you have seen me? Blessed are those who have not seen and
yet have believed.'[43]

From this account with Thomas, we see that Jesus actually invites us to examine him. He revealed evidence to Thomas, asked him to examine it, and the only thing Thomas could conclude was that Jesus was truly God. We sometimes give Thomas a bad reputation by ascribing the title of *doubting* to a man who did what any of us would have done in the same situation. Based on our own personal experience, we doubt Christ perhaps on a daily basis. Yet one thing remains to be understood; Christianity is not a system of philosophy but an evidence–based faith. Jesus invites us to examine him apologetically to see, understand, and believe that he is the one he claims to be. This is something we must emphasize to members of rival worldviews. Perhaps we should ask them whether or not their Jesus invites them to examine him?

When talking to members of rival worldviews, ask them how their organization would react if they brought them a list of what they thought were contradictions in the Qur'ān or the Book of Mormon. If they answer that their leadership probably wouldn't appreciate it then share the Doubting Thomas story with them. Show them that Jesus invites examination and exploration of his claims. Get the gears turning on why their organization doesn't smile upon them questioning what they have been told about Jesus, when the Jesus of scripture holds out his nail–scared hands for all to examine and see.

POLITICALLY INCORRECT

Wouldn't telling people to buck the system of their beliefs because they're wrong offend some people? The simple answer is yes; however, in modern society this requires more attention than simple answers. A major lie in today's overly ecumenical society is that offending someone's personal beliefs is wrong and a socially taboo practice. Because of subjective absolutes, everyone is entitled to his or her own beliefs and should be free from "offensive" proselytizing. To a certain point, there is some truth to this. If

---

[43] John 20:25–29

people do not want to hear what you have to say, then don't bother. However, if truth is offensive to someone, it doesn't make it any less true. We know through scripture that the gospel itself is offensive and will offend those who hear it.[44] Does that mean we shouldn't share it?

Being told we are no-good, wicked, lost, sinners who are in continual rebellion and subject to eternal punishment is not something we wake up in the morning and desire to hear first thing. The offensive parts of the Bible are offensive enough and definitely do not need our help with fire-and-brimstone preaching. At the same time, however, many people believe the simple act of evangelism is offensive in that a Christian is superimposing or pushing a certain worldview on another person who doesn't hold that view. No duh. If evangelism to non-Christians is offensive, then Jesus is more offensive than a steak dinner at a PETA event.

The fact of the matter is this – the gospel is offensive and it needs to be proclaimed. How this pans out in an ecumenical society depends on our willingness to contextualize, defend, and present the gospel. This is not something we *should* do, but something we are *commanded* to do through the Great Commission. Jesus instructed Christians to make more Christians. If you could not already guess, making Christians out of non-Christians might require evangelism, offensive as that may be in our society devoid of moral absolutism. Like Paul points out, "How then will they call on him in whom they have not believed? And how are they to believe in him of whom they have never heard? And how are they to hear without someone preaching?"[45]

If there is someone who has never heard about Jesus in your life, then tell them about him. If they have been taught a different Jesus, then tell them about the real Jesus. They may be offended because you are directly or indirectly telling them that their long-held beliefs are wrong (often times handed down to them by loved ones), but this needs to happen nonetheless. Never feel like you shouldn't talk to people about Jesus because it might be offensive. If what we believe is actually the truth about the way the world is, and people believe things contrary to the truth, would it not be eternally offensive neglecting to temporarily offend them in this life?

---

[44] 1 Pet. 2:8
[45] Romans 10:14

Note that there are emotional difficulties that come with evangelism. You may act as a catalyst that forces an individual to reconsider their beliefs.[46] When it comes to members of rival worldviews, conversations may not always be cordial. In fact, it may get awkward and uncomfortable to navigate through the emotional investment that an individual has in a gospel that does not quite line up with the gospel. For most people, this will hurt.

It takes a lot of wisdom to evangelize. We cannot simply tell a member of a rival worldview that they're wrong because their worldview, its founding leader, and everything he did was fundamentally wrong. Consequently, by extension, they are no better than their leader. I actually heard a conversation go a little something like this once. For this act, Jimmy will be playing a non-successful Christian apologetic evangelist trying to share the gospel with Ameed, who is a member of a rival worldview.

"Did you know your god is a demon?" Jimmy eloquently kicks off the conversation.

"Excuse me?" Ameed responds.

"Well, I noticed you were wearing headwear traditionally worn by people who worship a false demon god," Jimmy whips as he continues to shove his foot further and further down his mouth.

"I don't worship a demon; I worship the same god you do, just in a different tradition," Ameed says as his patience towards Jimmy quickly dissolves.

"No, your god is a demon. You don't realize it now, but you will in hell unless you pray to the real god for forgiveness." This is the apex of Jimmy's candor.

Ameed is quick to respond. "Why would I pray to your god when he produces [BLEEP] followers like you?"

Good point, Ameed. Well done, Jimmy.

The worst thing we could possibly do when dialoguing on the gospel is to tell people that they, along with their families, culture, history, and beloved leaders, have first–class tickets to eternal torment. What about befriending them, listening to them, loving them as a neighbor, and earning the respect to be heard? This is a point that some Christians fail to realize; more than anything, apologetics is love. We can argue all we want, and even win

---

[46] John 15:18

the arguments, but unless the people we are talking to love and respect us, the impact of our arguments will fall short of anything more than trivial.

THE BEST APOLOGETIC

Without a doubt, the best apologetic argument has always been and will always be love. Many basement blogging, armchair theologians will use apologetics as a means of satisfying their own prideful desire to outdo a person in debate, yet ignore the fact that human wisdom doesn't allow us to know our king, the Holy Spirit does. It's extremely important to understand that our job as gospel–sharing Christians is not to debate, but to love. If God is love, and we want to share him with people, we must show them love.[47] If we view our primary purpose in apologetics as being remarkable debaters who put their opponents in their place, then we will completely miss the point. This kind of apologist chases after self-promotion by seeming intelligent, and ironically they selfishly debate for the existence of a selfless God – one who was so humble that he would die for their sin of arrogance.

Our own intellect is nothing without the Holy Spirit, so how can we possibly believe that winning an argument with a non-Christian proves anything of our own worth? Paul tells us that the wisdom we receive from God or from scripture is not of our own doing but revealed to us spiritually.[48] Christians should seek for the promotion of God's name by loving his creation made in his own image. John tells us that, "anyone who does not love does not know God, because God is love."[49] If the goal is to show them God, and God is love, then the question deserves to be asked; what should we show members of rival worldviews? Love.

Simple answer, I know, but the fact remains that we can outwit, out smart, and out debate people until Jesus returns, but if we never show them love then nothing will ever change. When we evangelize apologetically to members of rival worldviews, we are committing to a long–term, loving relationship to show them the same love Jesus shows us daily. It is infinitely

---

[47] 1 John 4:8
[48] 1 Cor. 2:13
[49] 1 John 4:8

better to have love without words than words without love. Not only is it not our job to callously debate as if we can fully comprehend God, it's impossible. God wouldn't be God if we could completely explain him to people. Trying to describe an infinite, triune, trans–dimensional, omniscient, omnipresent, omnipotent being as a finite, limited being is absolutely impossible. We give thanks to God that he revealed himself in a way we could understand – as the god–man Jesus speaking to us in the language of love.[50]

OCEAN IN A VASE

Early church father Augustine of Hippo (354–430CE) understood the impossibility of explaining God in pure intellect or reason better than any of us could ever hope to in our lifetime. He understood that the sheer concept of God by definition demanded that God be a being incomprehensible to his creation. However, Augustine was not born with this understanding. He struggled deeply with the notion that God was incomprehensible and would frequently walk along the Mediterranean coast, trying to grasp the full concept of God in order to better explain him to opponents of Christianity.

If there were ever a guy who had the mind to comprehend God, Augustine would be him. He was a premier apologist against the false teachings of Arianism, Pelagianism, Donatism, and Manichæism – all fancy terms for belief systems that taught a different Jesus than scripture. He once served as the head professor of rhetoric in Rome, and penned invaluable books such as *Confessions*, *City of God*, and *On The Trinity*; works that are still studied today. He led many Christian churches as a bishop, an office reserved for only the brightest of Christian thinkers in his day, as well as founded a monastic order which still exists today. Yet in all his intelligence, he still felt as though he lacked complete understanding of the whole concept of God. If Augustine wanted to present a solid apologetic argument against his opponents, surely the way to do so would be through academic rigor and philosophical discipline. But academia was getting him nowhere. So, he took to long walks along the seacoast to pray and think about the nature of God.

---

[50] Col. 1:15

During one of his walks, Augustine came across a small boy knelt down over the lightly rolling waves. He was scooping water into a vase each time the swells rose around his legs. With every scoop of water he would look back out into the ocean and let out a disappointing sigh. Augustine asked the little boy what he was doing. Without stopping to scoop up the water, he explained that he was trying to take the ocean home with him to show his father. Augustine smiled and informed the little boy that the ocean was too large to be able to fit inside the small vase. The little boy eventually realized that his attempts would go unrewarded and decided to quit. Then it hit Augustine.

This was perhaps one of the most profound moments in his life. Augustine realized that we are the little boy with the vase and God is the ocean. We can try as hard as we can to completely grasp God, but it will always be as useless as trying to collect the ocean in a vase. Our minds, much like the vase, are simply too limited to comprehend the being that created the universe and holds it together. We can understand only what our minds will hold. You can only take as much of the ocean home that the size of your vase allows. From that time onward, Augustine resolved to be satisfied with never fully being able to comprehend God and continued defending the gospel to the best of his ability.

What we can learn from Augustine is invaluable to apologetics in dialogue on the gospel. The angle Christians should approach members of rival worldviews is not primarily intellectual arguments; rather, it's fostering a loving relationship and friendship with them for the expressed purpose of sharing the gospel. We should be gracious but uncompromising. Intellectual arguments for the faith should be secondary to showing them the love of Christ through our lives simply because intellectual arguments are as limited as taking the ocean home in a vase. Do they help? Sure. A part of the ocean did indeed go home with the little boy, but it does not do justice to understanding the power and immensity of the whole ocean.

We cannot completely understand God, and we cannot share him through intelligence alone. This means we must serve, understand, and love those we are dialoguing with. John says it best;

"Beloved, let us love one another, for love is from God, and whoever loves has been born of God and knows God.

Anyone who does not love does not know God, because God is love. In this the love of God was made manifest among us, that God sent his only Son into the world, so that we might live through him. In this is love, not that we have loved God but that he loved us and sent his Son to be the propitiation for our sins. Beloved, if God so loved us, we also ought to love one another."[51]

Loving members of rival worldviews means showing them Jesus. Showing them Jesus means learning their theology to explain away the misrepresentation of Jesus they may believe. Showing them the real Jesus is the *most* loving thing you can do, whether that means inviting them over for dinner, mowing their yard for them when they are away on vacation, or studying what they believe to clarify the misconceptions they have about Jesus. Just remember as you read this book – understanding a rival worldview's misrepresentation of Jesus in order to show them the real Jesus is the powerful tool for the desired outcome…

…showing them the love of Jesus.

---

[51] 1 John 4:7–11

CHAPTER TWO

Mormonism & Big Brother Jesus

"A large majority of the whole have stood by me. Neither Paul, John, Peter, nor Jesus ever did it. I boast that no man ever did such a work as I. The followers of Jesus ran away from Him; but the Latter-day Saints never ran away from me.."[52]

JOSEPH SMITH JR. (1805–1844)

It was early fall and I had just graduated from boot camp. Bubbling with excitement about being stationed in Monterey, California I couldn't help but resent the layover I had at Salt Lake International Airport. With backpack in hand, I walked down the corridor connecting my plane to the terminal where I was to spend the next few hours anxiously awaiting the Golden State. As I turned the corner in the jet bridge I glanced ahead toward the exit and saw two guys my age wearing identical outfits. Albeit, seeing people in the exact same uniform had been the norm the past few weeks what with boot camp and all, but this was different.

With white button–up shirts, black slacks, matching black ties, and what appeared to be small nametags on their chests, these guys were very easy to pick out in the crowd, like two penguins on the field during the Super Bowl. There was something in their hands that caught my eye – identical small, blue books with gold lettering on them. I thought I could make out the words *Jesus Christ* written on the cover, but wasn't sure.

Walking further up the corridor, I finally came within clear view of the two. I approached them slowly, trying not to betray my curiosity by looking as uninterested as possible. I avoided eye contact with them once I noticed they were stopping and speaking with anyone who gave them even the slightest glance. As I passed by, I overheard their conversation with an older woman who seemed less than interested in what they had to say. I could make out

---

[52] Joseph Smith, Jr., *History of the Church of Jesus Christ of Latter-day Saints*, Vol. 6, 2nd ed. (Salt Lake City: The Deseret Book Company, 1973), 408–409.

Christian buzzwords like 'Heavenly Father' and 'salvation' under the dull, ubiquitous roar of the airport terminal. It was obvious to me at this point that they were somehow affiliated with a Christian organization of some sort. Perhaps they were a type of salesmen. But *Jesus* salesmen?

Maybe this was a new approach to evangelism that some church with absolutely no finger on the pulse of our culture was trying. "That has to be it," I callowly thought to myself, "there's no other explanation." In a sure sign of my youthful nescience, I assumed these guys were just some poor saps duped into performing a weird form of evangelism that was obviously not working. But what was the name of their organization? I had to know.

Inching a little closer I squinted my eyes to read their name tags at a distance; *Church of Jesus Christ of Latter-day Saints.* "Latter-day Saints? What's a Latter-day Saint?" Now my interest was piqued. Amidst all the hustle and bustle of the busy airport, I waited for them to finish what seemed to be a sales pitch while continuing to watch them discretely from a distance. As one guy did all the talking the other guy scanned the crowd looking for their next potential target.

Determined to speak to them on my terms I turned my head every time the lookout guy glanced my way – a game of visual cat and mouse. They finally finished with the older woman and I made my way towards them. I kept my head down until the most opportune moment. I was resolved to start the conversation and had no interest in their strange proselytizing sales pitch. I was going to meet them on my terms and not let them lead me in their...

"Uh, sir! Excuse me," one of them said, "have you ever heard the gospel of Jesus Christ?"

I looked up to discover he was talking to me; my plan had failed. Taken a little off guard, I fumbled for a reply.

"Um, yeah. But..."

"Well that's great to hear," he interrupted me. "My name is Elder Croft and this is Elder Hendricks. We're missionaries with the Church of Jesus Christ of Latter-day Saints."

Again, I was bewildered by what a *Latter-day Saint* was, but the only thing I could think about was how awkwardly unusual this conversation was and it was only five seconds old.

Elder Croft's enthusiasm seemed misplaced considering the task he was given to perform. Speaking with complete strangers about Jesus in a busy airport did not strike me as a happy assignment. Both of these guys were clean-shaven, neatly dressed, and confident representatives of their church. The dichotomy of being professionally joyful in such a dull task captivated my interest. Indeed, there was something to be said about the motivation behind their work. Was it because they were being paid? Were they receiving some type of reward? Neither of these explanations seemed adequate, so I figured it must be the organization that they worked for.

"Latter-day Saints," I inquired, "I've never heard of that church before." Slowly, their smiles grew simultaneously larger. It was one of those smiles where you know they have you right where they want you. Elder Hendricks told me about how the Latter-day Saints are God's restored church on earth. He told me the Christian church as a whole had gone astray. Thankfully, under the guidance of a man named Joseph Smith, God was able to rear his church back into the institution he had originally planned it to be.

They asked if I had any other questions, which of course I had, but given the information overload I simply told them no. The young missionaries handed me a copy of the little, blue book with gold writing on it, told me to read it over, and to perhaps get in contact with other Latter-day Saints upon settling down in California. I looked down at the little, blue book as I walked away and read the title *The Book of Mormon: Another Testament of Jesus Christ*.

Another testament of Jesus Christ?

Book of Mormon?

Joseph Smith?

"Well," I thought to myself, "this was definitely the most interesting layover I've ever had."

WHAT IS MORMONISM?

I later learned the two elders were Mormon missionaries. Being smart enough to put two and two together, I gathered that the *Book of Mormon* might have something to do with *Mormonism*. Mormons, or *Latter-day Saints* as they are properly called, belong to an organization that claims to be the only true and restored church of Jesus Christ. This was something not only told to me by the missionaries in the airport, but is a universally accepted truth within Mormon belief.

With a membership of over 15 million worldwide, Mormonism teaches that the greatest and fullest expression of salvation is impossible absent the Church of Jesus Christ of Latter-day Saints, or LDS Church, and its revelations.[53] It teaches that the Christian church as a whole has never truly been what Jesus intended ever since the death of John the Apostle. It hit some high point here and there (such as the Protestant Reformation in Europe and perhaps the Great Awakening in America), but it was never fully realized until God chose a man named Joseph Smith to restore the church.

Joseph Smith. Herein lies the majority of the LDS story – where they came from, why they are here, and where they are going. The vast majority of Mormon philosophy and theology comes from this one man who is viewed as the greatest apostle that ever lived. More importantly, Latter-day Saints believe they cannot fully know Jesus outside of the revelations of Joseph Smith. From him they are taught that God, or Heavenly Father, is the creator of this planet and governs it with the Holy Spirit and his son Jesus Christ. Heavenly Father came to this godly position through obedience of the ordinances set in place by his god (or God's god) earlier in his existence.

Once a man himself, Heavenly Father now rules and reigns in heaven as God. With Heavenly Mother, he created all people in the heavenly realm where they previously existed in a premortal state. At some point in history past, a counsel of gods convened to discuss the formation and governance of earth. Jesus Christ, our spirit brother, proposed a plan of salvation that was accepted by Heavenly Father. Satan, our other spirit brother, despised the plan

---

53   The Church of Jesus Christ of Latter-day Saints, "Church Grows Rapidly," http:/www.lds.org/ library/display/0,4945,40-1-3474-2,00.html (accessed January 8, 2012).

and rebelled against Heavenly Father; however, Jesus' plan won out in the end.[54] Now, through faith in Jesus Christ and our obedience, we may also attain perfection like our Heavenly Father. Through enough good works and faithfulness to Heavenly Father, we may become gods like him one day.[55]

JOSEPH SMITH AND THE FIRST VISION

It goes without saying that even this small bit of Mormon theology is very different from orthodox Christianity. A blurring of the line between the Creator and his creation, questions over the nature of Jesus, and the apparent dissolution of the unique oneness of God are just a few thoughts that may have popped into the mind of a non-LDS reader at this point. So, where did these differences between Mormonism and orthodox Christianity arise?

As stated before, the majority of Mormonism's story lies with Joseph Smith. While orthodox Christianity ends revelation concerning Jesus at the apostles, Latter-day Saints continue the apostolic tradition all the way to 19th century America being restored with Joseph Smith. This is where differences between Christianity and Mormonism arise, and where Christians who wish to dialogue with Latter-day Saints should begin their study of the Mormon faith. It is nearly impossible to hold a conversation about Mormonism with a Latter-day Saint without first visiting the life and works of Joseph Smith.

Joseph Smith was born on December 23, 1805 into a large Vermont family. The Smiths would later relocate to Palmyra, New York in 1816 and provided Joseph with a modest upbringing.[56] He assisted his agrarian family through farming, and by many accounts young Joseph had a very active and creative imagination during his adolescence.[57] This imagination also presented itself in a form of maturity as Smith often contemplated issues that other children did not concern themselves with.

---

[54] Brent L. Top, 'Satan,' *LDS Beliefs: A Doctrinal Reference*, eds. Robert L. Millet, et. al. (Salt Lake City: Deseret Book Co., 2011), 562.
[55] 2 Nephi 25:23; *History of the Church*, 6:302–17
[56] Joseph Smith, Jr., *History of the Church of Jesus Christ of Latter-day Saints*, Vol. 1, 2nd ed. (Salt Lake City: The Deseret Book Company, 1973), 2.
[57] Fawn M. Brodie, *No Man Knows My History: The Life of Joseph Smith* (New York: Vintage Books, 1995), 11.

At a young age, he recalls being spiritually confused by the quarreling of certain Christian denominations during a local revival.[58] Eventually, after a long period of time wrestling with this issue, Smith decided to ask God which denomination he should join in order to end his own confusion. The idea came to him after reading James; "If any of you lacks wisdom, let him ask God who gives generously to all without reproach, and it will be given him."[59]

Smith took this verse as a bidding to bring his struggles with Christian denominationalism before God in prayer and to ask him which body represented the true church. This was a major turning point in his life since the answer he received would eventually give birth to Mormonism. Yet, admittedly, I find asking God which bickering denomination you should join a bit like asking a dad which bickering child he loves best. He loves them all equally, despite their flaws, because they all contain people God loves. God does not want people to join a church to become a Christian; he wants us to become a Christian who joins a church. Then, when Jesus has given us a new heart, perhaps you could be the one he uses to end the fighting.

Regardless of his intentions, Smith decided to make the attempt in the woods solitarily. So, in 1820 at the age of fifteen, he retreated into a nearby forest to pray by himself.[60] What followed would become known as the First Vision.

It was on the morning of a beautiful, clear day, early in the spring of eighteen hundred and twenty. It was the first time in my life that I had made such an attempt, for amidst all my anxieties I had never as yet made the attempt to pray vocally. After I had retired to the place where I had previously designed to go, having looked around me, and finding myself alone, I kneeled down and began to offer up the desires of my heart to God. I had scarcely done so, when immediately I was seized upon by some power which entirely overcame me, and had such an astonishing influence over me as to bind my tongue so that I could not speak.

---

[58] Joseph Smith, Jr., *History of the Church of Jesus Christ of Latter-day Saints*, Vol. 1, 2nd ed. (Salt Lake City: The Deseret Book Company, 1973), 2–4. No record of a revival in this part of New England at this time exists outside of Smith's account; however, it may easily be taken for granted that Smith was questioning his faith considering his maturity for his age. Fawn M. Brodie, *No Man Knows My History: The Life of Joseph Smith* (New York: Vintage Books, 1995), 14.
[59] James 1:5
[60] Joseph Smith, Jr., *History of the Church of Jesus Christ of Latter-Day Saints*, Vol. 1, 2nd ed. (Salt Lake City: The Deseret Book Company, 1973), 3–4.

> Thick darkness gathered around me, and it seemed to me for
> a time as if I were doomed to sudden destruction.[61]

Two interesting aspects of Smith's account are the frightening picture of his forcibly bound tongue and his fear of sudden destruction. These should cause some concern since muteness, in particular, is not good for myriad reasons. Smith recalls an unseen power that overcame him so forcefully that it rendered him mute. This may seem like a minor detail; however, when taking biblical teaching about muteness into consideration we may draw an unsettling inference that young Joseph was dealing with something more than he obviously anticipated. Consider the following verses on muteness in scripture:

- As they were going away, behold, a *demon-oppressed* man who was *mute* was brought to [Jesus].[62]
- Then a *demon-oppressed* man who was blind and *mute* was brought to [Jesus], and he healed him, so that the man spoke and saw.[63]
- And someone from the crowd answered [Jesus], "Teacher, I brought my son to you, for *he has a spirit* that makes him *mute*."[64]
- And when Jesus saw that a crowd came running together, he rebuked the *unclean spirit*, saying to it, "You *mute* and deaf spirit, I command you, come out of him and never enter him again."[65]
- Now [Jesus] was casting out *a demon* that was *mute*. When *the demon* had gone out, the *mute* man spoke, and the people marveled.[66]

According to scripture, then, it would seem that muteness is symptomatic of demonic oppression or possession. At the very least muteness is not something one would want any association. Yet, Smith viewed his muteness as a critical detail to divulge in his memoir. By his own admission, it seems that Smith's attempt to ask God about Christian denominationalism was met with an

---

[61] Pearl of Great Price, *Writings of Joseph Smith*, 2:14–15 and Joseph Smith, Jr., *History of the Church of Jesus Christ of Latter-Day Saints*, Vol. 1, 2nd ed. (Salt Lake City: The Deseret Book Company, 1973), 4–5.
[62] Matt. 9:32, emphasis added.
[63] Matt. 12:22, emphasis added.
[64] Mark 9:17, emphasis added.
[65] Mark 9:25, emphasis added.
[66] Luke 11:14, emphasis added.

extremely unwelcomed demonic presence while he was alone. Still, the story moves past impending destruction to spectacular redemption.

> But, exerting all my powers to call upon God to deliver me out of the power of this enemy which had seized upon me, and at the very moment when I was ready to sink into despair and abandon myself to destruction—not to an imaginary ruin, but to the power of some actual being from the unseen world, who had such marvelous power as I had never before felt in any being—just at this moment of great alarm, I saw a pillar of light exactly over my head, above the brightness of the sun, which descended gradually until it fell upon me. It no sooner appeared than I found myself delivered from the enemy which held me bound. When the light rested upon me I saw two personages, whose brightness and glory defy all description, standing above me in the air. One of them spake unto me, calling me by name, and said – pointing to the other—"This is my beloved son. Hear him!"[67]

Miraculous visions such as these, commonly referred to as *theophanies*, were actually very commonplace during Smith's day. Many people reported similar experiences of personal divine encounters with God throughout the frontier country. In the new world of individualized religion, free from the shackles of centralized European Christianity, one's authority to preach and baptize no longer came from a bishop or pope, but directly from God himself. Yet, Joseph's encounter was unique in that moved beyond a simple conferral of divine approval to his calling into a radical redefinition of Christ.

We see this in Smith's use of the word *personage*. The term is introduced here early in the story of Mormonism as a first glimpse of the Mormon doctrine of God. Here the Father and the Son are not the same God, as with classic trinitarianism, but two separate personages belonging to one Godhead. Smith differentiates the Father from the Son as separately distinct *personages*, which he views as separately distinct beings altogether. In other words, there were two gods speaking to the young prophet in the forest that day, not one God in three persons. This marks a radical departure from orthodox Christianity, and Smith would have it placed at the earliest possible event in the history of Mormonism.

---

[67] Pearl of Great Price, *Writings of Joseph Smith*, 2:16–17 and Joseph Smith, Jr., *History of the Church of Jesus Christ of Latter-Day Saints*, Vol. 1, 2nd ed. (Salt Lake City: The Deseret Book Company, 1973), 5.

Interestingly, this version of Smith's encounter with the two personages is not the original version. The first time Smith penned the account was in 1832, two years following the publication of the Book of Mormon. In the original version Smith was met not by two personages but one; "the <Lord> opened the heavens upon me and I saw the Lord [who] was crucifyed [and] in the glory of [his] Father."[69] This original theophany followed the familiar pattern of similar visions by other 19th century religious leaders; an appearance by Christ alone, forgiveness of sins, and the ordination of divine authority to minister. Three years later, however, Smith expanded the vision to include both the Father and the Son. Some explain this change as evidence that Smith's understanding of God's nature evolved from one strict monotheistic being (the Father and Son as literally one being) to Mormonism's current form of bitheism (the Father and the son as literally two separate beings).

THE GATES OF HELL PREVAILED

Continuing in Smith's vision we see him move away from awe to inquiry. The young prophet had a question and the personages had an answer.

> My object in going to inquire of the Lord was to know which of all the sects was right ... No sooner, therefore, did I get possession of myself, so as to be able to speak, then I asked the personages ... which of all the sects was right (for at this time it had never entered into my heart that all were wrong)—and which I should join. I was answered that I must join none of them, for they were all wrong; and the personage who addressed me said that all their creeds were an abomination in his sight; that those professors were all corrupt; that: "they draw near to me with their lips, but their hearts are far from me, they teach for doctrines the commandments of men, having a form of godliness, but they deny the power thereof." He again forbade me to join with any of them; and many other things did he say unto me, which I cannot write at this time.[70]

---

[68] 1 Cor. 6:11

[69] Joseph Smith, "Letter Book A," *JS Letterbook 1*, in Joseph Smith Papers, 3.

[70] Pearl of Great Price, Writings of Joseph Smith, 2:18–20 and Joseph Smith, Jr., *History of the Church of Jesus Christ of Latter-Day Saints*, Vol. 1, 2nd ed. (Salt Lake City: The Deseret Book Company, 1973), 5–6.

Smith finally gets his answer, but it wasn't what he was expecting. The personages tell him not to join any church since they were completely corrupt. In fact, the churches were so corrupt that all their creeds were an abomination in the personage's sight. The Christian church as a whole had failed and needed complete restoration.

Personally, this is a hard accusation to swallow as an evangelical. It comes across as a dismissive affront on an institution that Christ himself promised would not suffer defeat. If we are to take his promises seriously, both LDS and non-LDS alike, then we must compare the personage's words in Smith's vision with Christ's words in the Gospels where he declares that "the gates of hell [would] not prevail against it."[71] It is hard to envision a complete and utter failure of the Christian church as a whole – a "Great Apostasy" as some LDS leaders have called it – when we peer into church history. For all its warts and wrongs, this is still Christ's bride we're talking about. The First Vision rings more as a clarion call for Smith's self-produced apostolic authority in my ears than it does a cry for restoration, and any LDS that truly believes the Great Apostasy must reconcile it with Christ's promise against that very pitfall.

The importance of the First Vision to Mormonism cannot be overstated. Essentially, it is the anchor of the entire faith and worldview. When dialoguing with Latter-day Saints on faith, should Smith's account of this vision arise, practice sensitive timing and tact in discussion of this most important and sacred event. Take care to clarify that they are not being attacked, but Mormonism as a whole is being examined. If the First Vision is true, then the world was forever changed in the woods that day. If this is not true, then much of Mormonism begins to unravel.

Remember to discuss Smith's legitimacy as a prophet with gentleness, meekness, and respect. Always keep the conversation on Jesus. Ask them if Smith's account contradicts the Jesus of scripture. If they respond positively, unpack that idea with them. If not, just move on to another topic for the sake of being a non-contentious and loving neighbor.

---

[71] Matt. 16:18

JOSEPH SMITH AND THE SECOND VISION

A few years passed after Smith's encounter with the personages in the woods. Many local church leaders heard of Smith's experience and grew increasingly concerned for him. They attempted to counsel Smith on the matter but he ultimately held to his belief that what he saw was a genuine message from Jesus.[72] Then, in 1823, Smith described a second vision, this time in the privacy of his home. He claimed to have been awakened by bright light during the night.[73] When he opened his eyes, he saw an old man standing next to his bed who told him that he was an angel named Moroni and had been sent from heaven to deliver a message.[74]

Moroni informed Smith that hidden among the hills near his home were buried golden plates that contained the true and complete gospel message preached by Jesus to the earlier inhabitants of the American continents – a gospel that had been lost over time. These early inhabitants, as Smith would later learn, were ancient Jews who migrated to the Americas well before Christopher Columbus discovered the New World for Europeans.

The angel also informed Smith that two "interpreters," called the Urim and the Thummim, were buried with the golden plates and were required for translating their contents. After leaving for a brief moment, Moroni returned shortly thereafter to retell the same message to Smith adding only that great desolations by "famine, sword, and pestilence" were swiftly coming to his generation, an apocalyptic message Smith would frequently preach throughout his career.[75] According to Moroni, it was now Smith's job to discover the plates in order to learn and preach the restored gospel of Jesus.

As with the First Vision, it is important to process the full implications of what Smith is recounting. The most obvious point of concern from an orthodox Christian perspective is the claim that an angel testified to the insufficiency of the gospel message. This seems to fit Paul's warning that if "we or an angel from heaven should preach to you a gospel contrary to the one

---

[72] *History of the Church of Jesus Christ of Latter-Day Saints,* Vol. 1, 2nd ed. (Salt Lake City: The Deseret Book Company, 1973), 10.
[73] Ibid., 11.
[74] Ibid.
[75] Ibid., 14.

we preached to you, let him be accursed."[76] Ponder this verse for a moment. Paul commands us to ignore any contrary gospel to the one he originally preached even if he himself preached a different message later. This is Paul we're talking about, the guy who wrote a huge chunk of the New Testament.

Additionally, Paul warns against angels introducing contrary gospel messages. Therefore, it's safe to say that absolutely no one in the universe should come and teach a gospel contrary to the one taught in the New Testament, especially if they are introducing a gospel from a Jesus who is foreign to scripture. Of course, a Latter-day Saint would view Moroni's gospel as the same message that Paul preached. However, comparing the two gospels, as we will later survey, shows differences that are important enough to render Paul's warning applicable to Moroni's message.

THE BOOK OF MORMON IS BORN

It took Smith quite some time before he managed to find the promised golden plates. In 1827, at twenty-three years old, Smith claimed to have discovered plates containing a written record of America's earliest inhabitants.[78] To critic and believer alike, the four year delay in finding the plates deserves an explanation. According to Smith, he had in fact found the plates in 1823 but was forbidden from excavating them until 1827.[79] But why such a long period of time? Four years passed and Smith supposedly knew the whereabouts of a completely new and fulfilled gospel. Why keep that a secret for four additional years? Smith gives a simple answer – he wasn't allowed.

However, his fascination with treasure hunting at that time likely contributed to the delay. There are recorded accounts of Smith hiring himself as a treasure-seeker, possibly swindling people in exchange for his services of searching for rumored Spanish gold in the local region. This was so well known to the public that Smith felt it necessary to address his "foolish errors" in his memoirs. This treasure hunting was accomplished through his use of a

---

[76] Gal. 1:8
[77] Ibid.
[78] Smith also married his first wife Emma Hale in 1827.
[79] *History of the Church of Jesus Christ of Latter-day Saints,* Vol. 1, 2nd ed. (Salt Lake City: The Deseret Book Company, 1973), 17–18.

magical seer stones to guide him, similar to those he would later use to translate the Book of Mormon.[80]

Researchers have noted the significance behind Smith's use of seer stones as it relates to early American mysticism and divination.[81] Joseph employed himself in an culture that (as strange as it may sound) secretly placed high faith in the value and utility of occultic practices. Folklore whispered promises of fabulous wealth in money-digging, a process that would grow exponentially with magical seer-stones paired with a talented diviner.[82] Smith was one such diviner, and those "foolish errors" came to defined much of his adolescence. But divining was not limited to his youth as the "seer stone," a media through which Smith previously utilized to discover buried treasure, would later assist in the transcription and formation of the Book of Mormon.[83]

With assistance from his "seer-stone," Smith repurposed his divining talents of money-digging to translating the golden plates from their native language into English following their excavation.[84] At the outset, one might expect a Native American document to be written in a known language given that the plates were an account of ancient Jewish–Native American history. If this were the case the golden plates would be subject to scholarly scrutiny to ensure proper translation. However, the language in which these golden plates were written is what Smith referred to as 'reformed Egyptian.'

This language, wholly unknown outside of this one instance, is purportedly a truncated version of Egyptian hieroglyphics. No archeological evidence for this language exists, which is peculiar for a culture said to have prudently recorded their history onto metal plates so as to require someone, Mormon, to abridge it all. Even if it were simply hieroglyphs, one historian points out, in the 1830s, "no one in America at this time could provide reliable

---

[80] Fawn M. Brodie, *No Man Knows My History: The Life of Joseph Smith* (New York: Vintage Books, 1995), 18–25.

[81] John L. Brooke, *The Refiner's Fire: The Making of Mormon Cosmology, 1644-1844* (Cambridge: Cambridge University Press, 1994), 152-53. Brooke notes that Joseph's "reputation as a diviner emerged in a culture of historically rooted magical practice," which he later identifies as money-digging via the assistance of seer-stones "perhaps bordering on the divine powers of the hermetic *magus*."

[82] Ibid., 153.

[83] Ibid., 154.

[84] Lucy Mack Smith, *Biographical Sketches of Joseph Smith, the Prophet, and His Progenitors for Many Generations* (Liverpool: S. W. Richards, ltd., 1853).

English translation of these or any other Egyptian hieroglyphs."[85] For vindication of his reformed Egyptian hypothesis, Smith had a facsimile of the language sent to Charles Anthon of Columbia University, who in turn denounced it as a hoax.[86] Despite this, many people believed Smith concerning the golden plates. One believer, Martin Harris, became a close confidant and partner of his.

Harris financed the transcription project of the Book of Mormon. Without Harris it could be argued that the Book of Mormon would have never been printed as Smith had little means to fund it himself. Indeed, much is owed by the LDS Church to Harris for his part in the transcription process. "Don't you mean *translation?*" you may have asked yourself. *Transcription,* according to Smith's account, is a more accurate way of describing the birth of the Book of Mormon. Smith would read aloud from behind a curtain that divided the room between himself and a scribe. He then donned the "interpreters," the Urim and the Thummim, which were bound by a metal rim, or used a transparent "seer stone," or a combination of both. Some accounts then have him placing the plates and seer stone into a hat to provide darkness.

It was in this darkness that the reformed Egyptian would mysteriously illuminate into an English translation. Finally, Smith would read aloud for Harris to transcribe. Integrity was ensured through an instant error-checking technique that stopped the illumination if a mistake was made, restarting only when it was corrected. For example, had a scribe written down something contrary to what Smith spoke the illuminated text would pause at the place of error until the correction was made. It was a 100% error-proof method of transcription.

---

[85] The Rosetta Stone had finished being translated by Jean-Francois Champollion in 1822 when Smith was seventeen. The Book of Mormon was fully "translated" and published by 1830 when Smith was twenty-five. This means that in just eight short years the research of Champollion was published in Paris, translated into English, made its way to the U.S., and became public knowledge that ancient Egyptian hieroglyphs were no longer cryptic mysteries. The timing lends credibility to the idea that Smith could have taken advantage of the public's interest in the newly deciphered language. When public interest is stirred in a specific topic it is easy to ride on the wave of that interest for one's own benefit. This is, however, purely speculative. See H. Michael Marquardt, 'Joseph Smith's Egyptian Papers: A History,' *The Joseph Smith Egyptian Papyri: A Complete Edition*, ed. Robert K. Ritner (Salt Lake City, Utah: Signature Books Publishing, LLC.: 2011), 13.
[86] Terryl Givens, *By the Hand of Mormon: The American Scripture that Launched a New World Religion* (Oxford: Oxford University Press, 2002), 29.

THE FIRST MORMON SKEPTIC

Doubtless, it was an exciting time for Martin Harris. In his mind he was a key instrument in bringing about God's truth into the world by working side-by-side with the true reformer and greatest prophet of the entire Christian church. One can only imagine the exhilarating delight he must have felt. In his elation Martin impulsively decided to share a part of the project with his wife, Lucy Harris. He wanted to assure his wife that the project they were financing was legitimate. So, Martin took 116 pages home in anticipation of her approval and admiration.

After being presented with the pages and learning how they were produced, Lucy decided that it was a scam. The response from his wife was not what Martin had expected. Instead of excitement Martin was met with skepticism and frustration that boiled to a point of Lucy demanding to see proof of the project's validity. As some have theorized she devised a small test in an attempt to persuade Martin of her suspicion of Smith's intentions.[87] Lucy withheld the 116-page manuscript Martin brought home until he was due to meet with Smith a few days later. According to the plan, if Smith were a prophet he could easily reproduce the 116 pages. If the Book of Mormon was a hoax, however, then he could not. This would provide irrefutable proof of whether or not Smith was truly a prophet.

Harris later met with Smith and confessed that he had misplaced the 116 pages. Smith became furious at the news and informed Harris that he needed solitude to pray about the situation. Naturally, God was displeased. Smith, whose divine transcription privileges were revoked for a season, was promised that a time would come when the project could start again. However, God warned that the 116 page manuscript, now in the hands of wicked men, would be altered and published so as to discredit Smith. To circumvent this catastrophe Smith would not retranslate the original plates, but new ones that covered roughly the same events as the originals were substituted.

At some point in time Harris informed his wife of the re-transcription process. He told her the news that God was angry with him because of her and

---

[87] Leonard J. Arrington and Davis Bitton, *The Mormon Experience: A History of the Latter-Day Saints* (New York: Alfred A. Knopf, Inc., 1992), 13.

that God would allow for a slightly varied version of the previous 116-page manuscript. Martin reaffirmed his belief that Smith was a prophet and his devotion to the Book of Mormon project, but Lucy protested. She held to her belief that it was a hoax. An argument erupted between the two and was overheard by Martin's sister-in-law, Abigail Harris. She would later recall Martin exclaim during the argument; "What if it is a lie; if you will let me alone I will make money out of it!"[88] The project would cost Martin his marriage as the two eventually separated. Smith, along with various scribes, published the Book of Mormon on March 26, 1830.

CAN I GET A WITNESS?

Smith quickly realized that similar criticism of the Book of Mormon was on the horizon. He acted preemptively by acquiring eyewitness testimony of the golden plates. This begs the question as to why he needed witnesses if the plates were in his possession anyway. Smith would simply need to produce the plates as irrefutable proof should criticism arise; however, the plates had eventually left Smith's possession. Where the plates ended up is debatable.

According to some accounts they were taken into heavenly custody by an angel.[89] Other accounts have Smith placing them in a cave near the Hill Cumorah.[90] Still to this day the LDS Church has not recovered them and has not excavated their property on the Hill Cumorah where Smith discovered and potentially returned the plates. Nevertheless, Smith believed that identifying eyewitnesses to the golden plates would silence critics long enough to foster confidence in the Book of Mormon with his new followers.

Every copy of the Book of Mormon has two lists of witnesses who testify to having seen and handled the golden plates. One list is comprised of three early leaders of the LDS movement. The other includes a man who later left the LDS Church to join a Methodist congregation in Ohio, five members of the Whitmer family, three members of Joseph Smith's family, and Martin

---

[88] Charles A. Shook, *The True Origin of the Book of Mormon* (Cincinnati, Ohio: Standard Publishing Co., 1914), 48.

[89] Dan Vogel, *Early Mormon Documents*, Vol. 5 (Salt Lake City: Signature Books, 2003), 21.

[90] Cameron J. Packer, "Cumorah's Cave," *Journal of Book of Mormon Studies*, 2004, Vol. 13, No. 1, pp. 50—57.

Harris himself who would eventually confess that he had not seen the plates with his naked eyes, but rather with his "spiritual eyes."[91]

These witnesses, along with a handful of other people, constituted Smith's new church. They packed into homes to listen to the charismatic modern prophet expound from a new and exciting religious text. But with growth came persecution. Since Smith had yet to develop a firm theological framework from which to defend his new movement, many arguments from non-Mormons centered on the authenticity and authority of that new and exciting text, the Book of Mormon.

It is easy to understand where the persecution might have originated as Latter-day Saints began to convince people that Native Americans were actually Jews from the lost tribes of Israel. (Although this sounds strange to 21st century ears, many contemporary North American and English pastors and theologians of Smith speculated as to whether Native Americans were in fact the lost tribes of Israel.)[92] This no doubt sparked a few debates and family feuds at dinner tables. The persecution eventually became too much for the small group of "Mormonites," so in 1831 Smith's followers packed up and left New York for Kirkland, Ohio in search of refuge from oppression.

MR. & MRS. & MRS. SMITH

Ohio offered Smith and his followers a small respite for about seven years. During this time, Smith was able to sharpen some of his theological ideas for the church and also introduced a more notorious aspect of Mormonism, polygamy.[93] At some point Smith had taken an inappropriate interest in a woman other than his wife. The woman's name was Fanny Alger.

Fanny, who was sixteen years old at the time, had been living with the prophet and his wife, Emma Smith, to assist with the household duties. As time

---

91 Lester L. Grabbe, "Joseph Smith and the Gestalt of the Israelite Prophet," *Ancient Israel: The Old Testament in Its Social Context* (Minneapolis, Minn.: Augsburg Fortress, 2006), 120.
92 Mordecai Manuel Noah, *Discourse on the Evidences of the American Indians Being the Descendants of the Lost Tribes of Israel* (New York: James Van Norden, 1837)
93 While polygamy was official denounced by the Church of Jesus Christ of Latter-day Saints prior to the statehood of Utah in 1890, it was nonetheless practiced by Smith and many Mormon leaders to include Brigham Young who had 27 wives, 56 children, and 306 grandchildren. Some Mormon sects still practice polygamy to this day.

went on, Joseph and Fanny grew closer and closer until finally Joseph held a secret 'celestial marriage' ceremony sometime in 1833 presided by Levi W. Hancock, an early LDS leader. Accounts of what happened next are difficult to wade through. Some believe Smith received a revelation from God to begin practicing polygamy as early as 1831, but the command may have come well after Fanny. Ultimately, Smith and Fanny were unable to keep their 'celestial marriage' a secret as they were eventually caught together. Oliver Cowdery, one of the original witnesses to the golden plates, described their relationship as "a dirty, nasty, filthy affair"[94] and was later excommunicated for "falsely insinuating that [Smith] was guilty of adultery."[95] When Emma learned of the relationship, she did not take the news lightly. Neighbors reported her driving Fanny from the Smith's residence in a fit of rage.[96]

The scandal grew too large for Smith to ignore as more and more criticism threatened to destroy the already fragile Mormon community. Around this time – precisely when is unknown – Smith began to teach a few associates that God was reinstated polygamy as it was practiced in the Old Testament period. This was despite the fact that God only tolerated the sin of polygamy with the Old Testament saints having never once condoned the practice.[97] Eventually, by 1843, Smith's teaching was recorded as a revelation and canonized in the Mormon scripture Doctrine & Covenants (D&C).

> God commanded Abraham, and Sarah gave Hagar to Abraham to wife. Was Abraham, therefore, under condemnation? Nay; for I, the Lord, commanded it. Abraham received concubines and they bore him children; and it was accounted unto him for righteousness. I am the Lord thy God, and I gave unto thee, my servant Joseph, an appointment, and restore all things.[98]

And to ensure cooperation from his first wife, Emma;

---

[94] Fawn M. Brodie, *No Man Knows My History: The Life of Joseph Smith* (New York: Vintage Books, 1995), 182.

[95] *History of the Church of Jesus Christ of Latter-day Saints,* Vol. 3, 2nd ed. (Salt Lake City: The Deseret Book Company, 1973), 16.

[96] Fawn M. Brodie, *No Man Knows My History: The Life of Joseph Smith* (New York: Vintage Books, 1995), 182.

[97] Although Old Testament prophets and kings were men of God who practiced polygamy, the practice was never once ordained by God and usually resulted in trouble for the men who practiced it. God established marriage as a covenant between one man and one woman at the very beginning. See Genesis 2:22–25.

[98] Doctrine & Covenants 132:37–40

> I say unto you: A commandment I give unto mine handmaid, Emma Smith, your wife. Let [her] receive all those that have been given unto my servant Joseph...to abide and cleave unto my servant Joseph, and to none else. But if she will not abide...she shall be destroyed, saith the Lord; for I am the Lord thy God, and will destroy her if she abide not in my law.[99]

While Joseph was now free to marry whomever he desired so long as it was under the guise of 'celestial marriage,' Emma was bound to him by the direct order of Heavenly Father himself. She would die if she did not obey. Smith took this new liberty to heart and would marry a total of forty-eight women, one as young as fifteen years old when Smith was thirty-nine years old.[100]

THE PERSECUTED DRIVEN MORMONS

Smith's preaching continued to attract more converts despite mounting criticism for his polygamous reputation. Similar to the unrest in Palmyra, Kirkland eventually did not take kindly to the Mormon group. Smith's church was tolerated to a certain degree, but he suspected future persecution and, in accordance with another vision of expanding further westward, Smith divided the church into two groups. One remained in Kirkland while the other traveled to the frontier of Jackson County, Missouri.

Local Missourians met these frontier Mormons with fierce resistance. Murder, strife, economic failure, and civil unrest on both sides forced the Latter-day Saints out of Missouri despite Smith's persistence for a Mormon settlement there. His reluctance to abandon the Missouri settlement may be due, at least in part, to his prophecy concerning the building of a great temple within Missouri borders.[101] This prophecy, however, ultimately failed as Smith would not live to see a single temple built in Missouri.

---

[99] Doctrine & Covenants 132:51–54

[100] Fawn M. Brodie, *No Man Knows My History: The Life of Joseph Smith* (New York: Vintage Books, 1995), 488.

[101] Doctrine & Covenants 84:2–5, 31

The Latter-day Saints were eventually driven out of Missouri in 1838.[102] The newly reassembled LDS Church, now accompanied by the Kirkland Saints, headed northward in search of yet another place to call their home. They finally settled in a small Mississippi River community in Illinois. Dubbed *Nauvoo* by Smith, here the Mormons enjoyed relative peace, prosperity, and growth. The Latter-day Saints became a medium-sized community for that time and location. By 1844, Nauvoo had swollen to over 11,000 citizens, well over twice the population of the up-and-coming city of Chicago in the same state.[103]

The Latter-day Saints were even afforded the opportunity to build a temple for sacraments and worship during this time. It must have seemed that Smith's community had reached a high point after years of turmoil and strife. They finally succeeded in building a Mormon community free from persecution and needed no one but themselves to prosper. Now, they could breathe a little easier. Smith continued to grow the church by sending missionaries across the country and overseas. He also bolstered the church's reputation with a bid for the U.S. presidency while in Nauvoo in 1844. This utopian era would not last, however, as persecution once again stood at their doorstep.

THE DEATH OF A LEADER

In 1844, a local news outlet, *The Nauvoo Expositor*, began running anti-Mormon articles to warn locals of spiritual and physical security threats posed by the Latter-day Saints. Smith was enraged by the slander. In June, the prophet ordered the destruction of the small press, a highly contentious move in a young republic that had just secured the right to free speech one generation earlier.[104] His order resulted in the arrest and imprisonment of Smith, his brother Hyrum, and some of the LDS leaders; however, this was not good enough for the local Illinoisans who wanted Smith dead and the Mormons gone.

---

102 Leland H. Gentry, "Missouri Conflict," in *Encyclopedia of Mormonism*, vol. 2, 4 vols. (New York: Macmillian Publishing Company, 1992), 927.
103 Laurel B. Andrew, *Early Temples of the Mormons: The Architecture of the Millennial Kingdom in the American West* (Albany, NY: State University of New York Press, 1978), 56.
104 Glen M. Leonard, *Nauvoo: A Place of Peace, A People of Promise* (Salt Lake City: Deseret Book Co., 2002), 114.

On June 27, 1844, a mob attacked and overran the jail holding Smith in the neighboring town of Carthage. This resulted in an armed shoot-out between the mob and the Mormon leaders in the jail to include Joseph Smith himself. He was fatally shot in the back while attempting to escape through a second story window after managing to shoot three assailants himself.[105] Smith's last words, "Oh Lord, my God,"[106] may have been a 19th century Masonic distress signal that fell on deaf ears.[107] The saints in Nauvoo received news of his death that night; "Joseph and Hyrum are dead. Taylor wounded, not very badly."[108] The Mormons had tragically lost their leader.

Today, many Latter-day Saints view the death of Joseph Smith as a heroic martyrdom leaving out altogether his contribution to the fight. In fact, the official LDS guided tour of the jail in Carthage, Illinois completely omits any violent involvement by Smith during the skirmish. This is, above most events in Smith's life, a sensitive topic for many Latter-day Saints to discuss. Should his death arise in conversation with a Latter-day Saint, it would be best not to dwell on his actions but shift the focus from Smith's asserted martyrdom to Jesus' death, burial, and resurrection – the greatest and most victorious martyrdom in history.

Compare Carthage to Calvary. Jesus' death is saturated with true martyrdom, forgiveness, and sacrificial love.[109] There is victory and triumph as he rose three days later, while Joseph Smith still lies in his burial. They will most assuredly agree, but establishing the crucifixion–resurrection event as the

---

[105] Fawn M. Brodie, *No Man Knows My History: The Life of Joseph Smith* (New York: Vintage Books, 1995), 393.

[106] *History of the Church of Jesus Christ of Latter-Day Saints*, Vol. 6, 2nd ed. (Salt Lake City: The Deseret Book Company, 1973), 618.

[107] The full Masonic distress signal was "Oh Lord, My God, is there no help for the widow's son?" A Mormon eyewitness to the event readily understood the meaning of Smith's last words; "Masons, it is said, were even among the mob that murdered Joseph and Hyrum in Carthage jail. Joseph, leaping the fatal window, gave the Masonic signal of distress. The answer was the roar of his murderers' muskets." (Orson F. Whitney, *Life of Heber C. Kimball* [Salt Lake City: Juvenile Instructor Office, 1888], 26). John Taylor who was jailed with Smith during the raid also recognized the significance of his last statement; "In Carthage jail Joseph Smith and Hyrum Smith gave such signs of distress as would have commanded the interposition and benevolence of Savages or Pagans. They were both Masons in good standing...Joseph's last exclamation was, 'O Lord, my God!'"(*Times and Seasons*, Vol. 5, No. 13, 15 July 1844, 585).

[108] *History of the Church of Jesus Christ of Latter-Day Saints*, Vol. 6, 2nd ed. (Salt Lake City: The Deseret Book Company, 1973), 621.

[109] Heb. 9:26; John 18:10–11

cornerstone of the Christian faith is vital for healthy dialogue with Latter-day Saints. Take any opportunity given to discuss it.

While Smith's life and death reveal much of his own character and the LDS Church's desire to glorify him, it is generally not something Latter-day Saints like to discuss. It reveals historical flaws in Smith's character that challenge their long held concepts of the Mormon prophet as an inspired man far above reproach. Attacking Joseph Smith's character can only prove that he was not a good man, rather than proving he was a fraud. Concentrate on the real issues surrounding Smith's theology as opposed to Smith's character when dialoguing with Latter-day Saints. As with any truth claim, at the end of the day it does not matter who devised it; although knowing their character may assist in formulating an opinion.

The person who invents a worldview or truth claim is irrelevant to the validity of the truth claim itself. What ultimately matters is not who said it but what was said. If Isaac Newton was a kleptomaniac would that invalidate his discovery of gravity? Likewise, simply because Joseph Smith lived a manner that many would view as trustworthy does not necessarily mean Mormon theology is wrong. We should emphasize what is actually being said about God, about the world, and about Jesus. This is where true transformation occurs – in the knowledge of the gospel.

WESTWARD HO!

A fierce debate arose among the Latter-day Saints as to who would succeed Smith as prophet immediately following his death. Due to his untimely departure he had not left behind marching orders for his successor. The clear choice among a majority of the Latter-day Saints was Brigham Young, Smith's closest friend and advisor. Others favored Joseph Smith's son while some sided with various LDS Church leaders. Young wanted to move westward to an envisioned promised land free of persecution where the church could continue to receive revelation from God. Other saints disagreed and believed that Smith was the final authority to be carried out in apostolic succession. In their mind the new leader's responsibility was to guide the church by utilizing the finished revelation of Smith.

This issue was never fully resolved as the LDS Church splintered into different factions. The largest group of saints accepted Young's leadership. These Mormons would come to adopt the name *Church of Jesus Christ of Latter-day Saints*, the group more commonly referred to today as Latter-day Saints. Only a fraction of the LDS Church stayed in the Midwestern states (Community of Christ, Fundamentalist LDS, Church of Christ – Temple Lot, etc.).

Under Young's leadership the Latter-day Saints packed up and headed west in 1846. This expedition was met with months of hardship traveling across the vast expanse of the Great Plains and Rocky Mountains. However, their endurance and adversity paid off as the LDS Church found a place to call home that still stands to this day. Salt Lake City was established in 1847 under the direction of Young, who was appointed governor of the Utah Territory by President Millard Fillmore.[110] Today, Salt Lake City is a bustling metropolis in the middle of what otherwise would have been an unforgiving landscape of desert and mountains.

---

[110] In February of 1849, Young drafted a proposal for the State of Deseret which would have encompassed all of modern Utah, Nevada, half of California, Colorado, Arizona, and parts of New Mexico, Oregon, Idaho, and Wyoming just one year after the United States gained this land from Mexico.[1] The State of Deseret's constitution, and ordinances finding their power in the constitution, reflected Mormon morality. One law passed placed a five dollar fine for using Jesus' name in vain.[2] Another law outlawed homosexuality, which was punishable by imprisonment.[3] To say Young was attempting to create a Zionist utopia would be an understatement – the State of Deseret, with Salt Lake City as its capitol, would be the new Israel and Jerusalem on earth from which the true gospel of Jesus Christ would flow. The term "deseret" comes from the Book of Mormon which means 'honeybee'. This is why today you have not only a honeybee's nest on the Utah state flag, but the hidden date of 1847 behind it, in between the two draped flags. The State of Utah was not officially accepted into the union until 1896. The result of Young's actions towards local Mormon sovereignty and against the United States government resulted in a peaceful intervention with the U.S. Army in 1858 when Young then lost his governorship. Ever since this event, Latter-day Saints have run into many state issues because of their beliefs. To the regret of almost every single Latter-day Saint today polygamy, racism, and violence have plagued the history of the LDS Church from the time they settled in Salt Lake City. Most notably, part of the reason Utah was not granted statehood earlier was the persistence of Latter-day Saints in practicing polygamy which began with Joseph Smith marrying a total of thirty-three women with some as young as fourteen.[4][5] By many accounts, Brigham Young had fifty-five wives.[6] Racism persisted within their community as the LDS Church did not accept blacks and Native Americans into full communion until 1978.[7] This despite the Book of Mormon's invitation of salvation to all humanity, "black and white, bond and free, male and female."[8] Violence also plagued the newly settled Latter-day Saints as they carried out the largest attacks on U.S. soil in the nation's history until September 11th, 2001. Mormon assailants disguised themselves as Native Americans and raided an emigrant caravan headed for California killing over 120 Americans.[9] At the time, this was the single deadliest terrorist attack committed on American soil. Ironically, the Mountain Meadows Massacre was also carried out on September 11th, 1857. Latter-day Saints are not proud of this history and are deeply repentant; however, they provide a warning flag to the underlying power behind the LDS Church's growth and expansion in spite of such atrocities.

MORMON SCRIPTURE: THE BIBLE

Now that we have a good idea of the origin of Mormonism, let's turn our attention to the origin of Mormon theology. Almost everything Latter-day Saints are taught originates from four main works – the King James Version of the Bible, the Book of Mormon, Doctrine & Covenants, and the Pearl of Great Price. These works will be examined in enough detail to assist us in Mormon evangelism, but a deeper study of the last three works will reveal much of why Latter-day Saints believe what they believe, which will give us a better understanding of how to dialogue with them. An important thing to remember is that many Latter-day Saints, for the most part, are faithful students of their scriptures.

In all honesty, Latter-day Saints tend to know more about the Bible than most evangelicals. It is my personal experience that Latter-day Saints are, generally speaking, more biblically literate than most orthodox Christians. While knowledge about scripture does not guarantee anything beyond knowledge, it most certainly helps to have intimate knowledge of scripture. The limitation with a Latter-day Saint's knowledge of scripture is, in my opinion, the restrictions placed on it by Mormon theology. They may know scripture well, but as G.I. Joe can attest, knowing is only half the battle. An understanding must always accompany biblical wisdom or else we study and learn in vain.

For the most part, Latter-day Saints know their Bible well and spend their entire lives studying the King James Version (KJV). They spend many hours of their youth in Mormon catechesis, called seminary. Latter-day Saints are most comfortable with the KJV, the translation that they believe is the closest English translation of the original Greek and Hebrew. Officially, the LDS Church does not accept other translations (with the exception of one) due to a fear of the corruption of biblical texts passed down to us since the original authors first penned their works. As it turns out, the KJV is one of only two English translations that have escaped corruption due to its translation. All other translations, to include the ESV, NIV, NASB, etc., are flawed and cannot be trusted as a reliable source of scripture. This is such an important belief for Latter-day Saints that their *Articles of Faith* declare,

"We believe the Bible to be the Word of God in so far as it is translated correctly."[111]

This article is frequently cited by Latter-day Saints to explain the Mormon belief that any Bible they utilize must be one that was not 'corrupted' by bad translations through the years by the historic Christian Church. This is a similar argument given by many atheists and skeptics who wholly reject the Bible on the grounds of faulty transcription of the texts. The argument accuses the historic Christian Church of having suppressed certain truths about scripture to fit orthodox theology. A good Mormon scholar might take you to 1 Nephi to support their argument that any version aside from the KJV is corrupted.

> And after they go forth by the hand of the twelve apostles of the Lamb, from the Jews unto the Gentiles, thou seest the formation of that great and abominable church, which is most abominable above all other churches; for behold, they have taken away from the gospel of the Lamb many parts which are plain and most precious; and also many covenants of the Lord have they taken away. And all this have they done that they might pervert the right ways of the Lord, that they might blind the eyes and harden the hearts of the children of men.[112]

This verse led the early LDS apostle, Orson Pratt, to ask, "Who knows that even one verse of the whole Bible has escaped pollution, so as to convey the same sense now that it did in the original?"[113] It could be suggested to Mr. Pratt that since scripture, being God's Word, is the foundation of the Christian faith, how can we expect to stand in confidence on an unstable and shaken foundation?

One may be quick to respond that Jesus is the foundation of our faith and scripture is just a part of it. Perhaps Paul had them in mind when he wrote that the Christian faith is, "built on the foundation of the apostles and prophets, Christ Jesus himself being the cornerstone."[114] Without knowing what the apostles and prophets taught, how can the cornerstone of our faith be confirmed and trusted?

---

[111] Joseph Smith, Jr., *History of the Church of Jesus Christ of Latter-Day Saints*, Vol. 6, 2nd ed. (Salt Lake City: The Deseret Book Company, 1973), 541.
[112] 1 Nephi 13:26–27
[113] Orson Pratt, *Divine Authenticity of the Book of Mormon* (Liverpool: 1850), 47.
[114] Eph. 2:20

Let us also remember, both LDS and non-LDS alike, the promise God made that his word would be preserved for all ages, not recovered in 19th century America. Jesus said that, "heaven and earth will pass away, but my words will not pass away."[115] This prophetic promise is further bolstered by over five thousand manuscript copies all testifying that the Bible we use today is a faithful witness to the original autographs.[116] This should provide ample evidence that the Bible we have today is the Bible God intends for us to have, one that does not require correction or is in some way incomplete. Regardless, Latter-day Saints still hold the notion that scripture has somehow been corrupted by those pesky medieval scribes and requires a divine translation to restore the spiritual truths left out by human error or sabotage.

The KJV fulfills this for the most part, but falls short of complete perfection since it tends to leave out important LDS doctrine purportedly removed sometime in the past. Latter-day Saints turn to the pinnacle of Mormon Bible translations to fill these theological gaps in the KJV – the Joseph Smith Translation (JST). The JST is the Bible of choice among many Latter-day Saints who view it as a spiritually fuller rendition of the KJV. In fact, the JST is simply the KJV with substantial editing rather than a direct translation from the original languages into English.

The JST is especially useful as an aid for Latter-day Saints to reconcile perceived inconsistencies between common English translations of the Bible and in Mormon theology. It is considered the most complete and proper translation of the Bible due mainly to Joseph Smith's "reintroduction" of Mormon theology into the text. With this in mind, the JST is a powerful apparatus of the LDS Church to reinforce Mormon theology and may cause some confusion or contention when dialoguing with Latter-day Saints.

Some years ago, while meeting with a wonderful Mormon family and some Mormon missionaries, our discussion led to the Genesis narrative about humanity's fall through Adam.[117] Up until this point, the KJV was the Bible of choice, and we were all happily dialoguing from it. The conversation took an interesting turn when the husband stated, "That's why Adam and Eve had to

---

[115] Mark 13:31
[116] Norman L. Geisler and William E. Nix, *A General Introduction to the Bible* (Chicago: Moody Press, 1986), 402.
[117] Genesis 3

sin. If not, we wouldn't have been able to exist. So, essentially, the fall of humanity was a good thing." In a nutshell, the husband was arguing in support of a Mormon idea that portrays the fall of humanity as good and necessary since humanity would not have come into existence given Eve's inability to bear children while in the Garden of Eden. The Mormon missionaries agreed with the husband's interpretation.

At the time this idea was completely novel to me, so the husband's passing comment stuck out. I began to think about how I could demonstrate that the fall was not only a terrible thing but that Eve would have been able to give birth in the garden. The idea of Eve's in-garden barrenness comes from a verse unique to the Mormon scripture; "And Eve [said]: Were it not for our transgression we never should have had seed."[118] I didn't know where to begin to push back against this idea, so I simply guessed and started scanning the third chapter of Genesis where this narrative occurs. After a bit, I found an interesting verse that seemed to speak against that idea. "Well, if that's true," I asserted, "then why did God tell Eve that he would greatly multiply her pain during childbirth? If you multiply something, doesn't that mean it had to exist in the first place in order for it to be multiplied?"

The young missionaries looked puzzled. The husband flipped his KJV to the beginning and scanned down the page with his finger until he came to the text I was referring to. He read Genesis 3:16 aloud so everyone was on the same page; "Unto the woman he said, I will greatly multiply thy sorrow and thy conception; in sorrow thou shalt bring forth children."[119] He pondered this for a moment, his eyes scanning back and forth over the passage. The missionaries sat staring into their Bibles. To me this seemed like the kind of push back that would result in continued fruitful dialogue.

The husband placed his finger on the page and closed the Bible. He looked up, smiled at everyone, and said, "You know, I think this might be something of a translation error." The missionaries readily agreed. I was confused. He turned to his wife; "Honey, would you grab the JST off my desk for me please?" She obliged and returned with a thick, leather-bound book. I

---

[118] Moses 5:11
[119] Gen. 3:16, KJV

would later learn this book was called a "Quad" – all of the Mormon scriptures in one book.

He opened it and reread the passage from the JST; "Unto the woman, I, the Lord God, said, I will greatly multiply thy sorrow, and thy conception; in sorrow thou shalt bring forth children."[120] It was different but not what he was looking for. Still troubled by the implications of Genesis 3:15, and with no help from the JST, he politely wrapped up the evening and wished me a good night.

That time the JST didn't help. This is not to say, however, the JST will always agree with the KJV. When dialoguing with Latter-day Saints, if the JST assists them in defending their theology, the KJV will quickly find itself obsolete. At this point it will be very difficult to continue the conversation. The JST did not help my LDS friends that night, but this serves as a good example of how the JST can sometimes assist Latter-day Saints in defending Mormon theology. It might be a good idea to have a copy of the JST on hand to know if the verses you plan to discuss have been altered. Also, the "Quad" is not a bad investment for those who meet with Latter-days Saints often.

IS THE JOSEPH SMITH TRANSLATION LEGIT?

Before we throw out the JST as a legitimate biblical translation it is only fair that we give it a good examination. To begin, a generally accepted rule is that Bible translations are only as reliable as their translators. Considering Smith's academic pedigree the initial prospect of the JST's legitimacy is bleak. Smith created the JST by revising bits in the Bible that he felt had been corrupted over many years of transmission. This was done despite his lack of any robust formal training in the ancient Hebrew and Greek, let alone English. Smith essentially retranslated the KJV through the Mormon hermeneutic.[121]

This is made apparent in many places throughout the JST concerning passages that contradict Mormon theology. For example, Mormonism rejects the orthodox concept of the Trinity. According to Mormon theology the Father and the Son are two distinct personages unified in will and desire alone. They are not the same God, but two separate gods. Yet, as we see in the Gospel of

---

[120] Gen. 3:22, JST
[121] A *hermeneutic* is a method or system by which one interprets a text like the Bible.

John (1:1,14), Jesus is not simply a god but God himself. However, the JST reinforces Mormon theology by stripping this passage of its trinitarianism.

This is not to say we cannot use John 1:1,14 to demonstrate Jesus' divinity and the JST's unreliability. A quick comparison of John 1:1 between the KJV and JST reveals that Smith deliberately targeted passages concerning the triune nature of God. John 1:1 in the KJV reads, "In the beginning was the Word, and the Word was with God, and the Word was God." Later, John 1:14 identifies the Word as Jesus; thus, Jesus is God. In the JST, John 1:1 reads, "In the beginning was the gospel preached through the Son. And the gospel was the word, and the word was with the Son, and the Son was with God, and the Son was of God."

Theological belief aside, is this a valid translation of this verse? The short answer is no. Accuracy for Smith's translation of John 1:1 demands the presence of the Greek word for *gospel* or εὐαγγέλιον (euaggelion). Unfortunately for Smith εὐαγγέλιον does not appear in the entire Gospel of John. Not once. In fact, John only uses εὐαγγέλιον once in the entire Bible.[122] For this reason, the JST translation of John 1:1 is absurd when one considers the original Greek. John meant to teach that Jesus is divine; he and God are ontologically the same.

Elsewhere, Smith strips the sovereignty of God's will in John 6:44 and replaces it with human exertion for their own salvation by works. The ESV renders this verse: "No one can come to me unless the Father who sent me draws him. And I will raise him up on the last day." Here, Jesus is teaching that God the Father is the ultimate source of our salvation. It eliminates the idea that we save ourselves in any form. It is by God's grace alone that we are saved, and we can in no way contribute to our salvation.

This contradicts the Mormon view of salvation, which blends grace and works for salvation. Consequently, in the JST we see substantial alteration; "No man can come unto me, except he doeth the will of my Father who hath sent me. And this is the will of him who hath sent me, that ye receive the Son; for the Father beareth record of him and he who receiveth the testimony, and doeth the will of him who sent me, I will raise up in the resurrection of the just."

According to this translation Jesus taught that salvation is dependent on our own obedience and works righteousness (obedience to the "will of him who sent me"). Again, theological beliefs aside, even as an academic exercise this translation falls short as it substantially adds to the original text. Smith introduces words into the verse that are simply not there in the original Greek. He literally made them up. This is because in the Mormon idea of salvation, that being a blend of grace and works for various postmortal rewards, a proper translation of John 6:44 makes no sense. Smith needed to change the meaning of this verse entirely to bring it in conformity with Mormon theology. With these small bits of information alone, the JST stands on dismissible grounds as even a poor English translation of scripture, let alone a misleading one.

Many Latter-day Saints recognize limitations of strictly using the JST on doctrinal issues and typically appeal to other works of Joseph Smith for theological justification of the differences in translation between the JST and all other English Bibles. When dialoguing with a Latter-day Saint, politely ask them to stick with the KJV for continuity sake. Otherwise, the JST may remove or alter some passages you rely on to discuss theology. If they stick by the JST, then use a translation of your choice but be prepared to hit major roadblocks in the conversation. Yielding to the JST is not only imprudent and dishonest to the original text of scripture but it is also severely limiting to genuine dialogue about the differences between our two worldviews.

Of course, a Latter-day Saint may feel uncomfortable departing with the JST. After all, they've been taught that even the KJV was subject to corruption by having plain and precious truths stripped from the translation. At this point, the discussion will orbit the issue of authority. If Joseph Smith is a trustworthy authority then perhaps God reinserted truth into the biblical text for the benefit of humanity. If he is not, however, then much is at stake given the implications of Smith's revision. Ultimately, we must hold a dialogue on who Jesus is from both perspectives. There is a recognizable difference between them, so the question becomes why that difference exists.

MORMON SCRIPTURE: THE PEARL OF GREAT PRICE

The Pearl of Great Price was first printed in 1851 as a means to teach British LDS about Mormonism. It is essentially a collection of five works; selections

---

[122] Rev. 14:6

from the book of Moses, the book of Abraham, Gospel of Matthew (JST), Joseph Smith – History, and the Articles of Faith. Two portions of the JST constitute the book of Moses and Gospel of Matthew (JST), offering the Pearl of Great Price's readers a glimpse of important verses retranslated by Smith. Joseph Smith – History is an excerpt from *History of the Church, Vol. 1* that recounts Smith's First Vision, which serves as a quick reference for the events that transpired according to Smith.

Finally, the Articles of Faith is the closest thing to a systematic theology that the LDS Church has ever officially published. It constitutes thirteen declarations of faith to which every Latter-day Saint should ascribe. This is a very good authoritative standard from which Mormon theology may be drawn. For example, the second article clearly places Mormonism into a camp that denies original sin.[123] The third article demonstrates the Mormon view of salvation as a blend of grace and works. The eighth article reaffirms the LDS Church's commitment to the Book of Mormon as scriptural.

Recently, one section in the Pearl of Great Price, the book of Abraham, has received a lot of attention. This work came about when, in 1835, a man by the name of Michael H. Chandler came in contact with Joseph Smith. Chandler was of particular interest to Smith because he owned a collection of ancient Egyptian artifacts. Smith persuaded Chandler to sell him the artifacts for a steep $2,400.[124] Then, the divining translator devoted a great deal of time to studying the artifacts and concluded that they were vessels of previously undiscovered scripture. By amazing luck or providence, Smith happened upon these ancient Egyptian artifacts which, when properly translated by him, would give way for unique Mormon theology. Yet, to call the book of Abraham a translation of Egyptian artifacts is a stretch, something even the LDS Church has recently admitted. Instead, a more reasonable assumption is that Smith created a unique text based on his own limited knowledge of ancient languages. For example, the text informs us that God resides near the star of Kolob.[125]

---

[123] *The Articles of Faith 2*, "We believe that men will be punished for their own sins, and not for Adam's transgression." Consequently, this view of humanity's sinfulness denies that we are guilty even before birth and asserts that everyone is born with a morally "blank slate". This is despite scriptural evidence that suggests that we are born into sin as sinners in need of God's redemption. See Ps. 51:5 and Rom. 5:12–14

[124] Osborne J. P. Widtsoe and Joseph F. Smith, *The Restoration of the Gospel: A Mormon Perspective* (Salt Lake City: Deseret Book Co., 1925), 116. *See also* Book of Abraham 3:9.

This word sounds strange, seemingly fabricated out of thin air. But there is logic behind "kolob." It is widely known that Joseph Smith received Hebrew language training at Kirkland, Ohio at the School of the Prophets during the mid-1830s near the time when the book of Abraham artifacts were acquired. It is very possible, then, that Smith put these new Hebrew language skills to work in constructing "kolob" by slightly altering the Hebrew word for 'star,' which is *kowkab*. Another example, from Abraham 3:13-16, is the word "kokaubeam" which, according to Smith, means "stars." This may also be an expansion of the Hebrew *kowkab*. Elsewhere, Smith translates the Hebrew word for eternity as "gnolaum," which is apparently an old transliteration of the Hebrew *owlam*, meaning 'eternity.'

Such pseudo-Hebrew words pepper the text in support of the main purpose of the book of Abraham, which is to give an emendated creation narrative as found in Genesis. This, of course, implies that the Genesis narrative is false or incomplete at best. Apparently missing from the Genesis account of creation, aside from Kolob, is the story about a counsel of gods who met together before the creation of the world in order to discuss how it would be made and function.

According to the book of Abraham, God, under the authority of an assembly of intelligences, took existing material and formed the earth. (Mormonism rejects creation *ex nihilo* in exchange for a radical materialism where even God is made of matter.) God created earth to provide preexisting intelligences, or premortal humans, the chance to follow his commands. Two intelligences, the Son of Man and Lucifer, both bade to assist in the planet's governorship, but God opted for Jesus, causing Lucifer to rebel. Immediately afterwards, the gods "organized and formed the heavens and the earth (Abr. 4:1)." What follows is a revision of the Genesis text with a consistently improper translation of the Hebrew *elohim* as "gods." While elohim can be the plural of *god* in certain instances, it is certainly not true that it must be plural in all cases. Take, for example, the monotheistic verse Deuteronomy 6:4, "Hear, O Israel: The Lord our God, the Lord is one." Following Smith's translation, we would end up with the absurdly confusing "the Lord our *gods*, the Lord is one."

---

[125] Pearl of Great Price, *Book of Abraham*, 3:9

It would seem, then, that the book of Abraham teaches a plurality of gods, which necessitates that Mormonism be described as polytheistic even if their worship is focused toward the Godhead and no other deities (or *monolatry*). For this reason, among many, the book of Abraham is an extremely important piece of Mormon scripture. Unfortunately, like the Book of Mormon, the artifacts from which the text were created eventually became lost to history, robbing us of the ability to confirm Smith's translation.

For a long time the papyri were thought the have been destroyed in the Great Chicago Fire of 1871 after having been sold in 1856 by Smith's family. Then, in 1967, ten fragments were discovered in the Metropolitan Museum of Art in New York City.[126] They were soon transferred to the LDS Church and published in a popular Church magazine.[127] Finally, researchers would be able to determine whether Smith provided an accurate translation of the artifacts based on the extant fragments. It was not long before the answer became clear – the book of Abraham was not a proper translation. None of the characters matched any of the book of Abraham, nor was Abraham's name even mentioned.

Instead, Egyptologists determined that the facsimiles were religious ritual instructions belonging to a work called the *Book of Breathings* that dated back to the Ptolemaic Era (305–30BCE).[128] As Mormon researcher Harry L. Ropp clarified the issue, "Joseph's translation in no way corresponds to the writing on the papyrus. From the 46 characters in the manuscript, Smith produces 1,125 English words, including over 65 proper names."[129] These manuscripts were said to belong to the same genre as the *Book of the Dead*, not Jewish antiquity.[130] Despite this, some within the LDS community contend that a final judgment cannot be made since we do not have the complete collection of artifacts available to Smith. A quick look at exactly how he used the extant material, however, casts a looming doubt over this hope.

---

[126] John Gee, *A Guide to the Joseph Smith Papyri* (Provo, UT: Foundation for Ancient Research and Mormon Studies, 2000), 2.
[127] Jerald Ray Johansen, *A Commentary on the Pearl of Great Price: A Jewel Among the Scriptures* (Bountiful, Utah: Horizon Publishers & Distributors Inc., 1985), 161.
[128] Robert L. Millet, *A Different Jesus? The Christ of the Latter-day Saints* (Grand Rapids, Mich.: Wm. B. Eerdmans Publishing Co., 2005), 156.
[129] R. Phillip Roberts, *Mormonism Unmasked* (Nashville, Tenn.: B&H Publishing Group, 1998), 114.
[130] Ibid., 113.

For example, it was discovered that Object 1 on the first artifact (*Figure 1.1*) was not an angel of the Lord as described by Smith, but a representation of a deceased person's soul. Object 2 on the same facsimile, which was said to be Abraham fastened to an altar, was actually a deceased Egyptian citizen. Finally, Object 3 was determined to be Anubis, the god of embalming, preparing a body for mummification. Smith understood this object to be a priest of Elkenah attempting to sacrifice Abraham.

Figure 1.1

Facsimile 1 as published in the book of Abraham. Reproduction with permission from the Church of Jesus Christ of Latter-day Saints, *A Facsimile from the Book of Abraham*, No. 1, (Salt Lake City, Utah), 28, © 1979 by Intellectual Reserve, Inc.

Figure 1.2

Facsimile 2 as published in the book of Abraham. Image above is a reproduction from *Times and Seasons* 3, no. 10 (Nauvoo, Illi.: March 15, 1842).

The second artifact (*Figure 1.2*) was the source of Smith's doctrine that Heavenly Father, who is the god of this planet, governs earth from a planet near the star of Kolob. Contrarily, Egyptologists determined this to be nothing more than a *hypocephalus*, a cloth placed under the head or feet of a deceased Egyptian to assist them in remembering what to say in their afterlife judgment. An English translation of the word "Kolob" could not be found anywhere on the artifact.

These findings were a source of criticism against Mormonism for years, and placed the LDS Church in the awkward position of explaining why their founding prophet did not actually achieve a proper translation of the text. Their solution is very unsatisfactory. Officially, the book of Abraham is Mormon scripture based on a text that has nothing to do with the text itself because it aligns with "saving truths." In other words, it does not matter that Smith did not provide a true translation so long as what he wrote was true.

Essentially, the LDS Church is saying, "Joseph Smith translated the German phrase 'Ich liebe dich' as 'The train station is blue,' even though the actual translation of that German phrase should read 'I love you.' Yet, in the end, this counts as revelation because the point of the translation is to inform us that the train station is blue." When compared to other scripture, this explanation is so bizarre as to render it practically risible. Imagine for a moment that we discovered that the Gospel of Matthew was not an account of Jesus' life, but was actually a collection of Roman tax documents, and you'll quickly realize the issue at hand. This is wholly unsatisfactory.

MORMON SCRIPTURE: DOCTRINE & COVENANTS

Unlike the other sacred texts in the LDS Church, Doctrine & Covenants (D&C) is not the divine product of miraculous translation. Instead, D&C is a collection of revelations, primarily given through Smith, in 138 sections and 2 declarations. While much of D&C is general instruction, it also introduces certain Mormon distinctives such as baptism for the dead and celestial marriage.

---

[131] Pearl of Great Price, *Book of Moses*, 5:10-11

The authenticity of D&C is unquestionably solid, unlike other Mormon scripture, which turns our attention towards content over origins.

Unlike the Book of Mormon, which raises myriad theological and historical questions, D&C contends against orthodox Christianity primarily in the arena of theology. Luckily, for the English-speaking world, D&C was originally written in English less than two hundred years ago. An argument of misunderstanding its meaning or faulty translation is rendered moot. D&C says what is says and means what it means to English speakers, particularly North American English speakers. This is of great advantage when dialoguing with Mormons on issues such as baptism for the dead and celestial marriage, both of which stand on shaky biblical grounds.

Baptism for the dead (or proxy baptism) in Mormonism seems to have developed gradually as Joseph Smith's theology evolved;

> As I stated to you in my letter before I left my place...I now resume the subject of the baptism for the dead...let me assure you that these are principles in relation to the dead and the living that cannot be lightly passed over, as pertaining to our salvation. For their salvation is necessary and essential to our salvation, as Paul says concerning the fathers—that they without us cannot be made perfect—neither can we without our dead be made perfect.[132]

The basic principle of proxy baptism is heavily influenced by the Mormon view of salvation, which is in turn heavily influenced by Pelagianism, and includes the postmortem possibility of atonement.[133] According to Mormonism there is still a chance for repentance and salvation after an individual dies. Therefore, it is not unusual for Latter-day Saints to celebrate private baptism ceremonies for late relatives, friends, or even people of no relation to them at all.

In fact, as an oftentimes unwelcome favor, the LDS Church has sanctioned postmortem baptisms for Napoleon Bonaparte, Christopher

---

[132] Doctrine & Covenants 128:1,15

[133] *Pelagianism* teaches the idea that humans are not born into original sin and have complete free will to choose between right and wrong without special divine aid. This view is incorrect since the very reason we need Jesus is that we are sinful and cannot help ourselves. "For it is God who works in you, both to will and to work for his good pleasure (Phil. 2:13)." and, "it is God who

Columbus, Albert Einstein, John Wesley, Abraham Lincoln, and even William Shakespeare.[134] More recently offended members of the Jewish community called for an immediate end to the practice upon the discovery of the LDS Church performing proxy baptisms on behalf of Jewish Holocaust victims, to which the penitent church graciously apologized and mended strained relations.[135] Proxy baptisms have gained even more recent criticism for the ceremony of Stanley Ann Dunham, the mother of U.S. President Barack Obama.[136]

For most Christians, proxy baptism is not practiced for one simple reason – it is extremely pagan. The ancient practice dates prior to the New Testament and has historically been associated with paganism. The need for ritualistic cleansing and renewal in the afterlife affords the deceased with an opportunity to square away their moral account on earth despite having passed on. This is not too far from the beliefs of Mormonism; however, according to scripture when we pass away, that's it. It's over. We are "at home with the Lord."[137] We also know that there is no second chance after death since "it is appointed for man to die once, and after that comes judgment."[138] There is no such practice of posthumous baptism taught in scripture outside of negative terms.

LDS leaders commonly employ 1 Corinthians 15:29 to biblically defend the practice, yet a close look at the verse reveals that Paul was not advocating proxy baptism. "Otherwise, what do people mean by being baptized on behalf of the dead? If the dead are not raised at all, why are people baptized on their behalf?"[139] Paul's entire argument prior to this verse was to demonstrate for the Corinthians that the resurrection is a fact. He gives the argument that even pagans believe the dead will resurrect since *they* perform baptism for the dead. Notice that the verse is written about *people* or *them*, a plural, third–person,

---

justifies (Rom. 8:33)." Also, "for by grace you have been saved through faith. And this is not your own doing; it is the gift of God, not a result of works, so that no one may boast (Eph. 2:8–9)."
[134] The Mormonism Research Ministry, "Prominent People Mormons Have Baptized by Proxy," http://www.mrm.org/prominent-people-baptized-by-proxy (accessed January 9, 2012).
[135] Melanie J. Wright, "Latter-Day Saints," *A Dictionary of Jewish–Christian Relations*, eds. Edward Kessler and Neil Wenborn (Cambridge: Cambridge University Press, 2005), 257.
[136] Cathy Lynn Grossman, "Is Barack Obama's mother a Mormon in heaven now?" USA Today, *Faith & Reason*, http://content.usatoday.com/communities/religion/post/2009/05/66469311/1 (accessed January 9, 2012).
[137] 2 Cor. 5:8
[138] Heb. 9:27
[139] 1 Cor. 15:29

personal pronoun. It was written about *them*, not *us*. Paul never rhetorically asks why we, being Christians, do not baptize on behalf of the dead.

Proxy baptism has also led many Latter-day Saints into a passionate pursuit of family history. If it is possible to baptize family members who have passed away, who wouldn't take the responsibility of getting as many family members into God's presence as possible? If you could be responsible for the eternal bliss and happiness of your family and ancestors, would you do it? Brigham Young acknowledged the Mormon obsession with genealogy as being motivated from God himself.[140] Contrarily, Paul viewed genealogy as promoting speculation and poor stewardship.[141]

Ultimately, proxy baptism as sanctioned by D&C is symptomatic of a heterodox view of salvation. If people are saved through a combination of grace and obedience in accordance with hearing a message, then it only stands to reason that if someone does not receive the opportunity to hear this message in their lifetime that they be awarded a second chance. Were salvation by grace alone through faith alone then proxy baptism is unnecessary.

Aside from proxy baptism, D&C teaches that those belonging to the Mormon faith should become married for now and eternity in order to achieve the highest state of perfection.[142] The term Latter-day Saints use to identify this idea is *celestial marriage*. You may have even heard the LDS Church slogan, "Families can last forever." One of the appeals to Mormonism is its high view of marriage and family, as they believe the covenant will last for eternity. And while this is a lofty and romantic aspiration, it is wholly foreign to scripture.

The subject of marriage in the afterlife was directly asked of Jesus who gave a straightforward response; "For in the resurrection they neither marry nor are given in marriage, but are like angels in heaven."[143] Despite D&C instruction to the contrary, scripture informs us that marriage ends at death – thus, 'til death do us part. It could be argued that because Jesus claimed there is no marriage in the resurrection (i.e., at the Second Coming of Christ), we are free to marry

---

[140] The Church of Jesus Christ of Latter-day Saints, *Teachings of Presidents of the Church: Brigham Young* (Salt Lake City, Utah: Church of Jesus Christ of Latter-day Saints), 309. "...there is a perfect mania with some to trace their genealogies...the Lord is prompting them."
[141] 1 Tim. 1:4
[142] Doctrine & Covenants 132
[143] Matt. 22:30

eternally before that event; however, Jesus clearly states that even after the resurrection we will be like angels in the aspect of marriage. And I am not aware of a Mrs. Michael the Archangel. The only marriage that will last for eternity is Jesus the bridegroom to his bride, the church.[144] This is not to say that married believers cannot spend eternity in each other's company, but certainly suggests that the institution will no longer exist.

MORMON SCRIPTURE: THE BOOK OF MORMON

The pinnacle of LDS scripture outside of the Bible is unequivocally the Book of Mormon. It is absolutely foundational to the Mormon faith. Most LDS hold the Book of Mormon as equal in authority only to the Holy Bible, perhaps slightly higher in some instances.[145] Without it Joseph Smith could not have started the Mormon movement. It was the catalyst in bringing about faith and confidence in Smith's leadership and prophetic office by his followers.

Rarely can a religious leader form a new religious movement on their own authority, and Smith was no exception. He needed an external source to testify of his apostleship, thus we find Smith's new revelation drawn from an external source in the Book of Mormon. Remember, the entire premise of Smith's ministry in the early years of the LDS Church was his calling by God to become the prophet who would restore the gospel to its fullness via the revelatory knowledge found in the Book of Mormon. Without the Book of Mormon there would be no Mormonism.

Having learned about the Book of Mormon's origin, it would be wise to examine what the text itself teaches. Much of our dialogue with Latter-day Saints will revolved around the content of the Book of Mormon – not where it came from but what it teaches. In fact, it is more beneficial to focus on the theology of the Book of Mormon rather than its origin. If we keep the conversation on the Book of Mormon's origin, then we will inevitably spur a heated argument of which both parties have little to gain from the outcome.

---

[144] Rev. 19:6–10
[145] "It is here. It must be explained. It can be explained only as the translator himself explained its origin. Hand in hand with the Bible, whose companion volume it is, it stands as another witness to a doubting generation that Jesus is the Christ, the Son of the living God. It is an unassailable

Genuinely helpful discussion can occur when sticking to what the Book of Mormon teaches rather than where it comes from.

With this in mind, learning what the Book of Mormon teaches should be done with the anticipation of dialoguing about Jesus as he is represented in both biblical and Book of Mormon sources. Ultimately, the person and work of Jesus should be the primary focus of spiritual conversation with LDS. At times there is agreement, at other disagreement. Yet, at all times the Jesus of the gospel must be placed over the entire conversation so that he receives glory in the dialogue. This is something – I'm sure – our LDS friends would agree.

It is important to understand at the outset that the Book of Mormon claims it completes, rather than compliments, the Bible. With few exceptions, it is strictly a historiographical work that describes multiple migrations of ancient Semitic and Hebrew families to the American continents. The first migration, under the leadership of Jared, ultimately failed, but a second migration, lead by a man named Lehi, succeeded.[146] This second migration began in Palestine ca. 600BCE shortly before the impending Babylonian Captivity.[147] Generations of Lehi's offspring grew and prospered as the people spread across the sparsely inhabited New World. Eventually, two distinct groups formed from Lehi's progeny, the Nephites and the Lamanites, and they turned against each other in quarreling and war.[148]

These two warring factions only set aside their differences briefly when visited by the resurrected Jesus who taught and ministered them.[149] Unfortunately, the two factions returned to warring and strife by which the Nephites were completely destroyed.[150] The last of these peoples, Mormon and his son Moroni, consolidated the events of the past millennia on golden plates and buried them for Joseph Smith to find in 1823.[151]

---

cornerstone of our faith." Gordon B. Hinkley, 2004. "Four Cornerstones of Faith." *Ensign* 34, no. 2 (February): 2–7.
[146] Ether 6:1–12; 15:13–32
[147] 1 Nephi 18:5–23
[148] 2 Nephi 5:14; Jacob 1:10; Enos 1:24
[149] 3 Nephi 11:8–10
[150] Mormon 6:4–5
[151] Mormon 6:6

THE LOOOOOONG VOYAGES

The Book of Mormon makes some incredible theological and non-theological claims. In some portions it speaks to the nature of God and salvation. In others, it speaks to historical events and places. These two types of claims are codependent on each other for the validation. Theological claims are dependent on non-theological claims to be verifiably true in order to bolster confidence in the reader. Just as when the Bible makes claims about the person and work of Jesus, it makes an equal amount of claims about historical events, places, and people, which bolsters the theological claims.

Imagine if the Bible made theological claims about Jesus without accurately describe historical events. Wouldn't this cause us to second-guess the text as a whole? As we will see, the non-theological claims in the Book of Mormon, such as historical notes on culture or events, are not met with supporting evidence (i.e., archeological, cultural, etc) that we would expect. This casts a looming cloud of doubt over the theological claims of the Book of Mormon, even those that seem to dovetail nicely with scripture. It is not enough to say good things about Jesus without saying right things about history.

The first claims to examine are two major transoceanic voyages made by emigrating peoples from the western hemisphere to the Americas. The first voyage by the *Jaredites* was accomplished under the leadership of Jared from the ancient near east to the Americas. The Jaredite journey is recounted in the book of Ether where we learn that the brother of Jared, who was present at the tower of Babel spoken of in Genesis 10 and pleaded with God to spare them from the confusion that was about to occur.[152] Fortunately, God felt compassion for this small tribe and allowed them to escape his judgment.[153] The Jaredites then, according to contemporary Mormon scholarship, set sail from the Arabian Sea, crossed the Indian Ocean, navigated through the Straights of Malacca, docked for a bit in modern-day Vietnam or Hong Kong, then sailed

---

[152] Joseph L. Allen and Blake J. Allen, *Exploring the Lands of the Book of Mormon*, revised ed. (American Fork, Utah: Covenant Communications, Inc., 2011), 495. *See also* Ether 1:33, 42–43
[153] Ether 1:35

clear across the Pacific Ocean until reaching the coast of Mexico somewhere near Chiapas.[154]

This is an extremely impressive feat when one considers that Jared commanded eight vessels across the Pacific Ocean from modern-day Oman for nearly a year during a time when the most advanced ships had difficulty making it across the Mediterranean Sea in one piece.[155] LDS apologists suggest that the Jaredite migration across the Pacific was similar to the Polynesian colonization of various islands and land masses. Yet, it must be pointed out, the Polynesians took hundreds of years to colonize because of limited seafaring technology. Regardless, the Jaredite migration to Mesoamerica eventually gave birth to the people group we commonly know today as Native Americans.[156]

The second migration was under the leadership of Lehi, a Hebrew. Strangely, despite advances in nautical technology, Lehi required divine navigational assistance see the trip through unlike his predecessor Jared. Lehi was able to make this voyage under the guidance of the *Liahona*, a small compass-like device that pointed in the direction he was to go. The strangeness of how a compass could exist hundreds of years before it was invented will be addressed a little later. For now another question deserves to be asked – why did Lehi need the Liahona hundreds of years after Jared already made the voyage?

Perhaps an argument for Lehi's successful voyage could be attributed to the Liahona, but what of Jared? According to Mormon scholars Jared would have set sail some time between 3100—2920BCE.[157] Lehi completed his eight-year voyage in 591BCE.[158] This means that there were around 2,332—2,512 years in between Jared's and Lehi's voyages. Two and a half millennia passed, shipwrights made leaps in sailing technology, yet it was Lehi, not Jared, who needed the Liahona to successfully sail across the globe. Such a strange detail may be explained, in my opinion, when one considers that the book of Ether appears to be an appendix to the greater Book of Mormon narrative.

---

[154] Joseph L. Allen and Blake J. Allen, *Exploring the Lands of the Book of Mormon*, revised ed. (American Fork, Utah: Covenant Communications, Inc., 2011), 495–511, 526–527
[155] Corethia Qualls, "Boats of Mesopotamia before 2000 B.C." PhD diss., Columbia University, 1981. See also Ether 6:11
[156] Ether 15:13–32
[157] John L. Sorenson, "The Years of the Jaredites," Neal A. Maxwell Institute, http://maxwellinstitute.byu.edu/publications/transcripts/?id=28 (accessed January 9, 2012).
[158] Joseph L. Allen and Blake J. Allen, *Exploring the Lands of the Book of Mormon*, revised ed. (American Fork, Utah: Covenant Communications, Inc., 2011), 525–529.

HORSES, ELEPHANTS, AND CIMETERS OH MY!

A second claim worth examining is archeological evidence. The Book of Mormon describes people, places, and things spread across the American continents for which there is no supporting archeological evidence. Mainstream academia has widely rejected alleged evidence that aims at proving the work's historicity to the protest of LDS scholars. In contrast, there is a copious amount of archeological evidence to support both the Old and New Testaments of scripture.

For example, if you were to turn to the end of a study Bible you would most likely find maps of the ancient Mediterranean countries and detailed maps of ancient Israel. Just about every single city listed in all of scripture either exists today, existed at one time, or exists under a new name. This is because the events that took place in scripture are historical and linked to physical locations. This is not true for the Book of Mormon. The lack of archeological evidence presents an insurmountable problem for Latter-day Saints because the book describes many inhabitants over a large amount of land throughout a long period of time without any evidence. Here are some examples of how the Book of Mormon described the ancient Americas. Keep in mind that the Book of Mormon is describing Native American or Mesoamerican culture.

- "The whole face of the land had become covered with buildings, and the people were as numerous almost, as it were the sand of the sea."[159]
- "[they] did multiply and spread … [they] began to cover the face of the whole earth, from the sea south to the sea north, from the sea west to the sea east."[160]
- "[they] multiplied exceedingly, and spread upon the face of the land, and became exceedingly rich."[161]
- "[they] had been slain … nearly two million."[162]

---

[159] Mormon 1:7
[160] Heleman 3:8
[161] Jarom1:8
[162] Ether 15:2

- "[they produced] fine workmanship of wood, in buildings, and in machinery, and also in iron and copper, and brass and steel, making all manners of tools."[163]
- "[they had] grain ... silks ... cattle ... oxen ... cows ... sheep ... swine ... goats ... horses ... asses ... elephants..."[164]

Despite this impressive list of economic and societal success, no archeological evidence currently exists to support these claims. LDS apologists typically retreat to questioning the Book of Mormon itself, opining that certain anachronisms (i.e., elephants) are simply poor translations of real things. A word of caution for LDS friends on this point – keep in mind that Smith was supposed to have been divinely assisted in his transcription. If the Book of Mormon contains words that do not mean what they say, then it is God, not Smith nor the Book of Mormon writers, who has chosen to author this confusion.

Another solution from LDS apologists is to ascribe Mesoamerican ruins to Book of Mormon people. This is, by far, the most popular explanation for where we may find archeological evidence in support of the Book of Mormon. However, there are currently no extant Incan or Mayan records of any Book of Mormon names, terms, or cities. If the Nephites and Lamanites were truly ancient Mesoamerican or Native American peoples, shouldn't we expect to see similar names of people, events, and locations in their writings, myths, and legends? The absence of evidence for Book of Mormon people and culture is a serious challenge to the work's authenticity. Consequently, some LDS opt to view the Book of Mormon as "inspired fiction."

THE BOOK OF MISTAKES MORMON

The first Book of Mormon you ever encountered was most likely a small, blue book with gold letters announcing its contents, "The Book of Mormon: Another Testament of Jesus Christ." This version is compact, cheap, and convenient for missionaries who carry a few with them as they tirelessly proselytize door-to-door on their two-year mission. It has, like so many books before and after it, gone through substantial revision. Thus, the version you were

---

[163] Jarom 1:8; 2 Nephi 5:15

given is different in significant ways from the one Joseph Smith held when he delivered his first sermon from the text. This is a mundane fact of life for many faithful Latter-day Saints.

Yet, it begs the question – should it be a mundane fact of life? Do these changes represent any cause for alarm among Latter-day Saints? Wouldn't substantial changes to the book testify to either its fallibility or the murky intentions of its editors? Besides, how do these revisions square with the transcription process that Joseph Smith and others spoke about? Surely, the revisions must be minor grammatical errors here and there given the divine error-checking technique with which the book was created. Oddly, this is not the case. There have been seven editions of the Book of Mormon since its initial publishing in 1830, four of which occurred at the hand of Smith himself.

Latter-day Saints are reassured by their leadership that these revisions are nothing to write home about. They are, after all, simple little errors that required simple fixes. This much is told to us at the beginning of each Book of Mormon. Do you remember the little blue edition you were given by those two kind, young missionaries? That edition is based on the latest revision of the text completed in 1981. The immediate greeting we receive upon opening its pages is a statement announcing the changes; "Some minor errors in the text have been perpetuated in past editions of the Book of Mormon. This edition contains corrections that seem appropriate to bring the material into conformity with prepublication manuscripts and early editions edited by the Prophet Joseph Smith."[165] Yet, it must be contended, why were these errors present in the first place? According to early LDS accounts, the transcription process from the golden plates into written manuscripts was said to have been divinely guided. Revisions would be expected were the text translated – Smith could have made some mistakes here and there moving the text from 'reformed Egyptian' into English. However, it was not Smith who translated the text. It was translated, as he reminds us, by "the gift and power of God."

An initial response from Latter-day Saints may be to flip the question – why are there so many different versions of the Bible? They may compare the many editions of the Book of Mormon to the many versions of the Holy Bible.

---

[164] Ether 9:17–19
[165] Book of Mormon, introductory notes

To respond, there is an important difference between an *edition* and a *version*. An *edition* suggests changes were made to the original text itself. A *version* simply means the interpretation or translation of an original text has changed, but not the original text itself. Thus, when a new *version* of the Bible is released the original Hebrew and Greek were not altered, but the English rendition was retranslated to assist native English speakers in understanding the original language. When a new *edition* of the Book of Mormon is released the original English is altered, sometimes resulting in meaningful or substantial changes to the original text, not simply the translation.

This is also when the difference between transcription and translation becomes extremely important. There is no need for translation if something is transcribed; therefore, mistakes should be severely minimal, if any at all. If something is translated, however, then the translator or translation committee is deciding how best to word something from one language to another, and in the case of scripture this means three dead languages into an ever-changing live language. Different versions (not editions) of scripture exist because scholars do their best to translate three dead languages into modern English, which is no easy task. Smith claims to have transcribed divinely illuminated English to English through the gift and power of God by using a seer stone and/or the Urim and Thummim. Biblical scholars translate ancient Greek, Hebrew, and Aramaic into English without divine intervention. Comparing the two as if they were similar tasks with similar challenges and issues is unhelpful.

So what were the "minor errors" that were corrected in the Book of Mormon? LDS leaders are quick to blame the printers. Smith's original faultless manuscripts were unfortunately tainted by sloppy publishers. Yet, if printers were to blame, it would be easy to identify errors of a misspelled word or improper formatting. Some of these changes, however, are theological in nature, not printing error in nature. In my opinion, this highlights the fact that Smith's theology evolved over the years, which required the Book of Mormon to be brought into conformity with his newer ideas. Here are some examples of "printers' errors" fixed from the 1830 edition from the first book of Nephi:

1Ne 11:18 (1830): "Behold, the virgin which thou seest, is the mother of God."
1Ne 11:18 (1837): "Behold, the virgin which thou seest, is the mother of *the Son of* God."

1Ne 11:21 (1830): "Behold the Lamb of God, yea, even the Eternal Father."
1Ne 11:21 (1837): "Behold the Lamb of God, yea, even *the Son of* the Eternal Father."

1Ne 11:32 (1830): "And I looked and beheld the Lamb of God, [...] yea, the Everlasting God."
1Ne 11:32 (1837): "And I looked and beheld the Lamb of God, [...] yea, *the Son of* the Everlasting God."

1Ne 13:40 (1830): "the Lamb of God is the Eternal Father and the Saviour of the world."
1Ne 13:40 (1837): "the Lamb of God is *the Son of* the Eternal Father and the Saviour of the world."

LDS apologists insist that these changes were made to clarify theological statements, not to conform the text to the evolving nature of God in Mormon thought at the time. Yet, if this is the case, the printers were oddly consistent with their mistakes. Is it really possible that they left out four counts of "the Son of" in 1 Nephi, which dramatically alters its meaning? Or is it more likely that Smith became uncomfortable with the modalism of 1 Nephi?[166] Perhaps the prophet's thoughts of Jesus literally being the Father changed. If so, the Book of Mormon needed to be brought into conformity.

JESUS HAD A SMART PHONE

A good historian reading the Book of Mormon might notice that a few things are a little out of place, particularly things existing in a time when they did not exist yet. These errors are called anachronisms. Think of Marty and Doc Brown with their 1980s DMC DeLorean in 1885 Southern California or a Tyrannosaurus Rex running amok in a modern museum building in Jurassic Park.

Remember the Liahona, the compass that directed Lehi to the Americas? Technically, it's an anachronism because neither the device nor the term for the device was invented until the first century.[167] The supernatural compass appears in 2 Nephi 5:12 (written between 588 and 570BCE); "And I, Nephi, had also brought the records which were engraven upon the plates of brass; and also the ball, or *compass*, which was prepared for my father by the hand of the Lord, according to that which is written." This means that Lehi's son, Nephi, possessed a compass about 600 years before compasses existed.

Some Mormon apologists have suggested that the Liahona was not a compass in the way we think of compasses today. It was uniquely different, but

---

[166] Modalism is the misconception of the Trinity as one single god who reveals himself differently throughout history. One consequence of this idea is that the Father died on the cross.
[167] Yinke Deng, *Ancient Chinese Inventions* (Cambridge: Cambridge University Press, 2011), 15.

functioned in much the same way. Yet, even the concept of the compass was foreign until the discovery of north-south magnetism in lodestones by the Chinese in the first century BCE.[168] Furthermore, the Book of Mormon describes the Liahona as a specific type of compass, the dry compass, which was not invented until the 14th century in Europe.[169] This widens the anachronistic gap to 1,600 years.

Moreover, in my opinion, simply because the Book of Mormon claims that God produced a compass hundreds of years before it was invented is not a sufficient explanation. He also could have supplied Elijah with a cell phone as his prophet and David with an electric guitar as his musician, but he didn't. If Nephi's father, Lehi, needed the compass to point the way the Lord wanted him to go, then why did God hold out on Moses when he was wandering in the desert for forty years?[170] Why go to all the lengths of supplying a flaming cloud if a compass would have done just as well?[171]

It seems oddly uncharacteristic of God to produce something from the future outside of visions or dreams. This would also be the only time in which God manufactured future technology for the private use of his chosen people. Latter-day Saints might also claim that the compass could have been another device with the same name. This would lessen the anachronistic offense, but the Book of Mormon specifically states that it was a compass.[172] And there should be no confusion as to what *compass* means in this passage since the Book of Mormon was transcribed from divinely illuminated English to English. Ultimately, the Book of Mormon claims that Lehi had a device hundreds of years before it was even invented regardless of how it came into his possession.

Another anachronism is found in Ether 9:19, which describes the American continents during antiquity; "And they also had horses, and asses, and there were elephants and cureloms and cumoms; all of which were useful unto man, and more especially the elephants and cureloms and cumoms."

---

[168] "And it came to pass that as my father arose in the morning, and went forth to the tent door, to his great astonishment he beheld upon the ground a round ball of curious workmanship; and it was of fine brass. And within the ball were two spindles; and the one pointed the way whither we should go into the wilderness." – 1 Nephi 16:10

[169] Anthony John Turner, *Early Scientific Instruments: Europe, 1400–1800* (London: Philip Wilson Publishers, 1987), 22.

[170] Num. 32:13

[171] Exod. 13:21

[172] 2 Nephi 5:12

Horses and elephants hadn't made it to the American continents at the time Ether was supposed to have been written. This is particularly difficult to explain given the Book of Mormon's emphasis of the usefulness of elephants prior to 600CE, an animal that would not see American shores until 1796.[173] Typically, LDS apologists have either requested patience from skeptics until the remains of these ancient animals could be discovered, or they choose to expand the definition of "horse" and "elephant" to mean horse-like and elephant-like animals. For many, though, both solutions are not satisfying.

Another anachronism follows a similar vein. Ether 2:3 claims that, "[the Jaredites] did also carry with them deseret, which, by interpretation, is a honey bee; and thus they did carry with them swarms of bees, and all manner of that which was upon the face of the land, seeds of every kind." In this passage, the Jaredites are preparing for their journey from ancient Palestine to the Americas. They begin gathering up all sorts of things to take with them, including honeybees.

Thus, the Book of Mormon claims that honeybees were brought to the Americas sometime between 3100—2920BCE; however, honeybees were not introduced to the Americas until European explorers brought them in 1622.[174] There were, of course, bees in the Americas, just not honeybees, or *deseret* as the Book of Mormon refers to them. Much like its emphasis on elephants, the Book of Mormon lays into the claim going so far as to invent a word to describe it, which is unsubstantiated by the evidence.

One final anachronism is a fascinatingly curious bit of information that often gets overlooked due to its surrounding narrative. If you recall, the Book of Mormon claims that the Jaredites emigrated from the Tower of Babel to Mesoamerica around 3000BCE in barges. While this in itself is difficult to accept, perhaps the more perplexing feature of this narrative is that those eight vessels were not only seaworthy barges, but are described as submarine-like. Ether 2:17–24, a section of the Book of Mormon that recounts the Jaredites emigration, painstakingly describes vessels that were created "tight as a dish," in order to "be as a whale in the midst of the sea," and were meant to sail both

---

[173] S. L. Kotar and J. E. Gessler, *The Rise of the American Circus, 1716–1899* (Jefferson, NC: McFarland & Company, Inc., Publishers, 2011), 67.
[174] Eric R. Eaton and Kenn Kaufman, *Kaufman Field Guide to Insects in North America* (New York: Houghton Mifflin Company, 2007), 346.

above and below water, perhaps like a submarine. When the Jaredites eventually set sail for the American continents these eight submersible barges proved seaworthy precisely because, according to Ether 6:7–10, "they were driven forth; and no monster of the sea could break them, neither whale that could mar them; and they did have light continually, whether it was *above* the water or *under* the water (emphasis added)."

While submarines may not seem so strange to us today, a person living in 3000BCE would have, assuming they could, conceptualized a submarine in the same manner we may think of a spaceship that could take us beyond the spiraling arms of the Milky Way and back before dinner time. So why are there submarines in the Jaredite emigration narrative? During the 19th century when the Book of Mormon was published submarine technology had just reached the point of reliable usefulness. It seems most likely that the author of the Book of Mormon was fascinated by the new technology and, with his or her limited knowledge, added it to an already incredible tale. This theory is bolstered by the fact that Ether 2:23 describes God being concerned with placing glass windows on the submersible vessels since they would, presumably at certain depths, "be dashed in pieces" due to water pressure.

THE BOOK OF MORMON VS. THE BIBLE

At this point it is my hope that the Book of Mormon has been demonstrated (if only briefly) as problematic for its inclusion as scripture. Currently, within the LDS Church there exists a movement to think of the Book of Mormon less as a literal account of historical events and more as "inspired fiction," a literary work that pushes humanity towards a clearer and more satisfying understanding of the Bible. If this is the case then we should expect to see strong correlation and agreement between the Bible and the Book of Mormon. Yet, as we will see, there are significant contradictions between the two works. This is especially true concerning the person and work of Jesus.

Initially, both works seem to be in concert. The Book of Mormon is replete with calls to repentance and faith in Jesus Christ. Much of this content, though, is painfully anachronistic, like Nephi's uncanny proclamation of the "gospel of Jesus Christ" in the 6th century BCE. Viewing the Book of Mormon as strictly "inspired fiction" can assuage our angst a bit. Yet, even the spiritual message of the Book of Mormon significantly challenges the Bible in many places.

As discussed earlier, Latter-day Saints are taught in the Pearl of Great Price that the fall of humanity was a necessarily good event. The idea is likewise found in the Book of Mormon as a pithy, succinct verse; "Adam fell that men might be; and men are, that they might have joy."[175] This verse teaches that the fall of humanity caused by Adam gave us the ability to exist and have joy. Consequently, Mormonism is presented with a problem since two inevitable conclusions of this theology force Latter-day Saints into a misunderstanding of God's plan of salvation. The first is that Satan played an integral part in humanity's ability to exist and have joy in the knowledge of *theosis*, or becoming gods. The second is that the fall of humanity was necessarily good.

Satan as a champion of human freedom is absolutely unbiblical. He acts as a luminary in Mormon thought, albeit a devious one, if Latter-day Saints hold the Book of Mormon verse above in serious regard. Scripture always describes Satan in negative terms, never positive: accuser, enemy, the son of destruction, the man of lawlessness, tempter, the evil one, and the father of lies to list a few.[176] While Latter-day Saints may agree with these descriptions, they cannot agree that he is completely evil in all that he does or has done without contradicting the Mormon view of the fall.

Also, aside from his assistance in teaching humanity the secrets of theosis, he is our spiritual brother. Mormonism teaches that every human existed as a spirit being prior to our physical existence with our brother, Satan.[177] In this way, he plays the role of the cosmic black sheep of the family, but nonetheless exhibits some redeeming qualities. Therefore, without Satan and the fall humanity would have never existed and would have never experienced the joy of existence. Scripture, however, would disagree.

The fall is not the reason for humanity's life – it is the reason for humanity's death. "For as in Adam all die, so also in Christ shall all be made

---

[175] 2 Nephi 2:25
[176] Rev. 12:10; Matt. 13:39; 2 Thess. 2:3; Matt. 4:3; 13:19; John 8:44
[177] Douglas J. Davies, *An Introduction to Mormonism* (Cambridge: Cambridge University Press, 2003), 74.

alive."[178] Scripture goes on to teach that the byproduct of the fall was the introduction of sin to humanity. "Therefore, just as sin came into the world through one man, and death through sin, and so death spread to all men because all sinned."[179] Not only was the fall of humanity a cosmically terrible event, it is the very reason we are separated from God. The fall is why Jesus needed to come rescue us, why we need redemption, and why we all start our lives saturated in rebellion from God.

To call this a good event that brings about joy is completely senseless and absolutely non-biblical. In fact, the Mormon view of the fall makes the cross of Christ a trifling matter when contrasted with our rebellion against God. Why do we need redemption from something that was not saturated in rebellion, sin, and depravity? The result of Adam's sin was not beneficial for our existence in any way, shape, or form. To the contrary, it destroyed and wholly corrupted what existence we did have.[180] I recognize the sternness of my words at this point, but the concept of the fall is no trivial matter. It ultimately dictates how we understand the atoning work of Jesus.

This leads us to another point of disagreement between the Book of Mormon and the Bible – salvation. We recognize as Christians, in relation to the fallen state of man, that humanity is completely dependent on the grace of God for our salvation. There is nothing we can do to add to it. In fact, the entire book of Galatians is written on that very subject. There is nothing we can do to add to the finished work of Jesus Christ on the cross. Period. The Book of Mormon, however, would disagree. 2 Nephi 25:23 states, "For we labor diligently to write, to persuade our children, and also our brethren, to believe in Christ, and to be reconciled to God; for we know that it is by grace that we are saved, *after all we can do*."[181]

Were in not for "after all we can do" there would not have been anything theologically wrong with that sentence; however, this passage clearly declares that salvation comes "*after* all we can do." Accordingly, the Book of Mormon teaches that there is something that must be done in addition to God's

---

[178] 1 Cor. 15:22
[179] Rom. 5:12
[180] Rom. 8:18–25
[181] 2 Nephi 25:23, emphasis added.

grace. Consequently, the work of the law has not been fulfilled in Jesus.[182] This leads Latter-day Saints to believe in a grace-works hybrid salvation that will be explored later in the chapter. Suffice it to say that according to scripture the law has been fulfilled in Jesus, and there is nothing (no work, no ordinance, no performance) that can be added to the work of salvation – Jesus has already accomplished it.[183]

Another contradiction stands out so visibly that its persistent presence in the different revisions is perplexing. Alma 7:10 states, "And behold, he shall be born of Mary, at Jerusalem which is the land of our forefathers, she being a virgin, a precious and chosen vessel, who shall be overshadowed and conceive by the power of the Holy Ghost, and bring forth a son, yea, even the Son of God."[184] Even before you study the scripture that this contradicts, one only needs to sing a few Christmas carols to know this is wrong. Perhaps the famous Christmas song *O, Little Town of Bethlehem* requires alteration to *O, Little Town of Jerusalem* in order for the Mormon Tabernacle Choir to sing it in good conscience.

Nevertheless, Matthew clearly states that Jesus was born in Bethlehem not Jerusalem.[185] Not to mention, Jesus' birth in Bethlehem was to fulfill a messianic prophecy of Micah.[186] Repudiation of this contradiction should be minimal – it's pretty obvious. But Mormon scholars have been quick to combat this contradiction by claiming that Jerusalem was a term that could have encompassed Bethlehem due to its geographic vicinity; however, in scripture Jerusalem is always described as just the city within the walls and never includes the cities in its region. Even the Book of Mormon describes Jerusalem as a singular city without mention of its "suburbs."[187] At the end of the day it's important to know that Jesus was not born and crucified just outside of the same city. He was born in Bethlehem to fulfill prophecy and was crucified near Jerusalem to defeat Satan, sin, and death in accordance with scripture.

---

[182] 2 Nephi 25:24, 30
[183] Matt. 5:17; Rom. 8:1–2
[184] Alma 7:10
[185] Matt. 2:1
[186] Micah 5:2
[187] 1 Nephi 1:4

BOOK OF MORMON ≠ MORMON THEOLOGY

Oddly, the Book of Mormon at times seems to contradict Mormon theology. Much of Mormon theology comes from the pen of Joseph Smith in the Pearl of Great Price, Doctrine & Covenants, and other sources. Sometimes, these sources contradict the Book of Mormon. This is perhaps due to the idea of continued revelation within Mormonism. God's word is never truly finished, so it is subject to change. Thus, at times the orchestra of Mormon scripture harmonizes while at other times it becomes cacophonous. In my experience, dialoguing about this with Latter-day Saints yields quite an interesting discussion. The conversation quickly finds itself standing on the issues of fallibility for either the Book of Mormon or the LDS religious tradition. If the Book of Mormon makes declarations that do not coincide, and even contradict, those made by the LDS Church, then one of the two must be in error.

These contradictions cover a wide array of theology from polytheism to the divinity of Jesus. For example, the Book of Mormon describes a scene with two characters, Zeezrom and Amulek, who were discussing polytheism. Zeezrom, a lawyer, was attempting to discredit the Jesus being preached by Amulek, an ancient Mormon prophet. "And Zeezrom said unto him: Thou sayest there is a true and living God? And Amulek said: Yea, there is a true and living God. Now Zeezrom said: Is there more than one God? And he answered, No."[188] It is reasonable to presume from this short dialogue that Amulek, a prophet of God, believes and teaches that there exists only one god. This is called monotheism, and, aside from its modalistic tendencies, the Book of Mormon as a whole teaches the existence of only one god.

Mormon theology, however, teaches something completely different – polytheism, or the existence of many gods. Joseph Smith taught that God the Father had a father as well, necessitating the existence of a god aside from God the Father. One example of this is found in Smith's the *History of the Church*; "If Jesus Christ was the Son of God, and John the Apostle discovered that God the Father of Jesus Christ had a Father, you may suppose that He had a Father also. Where was there ever a son without a father? And where was

---

[188] Alma 11:26–29

there ever a father without first being a son?"[189] This clearly rubs against the grain of the Zeezrom–Amulek dialogue on monotheism. Additionally, it also implies a never-ending pantheon of gods. God the Father must have had a father, who in turn must have had a father, who in turn must have had a father, ad infinitum.

Not only does this idea of polytheism contradict the Book of Mormon, it also severely contradicts scripture from which we learn that there is only one God. God declares in Isaiah that; "I am the first and the last; besides me there is no god."[190] God the Father does not have a father since he is the first and the last. There is literally no god beside God: no progeny of gods, no duality of god, no sub categories of gods, etc. Scripture teaches that God is literally and eternally the only god that exists.

Generally, in my experience, passages like these from Isaiah are met with the insistence that Latter-day Saints are just as monotheistic as orthodox Christians. They believe in the Godhead, which is Father, Son, and Holy Ghost. In response, it is good to ask for clarification on the being and person of the Father and the Son. They are, according to Mormonism, two distinct personages and two separate gods among many other gods like them. LDS may argue that humanity should only be concerned with the god of this planet even though other gods exist, an idea commonly referred to as *monolatry*.

Should this argument arise, discuss the meaning of Isaiah 44:6, "I am the first and the last; besides me there is no god." "...Of this planet," they might add, but we must remain steadfast that there is only one God of the entire universe, not simply this planet. A plurality of gods is foreign to scripture.[191] Not only this, but polytheism is also foreign to the Book of Mormon.[192] As strange as it may sound, the Book of Mormon contradicts Mormonism since it hints at a correct understanding of the Trinity, although it is still far from the orthodox definition.

---

[189] History of the Church 6:476

[190] Isa. 44:6

[191] *Old Testament* – Deut. 4:35, 39; 6:4–5, 32:39, 1 Sam. 2:2; 2 Sam. 7:22; 22:32; 1 Kings 8:59–60; Ps. 86:8–10; Isa. 37:20; 43:10; 44:6–8; 45:5; 46:9; Jer. 10:10. *New Testament* – John 5:44; 17:3; Rom. 3:30; 16:27; 1 Cor. 8:4–6; Gal. 3:20; Eph. 4:6; 1 Tim. 1:17; 2:5; 1 Thess. 1:9; James 2:19; Jude 25; 1 John 5:20–21.

[192] 1 Nephi 13:41; Alma 11:26–29, 35; 2 Nephi 31:21; Mosiah 15:1–5; Alma 11:44; 3 Nephi 11:27, 36; 3 Nephi 28:10; Mormon 7:7

Another contradiction between the Book of Mormon and Mormon theology is what Latter-day Saints refer to as the *doctrine of eternal progression.* Smith explains;

> The Father has promised us that through our faithfulness we shall be blessed with the fullness of his kingdom. In other words we will have the privilege of becoming like him. To become like him we must have all the powers of godhood; thus a man and his wife when glorified will have spirit children who will eventually go on an earth like this one we are on and pass through the same kind of experiences…We will become gods and have jurisdiction over, and these worlds will be peopled by our own offspring.[193]

This idea has other names: theosis, exaltation, etc., but they all describe the same idea. Mormonism teaches that we have the ability to become gods just as Heavenly Father and Mother exist now with similar powers, responsibilities, and abilities. This is accomplished through obedience to ordinances and laws.[194]

In fact, Jesus is just a little bit ahead of us in the process of becoming a god. As for *God* god, Heavenly Father, he is still progressing too. Soon his children will be gods who have people, then he will be a god whose people are gods who have people, etc. It is possible, according to Mormonism, that an infinite regression of gods exists in eternity past in a never-ending hallway of gods still working towards higher exaltation.

Holding this theology forces Latter-day Saints to admit that God exists in a continual state of change, which is contradictory of both scripture and the Book of Mormon.[195] Moroni 8:18 states, "For I know that God is not a partial God, neither a changeable being." If God is an unchangeable being, how has he gotten so far in his eternal progression? This presents a sizable challenge for Latter-day Saints to safely navigate between the straights of Mormon scripture and Mormon tradition. More will be discussed on this specific topic later.

---

[193] Joseph Smith, *Doctrines of Salvation*, 2:43–44, 48
[194] D&C 132:20, Joseph Fielding Smith, "The King Follett Discourse" *Teachings of the Prophet Joseph Smith: Taken from His Sermons and Writings as they are Found in the Documentary History and Other Publications of the Church and Written or Published in the Day's of the Prophet's Ministry* (Salt Lake City: Deseret Books, 1984), 342.
[195] Mal. 3:6

For now it is important to understand that the consequence of a changing God is the possibility that his love for us could change as frequently as his own being. God cannot love us more tomorrow than he did today or yesterday. This is crucial to understanding God's grace and mercy. Once we've experienced it we cannot earn or gain more. This is because God loves us as much today as he will love us into eternity. If God progresses, if he is in a perpetual state of change, then there is the very real possibility that he could actually love us more or less some time in the future.

There are many more issues with the Book of Mormon that deserve our attention, but cannot be explored in such a short as this book. Other issues include apparent plagiarism of the King James Bible into the Book of Mormon (compare Isaiah 2-14 to 2 Nephi 12-24) as well as literary curiosities such as allusions to 19th century American patriotism and anti-Masonry, racism against Native Americans (who were cursed by God with dark skin in Alma 3), geographical mysteries, and strong sentiments against the practice of polygamy, which is ironic given Mormonism's polygamous past (see Jacob 2:24).

It seems that our Latter-day Saint friends must reconcile the many competing voices within Mormonism to determine where truth may be found and where all else may be rejected. Our role in this is to lovingly and patiently, in gentleness and respect, journey with them through the murky waters of the Book of Mormon's history and message. If this is done well, then Jesus will ultimately be glorified.[196]

THE DOCTRINE OF ETERNAL PROGRESSION

It should be evident at this point that orthodox Christians and Mormons do not share the same belief in God. They are two very different beings. As such there are some basic aspects about the concept of *god* and *godhood* in Mormonism that should be known before dialoguing with Latter-day Saints. Initially, and perhaps most importantly, it is crucial to solidify the idea that the god of Mormonism, Heavenly Father, is an exalted man who became the god of our planet in accordance with his obedience to his god's ordinances on a

---

[196] Col. 3:14–17

planet in some other part of the universe. As previously mentioned, Heavenly Father was able to attain the state of godhood through the doctrine of eternal progression; however, he was not always god. Furthermore, Heavenly Father has not rid himself of his physical body; he has a corporeal body just like you and me. Joseph Smith taught that Heavenly Father, "has a body of flesh and bones as tangible as man's."[197] This is an extremely foreign concept for orthodox Christians and may take some time to reason out the implications of that belief in your mind – the God of Mormonism is a physical, exalted man.

When the doctrine of eternal progression is brought up with Latter-day Saints the typical response is usually along these lines; "We don't teach you can become gods, we teach that you can become *godlike*. Don't all Christians believe that?" This explanation shouldn't catch us off guard. The immediate answer is an emphatic "yes," and we should explain the Christian position on becoming perfect in the resurrection for clarification. Keep in mind that they may be attempting to intentionally divert the conversation away from eternal progression, not to deceptively conceal but to momentarily sidestep the issue.

Mormonism teaches that humans can literally become gods someday, not simply "godlike." Former LDS President Lorenzo Snow summarized the doctrine in one simple (and very well known) sentence; "As man is, God once was. As God is, man may become."[198] While Christianity teaches that humans may become perfect through God's grace and redemption in the resurrection of all saints someday, it does not teach that they can become gods themselves in the sense Lorenzo Snow is illustrating. There is a huge difference. One is ruling and reigning over their own creation; the other is worshiping and praising in the presence of God for eternity.

For the doctrine of eternal progression to make sense philosophically Mormonism teaches that Heavenly Father descends from a species of gods who infinitely existed prior to him.[199] Again, this absolutely necessitates a polytheistic (or, better, *monolatristic*) belief regardless of whether or not one worships the other gods. Since this theology is at odds with orthodox Christianity,

---

[197] Doctrine & Covenants 130:22
[198] In Eliza R. Snow Smith, *Biography and Family Record of Lorenzo Snow* (1884), 46.
[199] Brigham Young, *Journal of Discourses*, 26 vols. (Liverpool: The Church of Jesus Christ of Latter-day Saints), 6:227.

Latter-day Saints attempt to demonstrate from scripture that polytheism was originally taught but later discarded. In order to support this argument biblically, LDS leaders point to 1 Corinthians 8:5; "For though there be that are called gods, whether in heaven or in earth, as there be gods many, and lords many."

At the outset this does appear to teach that there are multiple gods in the universe; however, putting this verse in context, just one verse later Paul clearly teaches that, "to [Christians] there is but one God, the Father, of whom are all things, and we in him; and one Lord Jesus Christ, by whom are all things, and we by him."[200] One only needs to look at the next verse to understand that Paul was not teaching polytheism but was rather articulating what non-Christian Romans and Greeks believed at the time.

LDS leaders may also point to *elohim*, a Hebrew name for God, as proof of biblical support for polytheism and, consequently, the doctrine of eternal progression. *Elohim* (the plural form of *god*) is used in the Genesis narrative of creation. This is why Genesis reads plural when God is speaking; "let *us* make man in *our* image."[201] Latter-day Saints may see this as proof of polytheism, a council of gods as described in the book of Moses. However, in the very next verse scripture says, "So God created man in *his* own image."[202] Orthodox Christians may see this as proof of monotheism. So what's with the plural? If there is only one god, why describe God as many? Who's right in this instance?

The reason *elohim* is plural is to describe the fullness of God in the Trinity, not to describe other gods. God is three persons (Father, Son, and Holy Spirit) in one being. These three persons are distinct yet coexist in harmony, and are co-equal and co-eternal with one another. This trinitarian existence constitutes one being – God. Therefore, when God says he created us in his own image he is articulating that he created us in the fullness of his likeness.

Aside from some very shaky arguments, there exists no biblical scripture to support polytheism and, ultimately, the doctrine of eternal progression. Scripture is very clear – there is one God and we are not him, nor can we ever become him or even fully like him. The Bible offers a poor source

---

[200] 1 Cor. 8:6
[201] Gen. 1:26

of defending eternal progression, so Latter-day Saints may quickly turn to the highest Mormon authority for that defense, the office of the president and living prophet.[203] Brigham Young taught that, "after men have got their exaltations and their crowns – have become gods, even the sons of God – are made kings of kings and lords of lords, they have the power then of propagating their species in spirit."[204]

Citing Brigham Young to an orthodox Christian is not a satisfactory authoritative source of theology. Latter-day Saints will most likely realize this, but keep in mind that for them the words of their prophets are on par with the very words of God. We shouldn't be quick to discard Mormon prophets just because we don't believe them. Rather, we should take the time to wrestle and compare their ideas with the truth of scripture. Placing the ideas of Mormon prophets next to biblical ideas may spark a conversation over authority and, hopefully, produce fruitful dialogue about Christ.

Finally, we should ask them to think about the logical difficulties present in the idea of eternal progression. For eternal progression to work there would need to exist an infinite lineage of gods, most of whom have a beginning. By that very logic *gods* with a finite beginning are not gods at all – they defy the definition. *Demi–gods*, perhaps, but not *gods*. For something to have a beginning it cannot be truly eternal and, therefore, cannot be a god.

Also, if there has always been an eternal progression of gods, how did the first god come to be? Who is the first god? If there is an uncaused first god, then there exists a unique god above all gods who is not subject to eternal progression. If that god exists why aren't we worshiping him instead? Forget Heavenly Father, what about Heavenly Father's Grandpa? Wouldn't Heavenly Father's Grandpa be much wiser and more experienced than Heavenly Father?

Additionally, the doctrine of eternal progression must come to grips with the philosophical issue of infinite regression. At some point the physical

---

[202] Gen. 1:27

[203] Always keep in mind that the office of president and living apostle in the LDS Church is given the ability to speak ex cathedra, that is, from the very mouth of god himself. This is especially true of Joseph Smith who declared, "God made Aaron to be the mouthpiece for the children of Israel, and he will make me be god to you in His stead, and the Elders to be mouth for me; and if you don't like it, you must lump it." Joseph Smith, Jr., *History of the Church of Jesus Christ of Latter-day Saints*, Vol. 6, 2nd ed. (Salt Lake City: The Deseret Book Company, 1973), 319–320.

[204] Brigham Young, *Journal of Discourses*, 26 vols. (Liverpool: The Church of Jesus Christ of Latter-day Saints), 6:227.

aspect of the gods must have been created, as there is a point in history when the physical universe did not exist. If the gods are physical beings, then how did they exist prior to the creation of the universe? If the gods were spirit beings before the physical universe, when did they don physical bodies? If it was at a specific point in the physical universe's history, how does this change the dynamic of the gods' existence? Perhaps this may have been the uncaused first god who, again in my opinion, would be much more deserving of our worship and admiration considering that he created the universe and all that dwells within it, even our Heavenly Father.

There are many questions associated with the doctrine of eternal progression that can really get the gears turning and spark healthy dialogue. Emphasize that as polytheism derived from the doctrine of eternal progression is not only unfounded in scripture but even the Book of Mormon seems to disagree. Talk about the God of scripture as a loving God who rules and reigns as the only God. Make sure to explain that we can never become gods for a very good reason – we would be very terrible at it.

Stress that God is immutable and unchanging, unlike the Heavenly Father of Mormonism who is still learning even to this day. Moreover, the God of Christianity exists as the Son Jesus Christ who came to suffer, die, and rise again to conquer Satan, sin, and death. The god of Mormonism, however, cannot relate to humanity in the same manner.

MORMONISM & BIG BROTHER JESUS

The Jesus of Mormonism, much like the god of Mormonism, is very different from the Jesus of orthodox Christianity. This claim alone – that Mormonism teaches a "different Jesus" – has caused much feather-ruffling over the years. Yet, it must be admitted that there are significant differences. One Jesus is eternal and the other came into being. One is a spiritual big brother and the other is God himself in the truest sense. These differences aren't minor in-house debates – they are substantial doctrinal disagreements with incalculable consequences. According to Brigham Young, in a previous spirit life before the creation of the world, Jesus was produced by a sexual act between Heavenly

Father and Heavenly Mother.[205] This is also how we (our preexistence and souls) came into being. Every person who has ever lived or will live is the direct offspring of Heavenly Father and Mother. This makes Jesus our big brother. It also makes Satan our big brother. Not only are Jesus and Satan brothers but Satan is also our brother as well. (And you thought your family was bad before.)

This idea introduces a big problem. If Jesus is simply our spiritual big brother who was created and not begotten, then Jesus is not God in the trinitarian sense, which Latter-day Saints will readily attest. This is perhaps the most important thing to understand about Jesus in Mormonism – he is in no way truly God.[206] So, what does this mean for our dialogue with Latter-day Saints? Firstly, it is important to note that scripture hints at the denial of the preexistence of our souls. We were not created nor existed at any time prior to our physical bodies. As Paul explains, "Thus it is written, 'The first man Adam *became* a living being'; the last Adam became a life–giving spirit. But it is not the spiritual that is first but the natural, and then the spiritual."[207] Accordingly, humans do not exist prior to their physical conception and then never cease to exist as spiritual beings.

But what of Jesus' preexistence in eternity past? If there was no preexistence of humanity, yet Jesus existed prior to humanity according to scripture, the only conclusion one may reach is that of Jesus' divinity. How can the Bible speak of Jesus existing prior to creation yet also be born of Heavenly Father and Heavenly Mother, who needed to progress to godhood

---

[205] "According to Brigham Young, our spirit body was created via a sexual union of Heavenly Father and Mother. '[God] created man, as we create our children,' said Young, '[f]or there is no other process of creation in heaven, on the earth, in the earth, or under the earth, or in all the eternities, that is, that where, or that ever will be.'" Richard Abanes, *Inside Today's Mormonism: Understanding Latter-day Saints in Light of Biblical Truth* (Eugene, Oreg.: Harvest House Publishers, 2004), 157. This idea later took Young to its logical conclusion that God the Father engaged in physical, sexual relations with Mary in order to impregnate her with his spirit son. The prophet explained; "When the Virgin Mary conceived the child Jesus, the Father had begotten him in his own likeness. He was not begotten by the Holy Ghost," and, "The birth of the Savior was as natural as the births of our children; it was the result of natural action (Journal of Discourses 1:50, 8:115)." This, of course, denies the Holy Spirit's role in Christ's conception (see Matt. 1:18 and Luke 1:26–35). While Young's words do not represent an overwhelming consensus of Mormon thought on this point, he does represent the extent to which Mormonism's radical materialism takes the faith.
[206] Furthermore, the Mormon Apostle James Talmage taught that Jesus was born of Mary through literal conception between the two. Rulon T. Burton, *We Believe: Doctrines and Principles of the Church of Jesus Christ of Latter-day Saints* (Draper, Utah: Tabernacle Books, 1994), 330.

sometime in the past in order to give birth to Jesus?[208] As the old adage goes, you can't have your cake and eat it too.

For this reason, it's important to contend for Jesus' divinity. To do so, it may be helpful to use sources from both the Bible and the Book of Mormon, at least in the initial conversations. This will act as a helpful bridge between Mormonism and orthodox Christianity, and will demonstrate your sincere willingness to take time and understand their worldview.

To contend for Jesus' divinity from the Book of Mormon itself read 2 Nephi 31:21 without informing anyone of the source; "And now, behold, my beloved brethren, this is the way; and there is none other way nor name given under heaven whereby man can be saved in the kingdom of God. And now, behold, this is the doctrine of Christ, and the only and true doctrine of the Father, and of the Son, and of the Holy Ghost, which is one God, without end. Amen."[209]

Ask if they would agree that, according to this passage, Jesus is God. Should they answer affirmatively, tell them that this passage is actually from the Book of Mormon, and since this verse clearly teaches God is a triune being, ask them whether or not this agrees with Mormon theology, perhaps specifically the doctrine of eternal progression. Can Jesus exist as one god with the Father for eternity and have been created at some point in time? Could Jesus have been both eternal and created or eternal and temporal?

If the point is conceded, it may be helpful to discuss how the LDS Church teaches two aspects of Jesus' nature that are incompatible – that he is both eternal and temporal. This not only provides a display of contradictory Mormon beliefs but points suspicion towards the Book of Mormon. If the Book of Mormon, the earliest Mormon text, doesn't agree with sources such as the Pearl of Great Price and Doctrine & Covenants, which are later Mormon texts, then either Joseph Smith's theology evolved over time or the Book of Mormon had a different author(s). Either way, the LDS Church and the Book of Mormon seem to be at odds with one another and the Bible with these inconsistent truth claims.

---

[207] 1 Cor. 15:45–46, emphasis added.
[208] Mic. 5:2; John 1:1,14; 7:5, 24–25; Phil. 2:6,7; Col. 1:17
[209] 2 Nephi 31:21

The cross of Christ is another source of major difference between the Jesus of Mormonism and the Jesus of Christianity. The purpose of the cross in Mormonism is the enabling of salvation, not the enabling and finishing of salvation. According to Mormonism those two events are separate. The cross enables the ability for salvation through grace, but the individual must complete the process through obedience. According to scripture, however, Jesus taught that he had come to seek and save the lost; he did not come to add more to the law but to fulfill it.[210] He taught that humanity could find salvation through faith in him alone and finalized this promise at Calvary.[211] His work on earth would ultimately culminate in his death, burial, and resurrection.[212]

Mormonism disagrees. It teaches Christ's sacrifice on the cross by itself is insufficient for the greatest expression of salvation. The Jesus of Mormonism requires more work from the individual in addition to the work and sacrifice of his own life. Forgiveness of sin is achieved through a combination of Jesus' sacrifice and the individual's efforts of following Heavenly Father's ordinances (or laws). Mormon theologian James Talmage summarized this view well when he said, "The sectarian dogma of justification by faith alone has exercised an influence for evil," and, "the justice of the scriptural doctrine that salvation comes to the individual only through obedience."[213]

This stands in stark contrast to the Jesus of Christianity who freely gives the gift of faith and attributes his work for salvation to us.[214] Elsewhere, scripture makes it painstakingly clear that no work can add to the work of the cross.[215] The works Christians perform are not intended to bring about salvation but are the fruit thereof. Godly works are the great indication of Jesus at work in peoples' lives.[216]

At the end of the day it cannot be stressed enough – talk about Jesus. Dialogue with Latter-day Saints, or any member of a rival worldview for that matter, should revolve entirely around the person and work of Jesus. There is nothing greater than when a person meets Jesus for the very first time, especially

---

[210] Luke 19:10; Matt. 5:17
[211] John 14:6; 19:30; Col. 2:14
[212] 1 Cor. 15
[213] James E. Talmage, *The Articles of Faith*, (Salt Lake City: The Deseret News, 1919), 432; 81.
[214] Eph. 2:8
[215] Acts 13:38–39, Rom. 4:3–5; 5:1; 6:23; Eph. 2:8–9
[216] John 15:5, Phil. 4:13

when he's been near to their life the whole time. Jesus should always be the centerpiece of conversation. Try to return the conversation to Jesus should you feel yourself chasing rabbit trails or focusing on secondary issues.

WHAT MORMONISM TEACHES ABOUT MAN & SALVATION

Mormonism teaches a radically different concept of man and salvation from Christianity, and the topic of salvation will no doubt be raised in conversation. However, before diving into a discussion about salvation with a Latter-day Saint it is important to define terms early in the conversation. Remember, Latter-day Saints are taught that humanity is not fallen in the traditional sense of the term, and that salvation is a never-ending process. Latter-day Saints are on a works-filled journey towards salvation met by grace, not a celebration of salvation through the Holy Spirit's sanctification. If a Latter-day Saint wants to progress eternally, they must adhere to Heavenly Father's ordinances and laws. The work of their salvation is never finished.

According to Mormonism salvation is only a free gift in the initial phase open to anyone. It is like a door that everyone may walk through, but once you walk through the door, if you want to stay in the room of salvation you must continually work through Mormon missions, church service, evangelism, family life, pursuit of sinlessness, etc. This directly challenges the orthodox Christian understanding of salvation. Humanity cannot sustain individual salvation alone since it was never ours to begin with – it is a free and gracious gift from God alone.[217]

The Mormon view of a grace-works hybrid salvation is unquestionably bolstered by its understanding of the fall. As previously demonstrated Mormonism views the fall as a good event because it marked humanity's liberation from non-existence. Joseph Smith summarized this view when he said, "The fall of man came as a blessing in disguise, and was the means of furthering the purposes of the Lord in the progress of man, rather than a means of hindering them."[218] This idea is also reflected in the JST; "Adam [said]: Blessed be the name of God, for because of my transgression my eyes were opened, and in

---

[217] Gen. 49:18; Pss. 3:8; 37:39; 119:174; Heb. 5:9; Rev. 7:10; 19:1
[218] Joseph Smith, *Doctrines of Salvation,* 1:113–14

this life I shall have joy, and again in the flesh I shall see God. And Eve [said]: Were it not for our transgressions we never should have had seed."[219] Satan, therefore, is the protagonist enabler of this story as humanity is able to begin their trek towards godhood because of him.

Scripture, however, paints a different picture – one of corruption, sorrow, loss, and grief. "Therefore, just as sin came into the world through one man, and death through sin, and so death spread to all men because all sinned … *even* over those whose sinning was not like the transgression of Adam."[220] It doesn't matter who you are, you have been born into sin because of your relation to Adam.[221]

The fall of humanity is far from something we should embrace as good. It doesn't get us closer to becoming gods; rather, it gets us further away from worshiping the only God. We deserve eternal separation from the creator we rebelled against, but thanks be to God for his rich mercy, grace, and kindness that he sent his son to the cross for our substitutionary atonement. Because of Jesus' work as the Second Adam, reversing the curse of the First Adam by the fall, we can reconnect with our creator starting right now and lasting forever. Latter-day Saints may agree up until this point, but they are forced to depart from orthodox Christianity when they insist that each individual must finish Jesus' work of salvation for personal exaltation.[222]

In Mormonism each person contributes to the sustainment of his or her own salvation. Latter-day Saints are consequently inundated in a posture of good works in order to remain worthy of the highest level of salvation. No other Mormon leader was clearer on this subject than Brigham Young who emphatically declared; "Salvation is an individual operation. I am the only person that can possibly save myself."[223] Young elsewhere claims that, "salvation is an individual work; it is every person for himself."[224]

---

[219] Moses 5:10–11
[220] Rom. 5:12–14, emphasis added.
[221] This concept is what theologians call *original sin*. We are not born morally neutral; we are born sinners. A good example of original sin taught in the Bible is Ps. 51:5.
[222] "Jesus is laboring with [Heavenly Father's] might to sanctify and redeem the earth and to bring back his brethren and sisters into the presence of the Father." – Brigham Young. The Church of Jesus Christ of Latter-day Saints, *Teachings of Presidents of the Church: Brigham Young* (Salt Lake City: Church of Jesus Christ of Latter-day Saints), 296.
[223] The Church of Jesus Christ of Latter-day Saints, *Teachings of Presidents of the Church: Brigham Young* (Salt Lake City: Church of Jesus Christ of Latter-day Saints), 294.
[224] Ibid., 293.

Young's greatest justification for this doctrine most likely derives from the Book of Mormon, which promotes working towards salvation.[225] Consequently, many Latter-day Saints struggle with the dichotomy of presumptuous pride or destructive despair in their spiritual life because of this grace-works hybrid, which is addressed in LDS Brad Wilcox's helpful talk "His Grace is Sufficient."[226] People may presume they are in God's grace, becoming prideful because they think they can maintain God's standards, or they may become overwhelmed by despair, leading to destruction because they realize they can't maintain God's standards (a struggle many evangelicals know all too well). Young further added to this dangerous doctrine by insisting that works impress Heavenly Father, which is the only chance a person has of restoring community with him; "Cultivate righteousness and faithfulness in yourselves, which is the only passport into celestial happiness."[227] Young is wrong.[228] The only passport into celestial happiness is not our righteousness and faithfulness but rather Jesus' righteousness and faithfulness imputed to us by faith through his grace alone and by his finished work on the cross.[229] We cannot merit a single aspect of our salvation no matter how righteous or faithful we believe ourselves to be.[230] We cannot possibly mediate our own salvation with God because Jesus is the only one who can and does serve in that capacity.[231]

Paul summarizes this when he declares, "By grace you have been saved through faith; and that not of yourselves, it is the gift of God. Not by works, lest any man should boast."[232] There is nothing we can do to ever work our way to God because of our fallen state in sin.[233] We are absolutely and completely dependent on his grace, mercy, and redemption.[234] It's not our redemption, it's

---

[225] 2 Nephi 25:23
[226] During Wilcox's speech he pleads for his audience to understand that "Jesus doesn't make up the difference. Jesus makes all the difference. Grace is not about filling gaps. It is about filling us."
[227] The Church of Jesus Christ of Latter-day Saints, Teachings of Presidents of the Church: Brigham Young (Salt Lake City: Church of Jesus Christ of Latter-day Saints), 293.
[228] Rom. 10:3. Scripture seems to indicate that anyone who espouses self-righteousness in the sight of God is ignorant of God's righteousness.
[229] Rom. 5:16–17; 2 Cor. 5:21; Titus 3:7
[230] Matt. 5:20
[231] 1 Tim. 2:5
[232] Eph. 2:8–9
[233] Rom. 3:23; 8:7–8
[234] Eph. 2:4–5

his.[235] It's not our work in our lives, it's his finished work on the cross.[236] It's not our intercession through our righteousness; it's his substitutionary atonement that intercedes in spite of our unrighteousness.[237] We are completely helpless to merit community with God by ourselves, and we cannot have it any other way. The great preacher C. H. Spurgeon summarized this well; "Either Jesus bore all our sins, or none; and He either saves us once for all, or not at all."[238]

This is why the cross of Christ is so crucial. It's important to talk about grace with Latter-day Saints. They, along with us, need to understand that there is nothing they can do to make God love them any more or less than he already does. They cannot add nor take away from salvation – it's all or nothing. Latter-day Saints are saturated in a grace-works hybrid view of salvation, although grace-alone is given lip service by their leaders.[239] Talk to them about grace. Ask them if they really think their good works are good enough for an infinitely perfect and completely just God.

THE GOSPEL IN DIALOGUE WITH LATTER-DAY SAINTS

The most important conversation we can have with Latter-day Saints is about the gospel. Before we enter into that dialogue, however, we should make sure that we are spiritually ready. We should prayerfully consider what we should bring up in the dialogue, seeking after what God has placed on our minds to discuss. We should also pray that God's Word take root in our hearts and minds so we may stand firm when presented with Mormonism's take on Jesus and the gospel.

We should also keep in mind the spiritual state of the Latter-day Saint to whom we are speaking. Are they in a good position to dialogue with an orthodox Christian? Could we conduct our conversation in a way that is honoring to Jesus and productive for both sides? Or, will we simply talk past one another and cause a rift that will become difficult to repair? Remember,

---

[235] Eph. 2:10
[236] Col. 1:20; Rom. 3:28
[237] Rom. 3:10–11; 5:8, Isa. 53:12, 1 Tim. 2:5
[238] Charles H. Spurgeon, *The Soul Winner* (Grand Rapids, Mich.: Wm. B. Eerdmans Publishing Co., 1963), 33.

Mormonism is very holistic. It permeates every aspect of a Latter-day Saint's life from family to work, from friends to hobbies. A potential life change could be around the corner when we engage in dialogue about the gospel with LDS.

This is an aspect of Mormonism that is very difficult to overcome. Mormonism isn't simply a religion for most Latter-day Saints, it's their entire life. Should they choose to leave Mormonism they are often times choosing to leave family, friends, and jobs. It sometimes even means leaving their homes and towns. This can cause an immense amount of stress and emotional injury that, I think, orthodox Christians have a difficult time understanding. If we leave a church, there's typically only a few waves made. When a Latter-day Saint leaves Mormonism, their entire world is shaken. So, dialoguing with them about Jesus is not like talking to a Baptist as an Anglican. There is a lot at stake for them, which we need to continually bear in mind. The question for us becomes, How do we dialogue with Latter-day Saints about Jesus? How can we say with LDS Brad Wilcox, "Jesus doesn't make up the difference, he makes all the difference" while lovingly discussing the myriad issues that Mormonism presents in comparison to orthodox Christianity?

I would suggest to start by turning those home visits from Mormon missionaries into a time in which you can get your feet wet in dialogue about Jesus with Latter-day Saints.[240] The Latter-day Saints we dialogue with might not always be our neighbor or friend. You might get a knock on the door one Saturday morning to be greeted by two well-groomed, young men. Take advantage of this opportunity as it may only knock once. Pun *definitely* intended. Don't be afraid to talk to them about religion – that's their job! Remember, though, ultimately they'd like to see you join the LDS Church. They have no other focus for two years except to make more Latter-day Saints. Ask them first if they are willing to dialogue with you straight from scripture, perhaps on a set topic such as salvation, heaven, or the person and

---

[239] Doctrine & Covenants 18:31, 20:30

[240] On this point discernment is needed. John advises Christians not to allow people into their homes if they preach a different gospel than the one spoken of in scripture. He states in 2 John 1:10 that, "If anyone comes to you and does not bring this teaching, do not receive him into your house or give him any greeting." Keep this in mind – if the Holy Spirit convicts you not to have any member of a rival worldview over to you home for the purpose of evangelism, then meet with them elsewhere. However, some missionaries, such as Latter-day Saints and Jehovah's Witnesses, will appear at your doorstep. If you feel led, and have considered it prayerfully, use this situation to show hospitality and share Jesus.

work of Jesus. If they agree, go for it. If they agree but you feel the conversation derailing back to what seems to be a script they are following to control the dialogue don't worry, they are. Mormon missionaries are taught to stick to the script.

Should this happen your encounter with them will usually entail a lot of talking on their end with a sort of Q&A portion at the end. If they continue to press with the script, wait for the end and dialogue during the Q&A. Afterwards, be prepared to have the missionaries guide you to a passage from Moroni in the Book of Mormon. Their underlying goal, as they wrap up their pre-planned talk with you, is to evoke within you a feeling (or "testimony") about whether or not the Book of Mormon is true. Cue the passage from Moroni;

> And when ye shall receive these things, I would exhort you that ye would ask God, the Eternal Father, in the name of Christ, if these things are not true; and if ye shall ask with a sincere heart, with real intent, having faith in Christ, he will manifest the truth of it unto you, by the power of the Holy Ghost. And by the power of the Holy Ghost ye may know the truth of all things.[241]

When (not if) they ask you to pray with a sincere heart about the Book of Mormon, politely decline. When they ask why, tell them that scripture teaches the heart is not something to be trusted. Jeremiah says, "the heart is deceitful above all things, and desperately sick; who can understand it?"[242] Of course, having Jesus as Lord over our hearts as Christians curbs the sinful nature of our heart but doesn't make it trustworthy, especially on big decisions like whether or not something is the word of God. In this instance we need to use all of the tools at our disposal to make a decision – our heart, mind, and scripture.

Refusing to pray in the manner Moroni suggests might wrap things up for them, but one last opportunity will afford itself to share Jesus. Ask them if you could close the meeting in prayer. They'll never say no as it would be extremely rude and off-putting to the one they are trying to convert. This is a great opportunity to pray the gospel – literally. Thank God that we can fully

---

[241] Moroni 10:4–5
[242] Jer. 17:9

know him through the Bible and that he sent his only begotten son to die for our sins. Thank him that there is no work we can do to gain our salvation but that it's given to us freely by him. This closing prayer is a chance to share the gospel uninterrupted, a chance to see Jesus glorified and the gospel magnified.

Always remember that the best tool at our disposal is the gospel. Tell them there are no works involved for salvation, they only need to have faith in the person and work of Jesus Christ. They don't need to worry about whether or not they are properly following Heavenly Father's ordinances perfectly; Jesus already accomplished this for us. God knows we are fallen and even after we become Christians, we still sin. This is why scripture says, "even when we were dead in our trespasses, [he] made us alive together with Christ – by grace you have been saved."[243] There is no work of righteousness we can do to make God love us more than he already does now. Likewise, there is no work of unrighteousness we can do to make God love us any less. Jesus is the one who loves us unconditionally, is far beyond a spiritual family member as God himself, and wants nothing more for us than to be free from the chains of bondage and works.

---

[243] Eph. 2:5

CHAPTER THREE

Jehovah's Witnesses & Archangel Jesus

"Only this organization functions for Jehovah's purpose and to his praise. To it alone God's Sacred Word, the Bible, is not a sealed book." [244]

WATCHTOWER MAGAZINE (1973)

"Did you finish your homework?" Jamie asked me.

Sitting beside her in my Chemistry class, I responded, "You know me! Of course I finished my homework; in, uh, German class last hour."

She smiled.

"You know we have that lab next week so you better know what you're doing!" Jamie and I were lab partners for a good part of the semester that year.

"I will, I will. Geez Jamie, you don't have to be worried. When have we ever botched a lab?"

One of her eyebrows rose, "*We* have never botched a lab because *we* have *me!*"

I laughed.

"Right, and the almighty Jamie can do no wrong," I quipped. Her jaw dropped in an over–exaggerative, playful reaction.

"Did you just go there, Kyle?" she smirked as she prepared for another bantering argument.

"Oh, I just went there!"

"Alright, buddy. But you just remember when we end up spending half our lab time listening to you trying to prove that one plus one plus one equals one, then I'll remind you of how the 'almighty Jamie can do no wrong'!"

She was referring to our frequent discussions about the Trinity.

---

[244] *Watchtower Magazine*, July 1st, 1973, 402.

I smiled, shook my head, and shifted my attention to the teacher who was beginning that day's lecture. But, in the back of my mind, the gears began to turn.

How could I defend myself against Jamie when all her arguments about the 'illogicality' of the Trinity were so well thought out? How could I better explain to her that Christians do not worship three gods but one god in three persons? How could I better reconcile God to my good friend, Jamie – my Jehovah's Witness friend, Jamie?

WHAT IS JEHOVAH'S WITNESS?

Jehovah's Witnesses hold the exclusive claim that they are the only true church of Jesus Christ. With a membership of over 8.2 million worldwide, they hold the belief that there is absolutely no salvation outside Jehovah's Witness beliefs as articulated through the Watchtower Society. Witnesses maintain that the Kingdom of Christendom, which includes Roman Catholics and all Protestant denominations, have falsely taught a foreign gospel since the time of the early church. However, the gospel's fullness was rediscovered in the late 19th century when a young 18-year-old from Pittsburgh named Charles Taze Russell organized a Bible class. In his mind, Russell was able to uncover many truths concealed by the Kingdom of Christendom that allowed him to establish the only organization, the Kingdom of Witnesses, that could publish the true gospel for salvation among many counterfeits.

From Russell's teachings, Jehovah's Witnesses have come to believe that God, a solitary being named *Jehovah*, performed his first creative act by bringing Christ into existence through whom he subsequently created all other things.[245] From the time Adam fell into sin God has been represented through his visible, theocratic organization.[246] Prominent members of this society have included; Noah, Abraham, Isaac, Jacob, Moses, David, John the Baptist, Peter, James, John, and Charles Taze Russell, who officially named the theocracy the *Watchtower Society*. This theocracy, because it is angel-guided, is the only

---

[245] George D. Chryssides, *Historical Dictionary of Jehovah's Witnesses* (Lanham, Mary.: Scarecrow Press, Inc., 2008), 37.
[246] Edmond C. Gruss, *Jehovah's Witnesses: Their Claims, Doctrinal Changes and Prophetic Speculation*, 2nd ed. (Maitland, Flor.: Inc., 2007), 99.

organization on earth that can properly reveal the character and will of God.[247] Jehovah's Witnesses are taught that Jesus was installed as Jehovah's heavenly king in October 1914. When Jesus physically returns at his second coming he will be accompanied by 144,000 faithful Jehovah's Witnesses to defeat sin and rule with him over paradise earth. God will recreate the remaining Jehovah's Witness population to enjoy eternal existence on the paradise earth and annihilate all others. Until then, it is a sin to have a blood transfusion, run for public office, join the Armed Forces, attend religious services outside of weddings or funerals, or celebrate Christmas and Easter.[248]

CHARLES TAZE RUSSELL & THE WATCHTOWER SOCIETY

At first glance Jehovah's Witness theology appears to be a dynamic mixture of eschatological (or "End Times") speculation, 19th century Adventism, and the resurrection of an old Christian heresy called Arianism. So, where does this story begin? The answer is found with the birth of Charles Taze Russell.

Russell was brought into this world on February 16, 1852 through a Presbyterian family. He echoed the founding Mormon prophet, Joseph Smith, in that at a young age he seems to have struggled accepting or understanding orthodox Christian theology. In particular, the doctrines of hell, predestination, and historical trinitarianism were especially vexing to Russell. He was inspired to exhaustively comb through the scriptures looking for answers, but never found any that satisfied him. Eventually, having been deeply persuaded by Adventism, he came to reject the doctrine of hell as traditionally understood. Additionally, he began formulating a complex eschatology that described apocalyptic events occurring near the time he lived. Russell was renewed with excitement for scripture and soon gathered a group of like-minded people around him. These people eventually formed a Bible study known as the "Bible Students," and elected Russell as their pastor.[249]

---

[247] John Ankerberg, John Weldon, and Dillon Burroughs, *The Facts on Jehovah's Witnesses* (Eugene, Oreg.: Harvest House Publishers, 2008), 70.
[248] I. Hexham, "Jehovah's Witnesses," *Evangelical Dictionary of Theology*, 2nd ed., Walter A. Elwell, ed. (Grand Rapids, Mich.: Baker Academic, 2001), 625.
[249] Ibid., 624.

The Bible study and his new office of pastor served as a medium to teach his convictions concerning the existence of hell, the nature of Jesus, and the end of the world. Eventually, the Bible study grew so large that in 1896 it formed into a society called the *Watchtower Tract and Bible Society*.[250] This organization still exists today and had more than ten million copies of its periodicals, *Awake!* and *The Watchtower*, in circulation by the 1970s.[251]

Russell, despite never claiming to wield revelatory powers, nevertheless considered himself a mouthpiece for God to speak in the Last Days. His apocalyptic system was riddled with issues from its inception, causing him to make a number of faulty claims concerning the end of the world. According to him, 1799 marked "the time of the end," which would set the stage to usher in the end of the world.[252] Christ later made an invisible return to earth and had been reigning as King since October 1874.[253] A few years on, in 1899, Russell taught that the Battle of Armageddon had begun, which was strictly spiritual and would continue for years. The battle, he claimed, would end in 1914 "with the complete overthrow of earth's present ruleship."[254] For the Bible Students, 1914 was the end.

In fact, Russell was so convinced that the world would come to an end in 1914 that he sold his prosperous clothing store in 1879 and began printing *Zion's Watchtower*, a magazine to warn people of the impending doom.[255] In 1886 he wrote a six-volume work called *Millennium Dawn*, later retitled *Studies in the Scriptures*, which he believed were the only means of properly studying the Bible. Russell warned that studying scripture alone would inevitably lead to confusion or even spiritual death. His commentary and theological instruction would clarify confusing points in scripture and allow his followers a unique glimpse into their leader's thoughts.

---

[250] Paul A. Djupe, Laura R. Olson, *Encyclopedia of American Religion and Politics* (New York: Facts on File, Inc., 2003), 466.

[251] Philip W. Goetz and Margaret Sutton, *The New Encyclopedia Britannica: Volume 1* (Chicago: Encyclopædia Inc, 1983), 131.

[252] Tony Wills, *A People for His Name: A History of Jehovah's Witnesses and an Evaluation* 2nd ed. (Morrisville, NC: Lulu Enterprises, Inc., 2006), 47.

[253] Charles T. Russell, *Studies in the Scriptures*, Vol. 4 (London: International Bible Students Association, 1916), 621.

[254] Charles T. Russell, *The Time Is at Hand*, (Brooklyn, NY: Charles T. Russell, 1916), 101.

[255] M. James Penton, *Apocalypse Delayed: The Story of Jehovah's Witnesses* 2nd ed. (Toronto: University of Toronto Press, 1997), 339.

One such unique glimpse is Russell's methodology for deriving his eschatology. According to *Studies in the Scriptures*, his ability to construct an apocalyptic calendar was found in the pyramids of Egypt. Russell claimed that these monuments to Egyptian royalty were ordained and situated by God to act as a second witness to God in addition to the Bible. In essence, the pyramids were instruments of revealing great truths to humanity. The Watchtower pastor measured passageways in pyramids that allowed him to calculate the year that the world would end – 1914.[256]

The idea caught on and spread like wildfire. Tracts were produced to warn of the impending destruction, and many of the Bible Students sold their possessions to campaign full-time. The timing was perfect. Apocalyptic fanaticism was at a fever pitch after decades of millenarian groups warning of the imminent return of Christ. With World War I looming just around the corner, combat in the Balkan Peninsula was beginning to bring serious speculation of widespread war. And behind the backdrop of years of apocalyptic language from most Christian denominations in 19th century North America, the fears of war in Europe served as ripe soil for Russell's doomsday prediction.

Soon, 1914 came and went. Unfortunately for Russell and his followers, 1914 passed by without the complete decay of human authority and the end of human history. Russell concluded that he must have made a miscalculation or two and pushed the date back to 1915. Again, Jesus was nowhere to be found as 1915 came and went without so much as a plague of locusts or a bowl of wrath. So, Russell pushed the date back again to 1918.

He was never able to see if his prediction came true as the world came to an end for him in 1916 while traveling on a preaching tour in Texas. The Bible Students were shocked. Their visionary and leader had left them in a relatively abrupt manner at the age of sixty-four. They needed Russell's legacy to carry on, for Watchtower Society prophecies to continue, and for Jehovah to be faithfully represented as Russell had prescribed. Just when it seemed no one within the organization could carry on the torch, one legal clerk stepped up to the challenge and led the Watchtower Society farther than they could have ever imagined under Russell.

---

[256] Ruth A. Tucker, *Another Gospel: Cults, Alternative Religions, and the New Age Movement* (Grand Rapids, Mich.: Zondervan, 1989), 124.

THE END IS ~~HERE~~ NEAR! — THE JUDGE CARRIES ON

In 1917, Joseph Franklin "Judge" Rutherford was elected unopposed as the second president of the Watchtower Society. Rutherford had served Russell and the Society as a legal counselor after joining the Bible Students in 1906. Something of a succession crisis occurred shortly after Rutherford's election as president.[257] About a quarter of those within the Society who did not recognize the new president's authority splintered into various groups. Those faithful to Rutherford remained in the Watchtower Society, which officially adopted the name Jehovah's Witnesses in 1931 as a modern designation and, in my opinion, a way to distance themselves from the poor reputation that Russell had brought the organization with regard to end times predictions.

Despite the shaky transition of power and previously failed prophecies, the Jehovah's Witnesses pressed forward and their obsession with eschatology only grew. So, Rutherford honored Russell's commitment to the idea that Judgment Day was just around the corner. The judge revisited Russell's calculations and prophecies to determine that the true end of the world was actually in 1925.[258] This time you could take it to the bank, and many Jehovah's Witnesses did.

To warn the masses of their impending doom, Judge Rutherford wrote a famous pamphlet titled *Millions Now Living Will Never Die*, and launched a campaign with faithfully motivated Jehovah's Witnesses to spread the truth about the end... again. To add a twist to the normal apocalyptic scenarios Witnesses were used to, Rutherford also taught that Abraham, Isaac, and Jacob would be resurrected in order to rule as princes on the new Paradise Earth.[259]

Many Witnesses believed the judge. They sold their possessions and property, left their hometowns, and lived out of automobiles in order to spread the news. As with all the previous predictions, 1925 came and passed without the restoration of all things, so the judge asked for a mulligan. He was insistent

---

[257] George D. Chryssides, "Finishing the Mystery: the Watch Tower and the 1917 schism," in *Sacred Schisms: How Religions Divide*, (Cambridge: Cambridge University Press, 2009), 112.
[258] Tony Wills, *A People for His Name: A History of Jehovah's Witnesses and an Evaluation*, 2nd ed (Morrisville, NC: Lulu Enterprises, Inc., 2006), 125.
[259] M. James Penton, *Apocalypse Delayed: The Story of Jehovah's Witnesses*, 2nd ed. (Toronto: University of Toronto Press, 1997), 93.

that the end was near as Witnesses patiently heard Rutherford's rationale for the recalculated final date of 1927.

Again, the end came and went. This time, faced with multiple failed predictions in their past, the Witnesses realized that nailing down a date for Armageddon was unwise and imprudent. These dates marked the end of Witnesses predicting hard dates for the end of the world. Yet, their dedication to the end times narrative never wavered. The end was near, it just was not as near as they had previously suspected.

The longer Rutherford remained in power, the more troubling the reports of his poor leadership became. His tenure of leadership over Watchtower was the longest any single individual had led the Society, but it was also marked with accusations of domineering leadership, womanizing, and alcohol abuse.[260] Rutherford took the mantel of leadership from Russell and transformed it into something that closely resembled a theocratic organization rather than simply an ecclesiastical one. In fact, Rutherford openly referred to himself as the head of a theocracy. This stripped the organization of many democratic processes and replaced them with very centralized, top-down approaches to governance. Such centralized control over the organization can still be seen today.

In the 1930s, Jehovah's Witnesses experienced one of their darkest hours. For Witnesses, World War II was sparked by Christendom, a term that describes the mixing of religious and political ideals. They viewed such mixture as unholy, a sure sign that the prince of the power of the air is currently at work in the world's governments. During the 1930s, as with today, they refused to participate in civic duties. Naturally, this resulted in persecution from the National Socialists. Their refusal to swear allegiance to Hitler (or any world leader for that matter) and their denial to cease proselytizing activities sent many Witnesses to concentration camps.[261] They were branded with inverted purple triangles to identify them as *Bibelforscher*.[262] The Nazis viewed

---

[260] M. James Penton, *Jehovah's Witnesses and the Third Reich: Sectarian Politics Under Persecution* (Toronto: University of Toronto Press, 2004), 102.
[261] As many as 2,000 Jehovah's Witnesses were sent to Nazi concentration camps with many more facing arrest.
[262] German for "Bible Student." The official name for Jehovah's Witnesses in Germany at this time was *Bibelforscher*, but they were also informally known as *Zeugen Jehova's* (Jehovah's Witnesses).

Jehovah's Witnesses as unpatriotic enemies of the state, members of an organization whose sole goal was to promote subversion of governmental powers and to undermine National Socialism.

Thousands of Witnesses suffered indescribable injustice during World War II throughout Europe, and they also experienced persecution closer to home. Jehovah's Witnesses did not simply refuse to support one side of Christendom over the other – they rejected both sides, axis and allies. As a result, many Witnesses in the United States were imprisoned for refusing to fight or participate in the war. Their pacifism cost them not only the freedoms of certain male adherents, but also any social capital the organization had prior to the global conflict. Refusing to support the war effort tarnished the Witnesses' public reputation. It was a price they were willing to pay.

Rutherford, for his part, attempted to shield the Witnesses during this time, albeit in an extremely dubious manner. The Society wrote Hitler in an attempt to dissuade the *Reichskanzler's* persecution of Witnesses. In the letter, Rutherford argued that while the Jehovah's Witnesses had never publicly declared their support for Germany, neither had they spoken against National Socialism. The real culprits for religious denunciation of Nazi Germany came from "Jewish businessmen and Catholics," not Jehovah's Witnesses. In fact, those men represented a common enemy – both Nazis and Witnesses were victims of slander from Jews and Catholics. After all, the letter reminded Hitler, the Witnesses were "fighting for the same high ethical goals and ideals" as Germany in certain instances.[263] The irony here is almost palpable. Rutherford's argument for such a bizarre alliance is, in my opinion, a stain on Jehovah's Witness history.

Rutherford died, before the war ended, in January 1942. With his death came a shift in the organization that has largely shaped the organization that we know today. Most notably the Jehovah's Witnesses no longer (after Rutherford) ascribe specific dates to mark the end times. Instead of Christ returning invisibly in 1914 or physically in 1925, now Witnesses understand 1914 as the date in which Satan was cast down from heaven and assumed

---

[263] Joseph F. Rutherford, "Declaration of Facts," June 25, 1933. Translation mine.

authority over the earth. His rulership will only last until an unknown time in the future when Christ will establish his earthly kingdom or *Paradise Earth.* Thus, it is commonly misunderstood that the Jehovah's Witnesses continually predict and re-predict the second coming of Christ. They are accused of pushing the date back further and further, utilizing end times angst at various points in history in an attempt to lure people into their organization.[264] The truth, however, is that Witnesses believe an incredibly complex eschatological system which simply claims that we are living in the End Times. At any rate, the tired accusation that Witnesses habitually push back the date of Christ's second return should be put to rest.

JEHOVAH'S WITNESSES & ARCHANGEL JESUS

As with every other rival worldview, much of the difference between orthodox Christianity and the Jehovah's Witnesses centers on the person and work of Jesus. Unlike Mormonism, it is common for Jehovah's Witnesses to emphasize these differences in a bid to distinguish themselves from other streams of Christianity. This is especially true when it comes to the doctrine of trinitarianism and the deity of Christ.

Perhaps the greatest difference between orthodox Christianity and the Witnesses is the person of Jesus who, according to their thought, is a spirit being created by God. Jesus had a beginning and did not exist from eternity past. He was created as a type of super-angel with much higher power and responsibility than the rest of the angels. This angel Jesus, when in heaven, is named Michael the Archangel. In fact, the two are one and the same – both Michael the Archangel and Jesus are the same person and spiritual creature.

At some point, Jehovah willed that humanity should have an opportunity for salvation, which resulted in his selection of Jesus. He was sent to earth, having shed his angelic nature, through the virgin convention of Mary. At this time, Jesus was only a man. There was nothing divine about him;

---

[264] Zoe Knox, "The Watch Tower Society and the End of the Cold War: Interpretations of the End–Times, Superpower Conflict, and the Changing Geo–Political Order," *Journal of American Academy of Religion*, December 2011, Vol. 79, No. 4, pp. 1018—1049.
[265] Paul Grundy, "Jehovah's Witness Statistics," J.W. Facts, http://www.jwfacts.com/watchtower/statistics.php (accessed January 9, 2012).

he was simply a human being. He completely shed his divinity. This is a hard concept to understand if you are coming from an orthodox Christian background. To the Jehovah's Witnesses, there was nothing divine about Jesus in his life prior to his ministry. Of course, he was sent by Jehovah God and would exhibit a very godly life, but he was just a normal human being like you and me.

This normal human state only lasted until his baptism by John when he then became the Messiah, or the Christ.[266] At his baptism, Jehovah publicly announced that Jesus was now the Christ; yet, Jesus was still not divine in any way.[267] He was still a human being, only now he was the messiah. Before this baptism, however, Jesus was just a normal, run-of-the-mill, angel-turned-human, blue-collar kind of guy. (That was a lot of dashes.)

Reasons for Jesus' divinity, or his nature as both God and man, will be will be examined in detail later in this chapter. Suffice it to say now, however, that Jehovah's Witnesses understand Jesus as created by God, not begotten.

A CROSS BY ANY OTHER SHAPE

The means of Jesus' crucifixion is another point of difference between orthodox Christians and Jehovah's Witnesses, who teach that the t-shaped cross portrayed in many illustrations of Jesus' crucifixion is actually a pagan symbol.[268] Therefore, they reject the traditional understanding of the cross and teach that Jesus was crucified on a tall "torture stake."[269] Imagine the countless amount of artwork depicting Jesus on a cross with his arms stretched outward. This image, Witnesses believe, is a faulty understanding of first-century Roman execution. According to them, Jesus would have been crucified on a single "torture stake" with his hands nailed down, one on top of another, above his head.

The problem with this idea, among many things, is found in the Greek text of the New Testament. Should this topic arise in dialogue with a

---

[266] Matt. 3:13–17
[267] Luke 3:21–22
[268] Eugene, V. Gallagher, W. Michael Ashcroft, *Introduction to New and Alternative Religions in America* (Westport, Conn.: Greenwood Press, 2006), 75.
[269] Ibid.

Jehovah's Witness, the original Greek is one place we can go. The Greek term for the cross is most commonly σταυρός or 'stauros.' The "torture stake," which the Jehovah's Witnesses believe Jesus was crucified on, is μόνος σταυρός or 'monos stauros' (*an isolated stake*). The word 'monos,' meaning *one* or *single*, denotes a different type of cross from the common t-shaped cross called a σταυρός or 'stauros.' In scripture, we simply do not find 'monos stauros' anywhere, only 'stauros.'

This is not to say that 'stauros' alone expresses the t-shaped cross. 'Stauros' by itself does not definitively identify the t-shaped cross, but neither does it definitively identify the "torture stake." This is because ancient sources do not describe crucifixion or the shape of the instruments in much detail. It was assumed that the reader had knowledge of crucifixion since these executions usually occurred in public places. However, the most common form of execution with the use of a 'stauros' was *crucifixion*, from the Latin *crux* (cross) and *figo* (fixed to), or *cruci affigo* meaning "to fasten to a cross."[270] The common use of the cross was two pieces of wood fashioned together to resemble either a *crux immissa* or *crux commissa*, which took the forms '+' or 'T' respectively.[271] In the case of Jesus' crucifixion, he most likely carried the horizontal cross beam, known as the *patibulum*, until Simon of Cyrene assisted him. He was later tied and nailed to the *patibulum* and fashioned to the vertical beam, thus making the t-shaped 'stauros.'[272]

This is why Christians have held for centuries the belief that Jesus was crucified on a t-shaped cross, as seen in the fact that the early church adopted the t-shaped cross as an identification marking that they were Christians. If the New Testament writers wanted to ensure we knew Christ's crucifixion took place on a torture stake, they would have clarified with the words 'monos stauros' rather than simply identifying the cross as 'stauros.' This is as big of a difference as saying 'America' over 'South America' or even 'theism' over 'atheism.' The preceding word (or prefix) entirely changes the meaning of the second word. Since the New Testament authors didn't identify Jesus' cross

---

[270] David W. Chapman, *Ancient Jewish and Christian Perceptions of Crucifixion* (Tübingen, Germany: Mohr Siebeck, 2008), 8.
[271] Ibid.
[272] Matt. 27:32–35; Mark 15:21–24; Luke 23:26–33

with 'monos,' we can say with confidence that Jesus was crucified on the traditional t-shaped cross.

Oddly enough, Jehovah's Witnesses haven't always believed in the 'torture stake.' At one point in time, they had no problem with the traditional icon of the cross. Below is a cover of the *Watchtower* magazine from 1931. In the upper left-hand side of *Figure 3.1*, one can clearly see the symbol they consider pagan today. *Figure 3.2* is a magnified image of that symbol.

Figures 3.1 and 3.2

Furthermore, there is evidence to suggest that it was a widely known fact throughout the Roman Empire that Jesus was crucified on the traditional t-shaped cross. The evidence comes from a most unlikely source – ancient Roman graffiti (*Figure 3.3*). Discovered in 1857 on the side of an unearthed building in Rome, the graffiti depicts a man with a donkey's head being crucified on a t-shaped cross. Below the donkey-man stands a Roman citizen with his left hand raised towards the cross. A caption reads, "Alexamenos worships his god." It was meant as an insult, inferring that Christians are stupid for worshiping a jackass; however, it is invaluable evidence to support the traditional t-shaped cross because this graffiti was etched around the beginning of the 3rd century in Rome.[273]

Figure 3.3
Vector traced from Rodolfo Lanciani, *Ancient Rome in the Light of Recent Excavations*, 6th ed.
(Cambridge, Mass.: Houghton, Mifflin, & Co., 1888), 122.

But, honestly, what's the big deal? Who cares what shape the cross was? Some view the Jehovah's Witnesses disagreement with the shape of the cross as a trivial matter – it doesn't matter what shape the cross was so long as Jesus died on it and left it empty. However, Christians should not be so quick to throw out the importance of the cross' shape since it is the center piece of the entire redemption narrative, emphasized in Jesus' outstretched arms. Of course, if someone really believes that Jesus was crucified on a torture stake, so be it – that is not an argument we should get too involved in. But, denying the shape of the traditional cross may give some indications about one's view on salvation and standing before God.

---

[273] David L. Balch and Carolyn Osiek, *Early Christian Families in Context: An Interdisciplinary Dialogue*, (Grand Rapids, Mich.: Wm. B. Eerdmans Publishing, 2003), 103.

Denying the cross, even the shape of the cross, to fit your own interpretation, is indicative of one's heart. Numbers 21:4–9 is a perfect example of what it means to look upon the cross as it is. Here's the setup – God hears the cries of his chosen people under slavery in Egypt and redeems them by setting them free from slavery. God's people begin to become rebellious against God and complain to Moses about being brought out of Egypt into the wilderness to die.[274] They wanted to go back into slavery and sought a response from God about their request. In response to their complaints, God sends snakes which was probably not what they had in mind when they were complaining.[275] Some of them began to die from poisonous snakebites. This is when the people realized they needed God's help. They repented and asked that the snakes be taken away from them.[276] Moses took the request to God who told him to make a bronze snake and put it on a pole. Moses was then instructed to hold the pole up in the air. If the people would look at the pole, they would not die from the snakebites.[277]

From this story we catch a glimpse into the crucifixion of Jesus hundreds of years before it took place. God looks upon humanity (the Hebrews) mired in sin (slavery) and bound to the world (Egypt). He chooses to redeem us and calls us out of our sinful existence; however, sometimes to do so God needs to show us exactly how bad our situation is. He allows snakes (sin and depravity) into our lives and convicts us with the Holy Spirit (Moses) to demonstrate how bad the sinful situation really is. Ultimately, the Holy Spirit acts as our intercessor to God like Moses did between the Hebrews and God.

When we realize that we are spiritually dying, we call out to God to rescue us. So, God tells us if we can look at the bronze snake (embodiment of sin) on the poll (cross) we will be saved. The snake represented the sin–covered Jesus on the cross hundreds of years before Jesus was on earth and crucifixion was even invented. If you can look at your sin on the cross and realize that God sent his son to die for you – to be your sin for you – you will be saved.

---

[274] Num. 21:5
[275] Num. 21:6
[276] Num. 21:7
[277] Num. 21:8–9

Jesus himself taught this interpretation when he said, "As Moses lifted up the serpent in the wilderness, so must the Son of Man be lifted up."[278] Jesus would become the serpent, or our sin, and be lifted up on the cross. Then, if we look at him drenched with our sin and bearing our punishment, we will be saved just like the Hebrews were saved in the wilderness. It's an awesome picture of God's redemption.

Now, with the importance of looking at the cross for redemption coupled with the term for 'cross' in the New Testament, we must ask ourselves why the Witnesses are so adamant to describe the cross in such a different light. Why, after two-thousand years, do Witnesses feel the need to buck tradition in spite of supporting biblical evidence? Personally, it feels a bit like the organization is grasping for a narrative to distinguish themselves from Christian denominations. They have falsified charges of paganism against Christian tradition to justify their own heterodox beliefs. They *want* a different cross – they've not simply discovered a different cross. Yet, at some level, doesn't a desire to have a different cross meet a desire to have a different Christ?

Granted, a Jehovah's Witness could come back from this to argue that Moses lifted the serpent up on a pole, therefore Jesus was likewise lifted up on a pole. However, a quick look at the actual Hebrew word for *pole* in Numbers 21:9 (נֵס or 'nec') reveals that it was not simply a *pole* or *stake* on which the serpent was raised. Rather, it was a *standard* or *banner*. It was something *more* than simply a pole. Moses was ordered by God to raise the serpent up on a banner, a sign for all to see their own sin. This only furthers the imagery that Jesus brings to mind in John 3:14. Jesus was lifted up, in some aspects, as a sign, a banner to display our sin.

Regardless of what shape the cross took, it seems to be a good indicator of whether or not someone is comfortable with looking at the representation of their sin and understanding their need for repentance. Should this come up while conversing with a Jehovah's Witness, it may act as a good starting point to question why the Witness leadership rejects the traditional cross. Tell them the story of Moses and the bronze snake. Explain how significant it is to reject the cross in favor of our own image, but don't get hung up on this point. Allow the "torture stake" to open the conversation to why Jesus was tortured to begin with.

---

[278] John 3:14

ANNIHILATIONISM

Jehovah's Witnesses teach that Jesus was buried in a tomb after the "torture stake" crucifixion. Then, his body was completely destroyed and recreated by God some time between his burial and bodily reappearance. This leads Jehovah's Witnesses to challenge the resurrection of Jesus in the traditional sense, denying that God raised Jesus from the dead with the same body he was crucified.[279]

This heterodox version of the resurrection may be the necessary outcome of the their belief in annihilationism. Witnesses believe that Christ will complete destroy all the wicked who fall outside the Kingdom of Witnesses when he returns to establish his earthly millennial rule. This destruction is literal – he will annihilate the wicked and they will eternally cease to exist in both body and soul. There will be no eternal punishment, there will only be nonexistence.

If annihilationism is true, however, Jehovah's Witnesses are left with the burden of explaining the atrocity of not justly punishing sin, and why Jesus needed to be resurrected as the "firstborn from the dead," or the firstborn of the resurrection.[281] The first problem is not a new one. Many theologians throughout history have attempted to reduce punishment in the afterlife to either temporary chastisement or the absence of punishment altogether.

Witnesses opted for the later, but this leaves us to understand that God will not justly deal with sin. For example, tyrants like Hitler or Stalin will not be fully punished for the atrocities they committed during their lives. They will simply cease to exist for all eternity never having truly experienced punishment. Thus, the consequence of believing in annihilationism is that sin is not dealt with fully and God is, therefore, not a wholly just God. This is simply incompatible with scripture since God is the definition of justice.[282]

Secondly, the doctrine of annihilationism necessarily rejects the traditional understanding of the resurrection. People will either be annihilated or recreated, but certainly not resurrected. However, Jesus is referred to as the

---

[279] Rom. 8:11, John 20:26–28
[280] Edward Fudge and Robert A. Peterson, *Two Views of Hell: A Biblical & Theological Dialogue* (Downers Grove, Illi.: InterVarsity Press, 2000), 101.
[281] Col. 1:18
[282] Isa. 5:16; 30:18; Luke 18:7

"firstborn of the dead."[283] Biblically speaking, the "firstborn" implies an inheritance that is received, not simply birth order. This is why the Old Testament patriarch, Jacob, was referred to as the firstborn (despite being born second) after tricking his father, Abraham, for the paternal blessing.[284] Jacob knew what being the firstborn entailed – the blessing of the promise of Abraham and many descendants in that covenant, along with his father's possessions and land. "Firstborn," by its very definition, conveys the fact that there will be descendants or followers from the person with the title who will receive an inheritance. In Jesus' case, being the firstborn of the resurrection, Christians are the descendants of the inherited resurrection power, looking forward to the day when we, like Christ, will be resurrected to eternal life.

Even though Jehovah's Witnesses deny a total resurrection of the living and dead, they explain why Jesus is referred to as the firstborn of the resurrection by claiming that humans are spiritually resurrected while those outside of God's redemption are annihilated. If there is no total resurrection then the "firstborn" problem, like annihilationism, simply ceases to exist. But the problem still persists since, as Paul points out, "if there is no resurrection of the dead, then not even Christ has been raised."[285] And if Christ was not raised, "let us eat and drink, for tomorrow we die."[286]

In other words, if you don't believe in the eternal resurrection of all the dead, then you can't believe in the eternal resurrection of Christ. If you don't believe the eternal resurrection of Christ, then salvation is available to no one.[287] This is a formidable problem for Jehovah's Witness theology. If we cast aside the idea that Jesus lived, died, and resurrected in the same body, then we start to walk on shaky ground. In my opinion, this is a great example of how one idea (annihilations) affects the broader spectrum of our entire theology (resurrection and salvation).

---

[283] Col. 1:18
[284] Gen. 27:32
[285] 1 Cor. 15:13
[286] 1 Cor. 15:32
[287] 1 Pet. 3:21

THERE'S ONLY ROOM FOR 144,000

After God recreated Jesus' body, Jehovah's Witnesses are taught that Jesus returned to heaven as Michael the Archangel where he sat at the right hand of Jehovah and awaited his return. In 1914, the time came for his arrival. Archangel Jesus left his heavenly residence for the second time, returning to earth to rule invisibly until the future time of Armageddon when 144,000 faithful chosen Jehovah's Witnesses are selected to reign over the earth with him.[288]

At this time Jesus will annihilate everyone except for the privileged 144,000 and the remaining Jehovah's Witnesses, who will live for eternity under the combined rule of Jesus and the 144,000. Although there is no way to know who exactly the 144,000 include, a celebrity list can confidently be assumed: Abraham, Isaac, Jacob, David, John, Paul, Matthew, Charles Taze Russell, and Judge Rutherford, just to name a few.

So, why 144,000? Simply put, Jehovah's Witnesses find this number in the Book of Revelation and apply it to a select group of themselves. Revelation 7 describes 12,000 Jews from twelve different tribes of Israel, all of whom have been sealed into salvation by God.[289] Witnesses interpret the tribes of Israel as an allegorical picture of the divinely appointed theocracy that Rutherford spoke about. Later on in Revelation that same 144,000 (12,000 Jews from twelve tribes) are seen ruling with Jesus in chapter 14.[290] As a result, Witnesses interpret this picture as a literal amount of 144,000 Jehovah's Witnesses (throughout history's past) enjoying rulership of earth with Jesus for eternity after Armageddon.

Holding to the interpretation that these passages speak of a literal number of 144,000 Jehovah's Witnesses has a few problems. First, if Jehovah's Witnesses wish to assert they are the actual nation of Israel (as often taught in replacement theology) chosen by God to co-reign with Jesus through eternity, they must explain why the list in Revelation 7 omits the tribe of Dan

---

[288] John Ankerberg, John Weldon, and Dillon Burroughs, *The Facts on Jehovah's Witnesses* (Eugene, Oreg.: Harvest House Publishers, 2008), 34.
[289] Rev. 7:4–8
[290] Rev. 14:1

and includes the tribe of Manasseh instead.[291] Since the tribe of Manasseh replaces the tribe of Dan, the list of tribes mentioned in Revelation are not ethnic Israel – there is a difference. Thus, the Jehovah's Witnesses replacement theology, which teaches the church replaced Israel, begins to unravel.

Perhaps the safer interpretation of Revelation 7, among other safe interpretations, is an allegorical image of the collective body of God's elect throughout the history of redemption. In other words, the 144,000 does not represent a literal number of Jehovah's Witnesses (or even Jews), but the complete and perfect number of those called, both Jew and Gentile, to salvation throughout history by God.[292]

This coincides with the second problem that Witnesses run into – a disregard for the allegorical language found in Revelation. If Jehovah's Witnesses choose to literalize the representation of the 144,000, namely that it conveys a literal number of privileged Jehovah's Witnesses, they would be forced to completely ignore the fairly evident symbolism of the number itself. For example, take the fact that 144,000 could be calculated as 12 x 12 x 1,000. These two numbers, 12 and 1,000, are common in biblical literature as symbolic.

Earlier in the book of Revelation we are given a picture of God's throne surrounded by twenty-four elders.[293] The symbolism in this picture is of twelve elders from the Old Testament (leaders of the twelve tribes, or prophets) and twelve elders from the New Testament (leaders of the church, or apostles). Couple the twelve prophets and twelve apostles with the 1,000 year reign of Jesus spoken of in Revelation 20 and we have a very reasonable interpretation of the number 144,000 – (twelve Old Testament leaders of the saints) x (twelve New Testament leaders of the saints) x (the reign of Jesus Christ for a thousand years) = (the salvation of all the saints, better known as the collective church, both Jew and Gentile) or 12 x 12 x 1,000.

---

[291] The 12 Tribes of Israel are Reuben, Simeon, Levi, Judah, Dan, Naphtali, Gad, Asher, Issachar, Zebulun, Joseph, Benjamin. The 12 tribes mentioned in Revelation are Reuben, Simeon, Levi, Judah, Manasseh, Naphtali, Gad, Asher, Issachar, Zebulun, Joseph, and Benjamin.

[292] "It being therefore understood, that they, who are sealed, represent the *complete number* of God's servants from every nation under heaven." Christopher Wordsworth, *The New Testament of our Lord and Saviour Jesus Christ: In the Original Greek with Introductions and Notes* Vol. 4 (London: Rivingtons, 1862), 197.

[293] Rev. 4:4

This is but one interpretation of the 144,000 that finds consistency throughout the Bible. Other interpretations include viewing this number as converted Jewish evangelists sent out from Israel towards the end of the world or Jews who were sealed to salvation during the destruction of the temple in 70CE. Either one fits within an acceptable framework of understanding Revelation consistently; however, limiting the number to a literal amount of salvation does not. What we should conclude, at the very least, is that the meaning behind the 144,000 doesn't represent a literal number of people who will be reigning with Jesus in the future. Rather, in my interpretation, it is a symbolic number of all the people who have been saved throughout the years and who will be with Jesus for eternity.

JEHOVAH'S WITNESSES = MODERN ARIANS

At the center of the Jehovah's Witnesses departure orthodox Christianity is a system of theology called Arianism. This is not to be confused with Aryanism – Jehovah's Witnesses do not secretly believe Jesus is blonde haired and blue eyed. Arianism is an ancient theological idea named after its first proponent, Arius (ca. 250–336CE), who believed and taught that Jesus was not God. Instead, according to Arius, Jesus was the first and highest created being since God the Father is the only god and does not share his glory with anyone. Arius was not able to sustain popularity for his view as he was condemned a heretic at the Council of Nicaea in 325CE. This council was actually called in large part to discuss Arius' view of Jesus.

It was important in that day, when communication was limited to sharing letters between churches, to hold meetings or councils with pastors from all over the known world to discuss Christian theology and matters concerning the church. Keep in mind, up until 325CE Christians didn't even have a complete copy of scripture like we do today. One aspect of theology the Council of Nicaea discussed was the nature of Jesus – to answer the question Arius rose over whether Jesus was human, god, or both. After studying scripture and prayerful consideration, the council rightly determined that Jesus was both the Son of Man (human) and the Son of God (divine). Today, Jehovah's Witnesses have resurrected Arius' view of Christ as a created being.

This idea, unfortunately, has detrimental repercussions of how one view's Jesus' redemptive work on the cross.

At the core of Arianism lies a failure to grasp the concept of what theologians call the *hypostatic union*. It is a fancy term that communicates the truth that Jesus Christ is both one hundred percent God and one hundred percent human. Jesus isn't 50/50; neither is he either fully human with divine attributes or fully God with human attributes. Jesus is both fully God and fully human. He is the God-Man, the Son of God and the Son of Man. This is why sometimes in scripture Jesus shows submission to God the Father but at other times claims that he is God. In the Gospel of John, for example, Jesus says that the Father knows more than Jesus does. However, Jesus also claims the same title God used to identify himself to Moses.[294]

Scripture makes it clear for us that Jesus took on the human aspect of his nature; "Have this mind among yourselves, which is yours in Christ Jesus, who, though he was in the form of God, did not count equality with God a thing to be grasped, but made himself nothing, taking the form of a servant, being born in the likeness of men."[295] If Jesus is simply a created being and not God – even a created being of the highest order – how could he have even entertained the idea that his equality with God was not a thing to be grasped?

This is something that would be worthwhile to discuss while dialoging with Jehovah's Witnesses. Explain that Jesus, who was eternally in the form of God, took on the likeness of men. He did not fully become a man by shedding his divinity. Even though Jesus was divine, he chose to veil his glory on earth, not part with it, to accomplish his mission as a servant and redeemer. Witnesses have historically denied the hypostatic union, the divine nature of Jesus, and ultimately the Trinity, and have made this denial a central pillar of their theology in sharp distinction to orthodox Christianity.

Regrettably, often times it may feel as if both parties are talking past one another when it comes to the Trinity. While an orthodox position may confidently set forth various passages as proof-texts for Jesus' divinity, Jehovah's Witnesses will likewise counter in a similar fashion. For example, they might employ John 17:3 as evidence that Jesus is not God. In this verse Jesus prays,

---

[294] John 14:28; 8:58
[295] Phil. 2:5–7

"and this is eternal life, that they know you the only true God, and Jesus Christ whom you have sent."[296] Jehovah's Witnesses may argue that because Jesus calls the Father the "only true God" Jesus cannot himself be God. If Jesus were God himself, why would he refer to God in the third-person?

A counter-point may point out that this interpretation fails to take into account the whole corpus of scripture in context, thereby missing the opportunity to witness the beautiful mystery that is the Trinity. Within the entire context of both the New and Old Testament, Jesus is calling God, to include himself, the only true god of all the other "gods" in existence. Jude, Jesus' half-brother, would later go on to call Jesus the only Lord and Master.[297] Consequently, if the Father is the only one true God, Master, and Lord as the Jehovah's Witnesses may argue from John 17:3, then Jude must be confused as to who Jesus is. If the Father is the only true God and Jesus is our only Master and Lord, then it necessitates that Jesus is God. Thus, when Jesus prays to the Father that he desires for us to know the "only true God," he is speaking of himself as well. Jesus' desire is that we would know the Father through him.[298]

Furthermore, Isaiah 42 tells us that God does not share his glory with anyone. Yet, in John 17:5 Jesus claims that he shares in that glory; "And now, Father, glorify me in your own presence with the glory that I had with you before the world existed." Such a bold statement, even for an archangel, was enough to incite the Sanhedrin to charge him with blasphemy. It could be reasoned that if Jesus shares God's glory and God does not share his own glory, then Jesus is God. There is no contradiction; it's just a matter of trying to wrap our heads around a being whose existence is so far beyond our comprehension that he inserted himself into our world as a person for us to understand him.

Another verse Jehovah's Witnesses may use to defend the Arianism is Colossians 1:15. "He is the image of the invisible God, the firstborn of all creation." Here the argument may be presented that Jesus was the firstborn of all creation in the sense that he was the first thing created in all of creation. This verse, then, acts as a sort of timestamp, teaching that Jesus was created first and the rest of creation followed. Then, Jesus acted as an agent in assisting Jehovah's creation of everything else. However, the obvious concern

---

[296] John 17:3
[297] Jude 4

with using this verse to argue that point is in the verse itself. How can Jesus be the visible image of the invisible God without himself being the invisible God made visible?

Furthermore, Witnesses using Colossians 1:15 to prove Jesus was the first created being are unfortunately missing out on the entire point of the verse. We must keep in mind that the Bible was written mainly by Jews, for a Jewish audience, surrounded by a Jewish context. Therefore, the term *firstborn* is not necessarily restricted to the definition of who was born first, although it is implied. A Hebrew firstborn is not only a numerical position; rather, it is a term that infers birthright (as previously discussed).

In this particular verse, emphasis on the term *firstborn* is on legal rights, not timing. This is demonstrated well in the Old Testament. If you remember, Jacob was not the firstborn chronologically, but he received the firstborn rights.[299] There would have been no way Jacob could have legally taken Esau's birthrights from him if the term firstborn meant strictly the chronological timing of a birth. Jacob wouldn't have received Isaac's blessings, and the nation of Israel would not have come into existence. It would have altered the entirety of the Old Testament.

At the end of the day, Arianism doesn't stand up to the test of scripture. Jesus' divinity is demonstrated well throughout the Bible, but Jehovah's Witnesses have positioned themselves against this fact. Indeed, they go to extraordinary lengths to ensure that the Bible agrees with their view of Jesus. One such length includes altering the original text of the Bible itself.

THE NEW WORLD TRANSLATION — IT'S ALL GREEK TO ME

One passage that my come to mind when speaking of Jesus' divinity is John 1:1,14. It speaks powerfully and clearly to the person of Jesus as God, the Word become flesh. There's a catch, though. Long ago, the Watchtower Society presented a solution to this theological roadblock, which had become a severe point of contention between Jehovah's Witnesses and most biblical scholars.

---

[298] John 14:6; 1 Tim. 2:5
[299] Gen. 25:20–34

If you recall from the last chapter, the Joseph Smith Translation (JST) provides faithful Latter-days Saints with an unreliable translation of scripture that conforms to Mormon theology. The JST distorts and/or ignores the original Greek text to allow for the presence of unique Mormon ideas. This is due, perhaps, to Joseph Smith's evolving theology over the course of many years, which necessitated scripture revision to meet the needs of newer ideas in Mormonism. Specifically, Smith severely altered John 1:1, which may be due to its clear statement on Jesus' divinity. John 1:1, when coupled with John 1:14, clearly indicates that Jesus is God. Mormon theology teaches otherwise – that Jesus is a god among many – so the verse was altered to validate Mormonism.

Jehovah's Witnesses have an identical disagreement with the Latter-day Saints concerning John 1:1,14. Jesus wasn't always God – at some point he was created. So, like the LDS Church, the Watchtower Society published a revision of John 1:1 that better conformed to Witness theology. This has resulted in a serious mistranslation that renders the verse "and the Word was a God" instead of the proper "and the Word was God." The implications of this revision are obvious – the verse is completely stripped of its trinitarianism and subsequently offers evidence of Arianism.

At the outset, it may seem tempting to simply dissuade Jehovah's Witnesses away from the traditional Watchtower position by walking them through a basic Greek lesson. Well, maybe not *that* tempting, especially if you don't know Greek apart from that sweet gyros shop down the street. Alright, let's face it – it's probably not the best idea to bust out a chalkboard and lecture a Jehovah's Witness on ancient Greek from A to Ω. But, before moving on, let's briefly overview the difference between most English translations and the NWT for our own benefit. Then, we'll return to some helpful points to discuss with Jehovah's Witnesses on the deity of Christ.

So, what does the original Greek text say? Did John actually mean to tell us that Jesus is God? If John 1:1 can be translated as anything other than "and the Word was God," then Jesus would lose his divinity, and Jehovah's Witnesses are spot on in their theology. The problem that Jehovah's Witnesses find themselves faced with is a lack of company in their translation. By far, the vast majority of biblical scholars do not agree with the way the NWT renders this verse. This is seen in versions such as the English Standard Version,

New International Version, New American Standard Bible, King James Version, New King James Version, American Standard Version, Revised Standard Version, Common English Bible, and the New Living Translation, that all agree on "the Word was God" as a proper translation for John 1:1.

Essentially, this is why the New World Translation was needed in the first place. Had other translations, such as the King James Version, rendered John 1:1 in a way that fit Jehovah's Witness theology, there would be no need for revision. Alas, this was not the case. No major translation agreed (or currently agrees) with Jehovah's Witness theology, so the NWT fills in that gap. It renders John 1:1 as, "In the beginning the Word was, and the Word was with God, and the Word was *a* god." With one small addition of the letter '*a*', the Watchtower Society's NWT takes Jesus from being divine to being created.

Translating John 1:1 in this way, however, breaks a well-established rule in Greek, which has led many leading Greek scholars to reject it. The late Dr. Bruce M. Metzger (1914–2007), Professor of New Testament Language and Literature at Princeton Theological Seminary and board member of the American Bible Society, once stated; "As a matter of solid fact, however, such a rendering is a frightful mistranslation. It overlooks entirely an established rule of Greek grammar which necessitates the rendering '…and the Word was God.'"[300] He also went on to state that, "if the Jehovah's Witnesses take this translation seriously, they are polytheists."[301] Dr. Metzger articulates the overall opinion of professionals when given the NWT's translation of John 1:1. At the end of the day, there are few people outside Jehovah's Witnesses who would agree with their translation.

This may be why the Watchtower needed to commission the translation in-house with their own committee of translators. Oddly, the committee opted not to reveal the names of those who actually translated the manuscripts citing concerns that Jehovah would not receive the glory for the work. This places us in the unfortunate position of being unable to verify the qualifications of the

---

[300] Patrick Navas, *Divine Truth Or Human Tradition? A Reconsideration of Roman Catholic– Protestant Doctrine of the Trinity in Light of Hebrew and Christian Scriptures* (Bloomington, Indi.: ArthurHouse, 2006), 242.
[301] Ibid.

translators. However, it is thought that one man, Fred Franz, contributed to the project. Frankly, his qualifications are wonting.[302]

Let's look at how the NWT squares away with the original Greek to illustrate Dr. Metzger's complain. To begin, look at John 1:1 in both the Greek and English. Here, John 1:1 is presented with the Greek on top, pronunciation in middle, English on bottom.

GREEK

Εν αρχη ην ο Λογος και ο Λογος ην προς τον Θεον και Θεος ην ο Λογος

TRANSLITERATION

En Arche en ha'Logos, Kai ha'Lagas En Pros Ton Theon, Kai Theos En ha'Logos

TRANSLATION

In (the) beginning was the Word, and the Word was with (the) God, and the Word was God

There are two important words for us to learn – Λογος (*logos*) is the Greek word for 'word' and Θεος (Theos) is the Greek word for 'god.' At the end of the verse, you see transliterated 'Kai Theos En ha'Logos.' Literally, it means 'and God was the Word.' This is the text in question. In short, there is absolutely no room in the Greek to place an '*a*' before '*God.*' It would break the Greek grammatical rules governing this sentence. If we broke this rule here, we could just as easily break it elsewhere in John's Gospel to come up with mistranslations like these:

> **John 4:24** – "God is *a* Spirit: and those who worship him must worship in spirit and truth."
>
> **John 20:28** – "My Lord and my *a* god."

The question we must ask of the NWT in this one instance is why the translation committee chose to go against the vast majority of biblical scholarship and a well-established rule of Greek grammar? We are left with only two options; either the NWT translation committee stumbled upon one of the greatest mistakes in the history of biblical studies, or their theology took precedence over a faithful rendering of the text. The latter, in my opinion, seems to be the case.

---

[302] M. James Penton, *Apocalypse Delayed: The Story of Jehovah's Witnesses,* 2nd ed. (Toronto: University of Toronto Press, 1997), 174.

Hopefully, it has been demonstrated that the NWT is an unfaithful witness to the original Greek text of John 1:1. Yet, as stated previously, it is impractical to debate the finer points of the Greek language when dialoguing with Jehovah's Witnesses. It is great to know why the NWT isn't trustworthy, but this information does not translate well into a conversation with Jehovah's Witnesses. Instead, I believe it's best to stick to passages where the NWT renders the Greek faithfully. Here we will find mutually safe ground from which to dialogue. Therefore, the question to ask isn't necessarily who sat on the NWT translation committee; rather, we should ask in what ways does the NWT retain other passages that speak to the deity of Jesus? Here we find some very fruitful conversation.

I find it helpful to locate what I call "Jehovah passages" in the New Testament that are attributed to Jesus rather than Jehovah. Remember, Jehovah's Witnesses pride the NWT on restoring the proper name "Jehovah" where many other translations render YHWH as LORD. Ironically, though, their use of Jehovah becomes very inconsistent. For example, take Paul's use of "Jehovah passages" in his letter to the Romans. In Romans 9:10 (NWT), Paul declares that righteousness results from faith "if you publicly declare with your mouth that Jesus is Lord." Thus, we are to publicly declare Jesus as Lord if we are to count ourselves among his people. Yet, a few verses later in Romans 9:13 (NWT), Paul quotes Joel 2:32, a "Jehovah passage," and attributes the verse to Jesus – "everyone who calls on the name of Jehovah will be saved." Here, we clearly see that Paul associated Jesus with Jehovah (or, better, YHWH). Another example is found in 1 Corinthians 2:16 where Paul identifies the mind of Jehovah and the mind of Christ as one and the same; "For 'who has come to know the mind of Jehovah, so that he may instruct him?' But we do have the mind of Christ."

These are in stark contrast to other "Jehovah passages" that are attributed to Jehovah himself. For example, Romans 11:34 (NWT), speaking of God's "riches and wisdom and knowledge" quotes Isaiah 40:13; "For 'who has come to know Jehovah's mind?'" The New Testament writers were comfortable with attributing Jesus to Jehovah's identity and mind, which is actually displayed in the NWT to a certain extent. The question to ask, then, is why the NWT in some instances attribute "Jehovah passages" to Jehovah and others to Jesus?

A final point that may spur conversation deals with the reason why Jesus was crucified. They story actually starts all the way back in the Old Testament. There we learn that God does not share his glory with anyone; "I am Jehovah. That is my name; I give my glory to no one else (Isaiah 42:8, NWT)." Fast-forward to Jesus' day where he teaches his disciples about his second coming; "When the Son of man comes in his glory, and all the angels with him, then he will sit down on his glorious throne (Matt. 25:31, NWT)." If it is true that Jehovah does not share his glory with anyone, how then can Jesus claim to come in glory and sit down on his glorious throne? This is basically the same question that the Sanhedrin asked Jesus at his trial, which ultimately lead to his crucifixion. Jesus was executed for one reason – claiming to be God.

Admittedly, in my experience, speaking on these topics with Witnesses has a propensity to lead to heated debate. Terminate that as quick as possible – we must dialogue in gentleness and respect. Yet, at the same time, in order for any fruitful conversation to occur between orthodox Christians and Jehovah's Witnesses, we need to iron out the text we both claim.

JEHOVAH'S WITNESSES & THE TRINITY

Because the Jehovah's Witnesses deny Jesus' deity, they must also deny the Trinity. This is something about which they are unabashedly blunt. So blunt, in fact, that the Watchtower Society seems to posture itself towards wholesale campaigning against the doctrine of the Trinity. One aspect of this campaign is to attack traditional Christian beliefs about the Trinity in order to instill doubt in the minds of Christians. The Watchtower Society has produced a very popular pamphlet (now out of print) for Jehovah's Witness proselytism that contains reasons why people shouldn't believe in the Trinity. Its title *Should You Believe in the Trinity?* captures the attention of nominal Christians who grew up in a household where the Trinity was taught but never explained.

Since these Christians have always had questions about the Trinity but never received answers, Jehovah's Witnesses can be very persuasive in their anti-trinitarian arguments. Maybe the old theological adage about the Trinity is no help in these situations, "Try to explain it, and you'll lose your mind. But try to deny it, and you'll lose your soul."[303] When it comes to theology, especially the doctrine of the Trinity, if a person is unable to find an explanation, no foundation has been laid. Without a foundation people are liable to waiver over biblical truths and incline themselves towards finding answers regardless of their trustworthiness. Through literature, the Watchtower Society widely disseminates a few arguments to persuade Christians that the doctrine of the Trinity is unbiblical. Most of them are philosophical, so put your thinking cap on for the remainder of this section!

The first is an argument from ignorance – because the Trinity is unexplainable, it's unbelievable. This argument makes reasonable sense when one considers Occam's Razor; if given multiple explanations, the simplest of all possibilities must be true. However, if we applied that logic to every area of our knowledge we would be reduced to perpetual skepticism. Simply because we don't understand something does not mean it does not exist. Take gravity, for example. We know it exists and how it acts. But ask any physicist if we truly understand what gravity is and they will tell you that we do not. That's because gravity is a very mysterious thing. However, just because we don't truly understand gravity doesn't mean we should reject gravity's existence. Why? Because we see evidence of gravity all around us.

Like gravity, Christians know that God exists and how he acts, but we don't truly understand him. However, we see evidence of him and of his triune nature in scripture. His ways – even his being – are higher than our ways.[304] What Jehovah's Witnesses do in rejecting God's nature is done out of ignorance for simply not understanding. It is as foolish to reject the Trinity as it is to reject gravity simply because we don't fully understand it.

The second popular argument Witnesses use is from church history. It argues that the early church did not believe in the triune nature of God and that Arius' teaching was actually the majority opinion at the time. This is simply not true. As demonstrated earlier, the majority opinion of God's nature at the Council of Nicaea was rightly trinitarianism, and Arius was consequently denounced as a heretic.

---

[303] Author unknown
[304] Isa. 55:9

With a little bit of research, one can discover that Jehovah's Witnesses claim is unfounded in historical fact; however, it could be argued that since the Council of Nicaea was held in 325CE all scripture past that year is suspect because the church could have changed the text to reflect trinitarianism. The church *could* have decided on a trinitarian position and changed the entire Bible to reflect the Trinity. The only problem with this theory is extra–biblical evidence that suggests Christians were trinitarian as early as 100CE, well over two hundred years before the Council of Nicaea was called.

Such evidence can be found in a manuscript titled *The Didache* (did-ak-aye). The Didache is a well-known document used by early Christians as a sort of guide for the early Christian faith. The Didache, from the Greek for 'instructions,' was passed around from home to home or church to church much like the four Gospels and Paul's letters were before the Bible was formed. It contains instructions on how to baptize new believers, stating that the baptizer should, "baptize in running water, in the name of the Father and of the Son and of the Holy Spirit."[305] The source of this quote may be found in the Gospel of Matthew, which was written closer to the time of Jesus. "Go therefore and make disciples of all nations, baptizing them in the name of the Father and of the Son and of the Holy Spirit."[306]

The name in which Jesus instructed Christians to baptize new disciples is a trinitarian title for God. Notice that we are not called to baptize in the *names* of the Father, Son, and Holy Spirit, but the *name*, singular. If the early church taught that God was a separate god from Jesus or even the Holy Spirit, then why copy the trinitarian title for God in Matthew into your instruction manual? The Didache provides good evidence of the Trinity outside of the Bible in the early church.

A third argument that Jehovah's Witnesses employs is the illogicality of the Trinity. Since the concept of three beings in one person is not logical, the Trinity cannot possibly be the true nature of God. This is perhaps their weakest yet most persuasive argument. It is persuasive because most people have never really given the Trinity much thought. When they are presented with the

---

[305] *Didache* 7:1
[306] Matt. 28:19

argument that the Trinity is not logical, having never considered the logicality of the Trinity, they may be inclined to believe Jehovah's Witnesses.

Nevertheless, despite the argument's persuasiveness, it's also very weak. The belief that the Trinity is illogical is philosophically bankrupt. The Trinity cannot be said to be *illogical*. For something to be illogical it must violate a formal principle of logic, which the concept of the Trinity does not. For example, *something* cannot be *not-something* at the same time; or, *X* cannot be *non-X* at the same time. In other words, one's house cannot both exist and not exist at the same time. That would be illogical, violating a formal principle of logic.

If you pointed to an empty field and said, "There's my house, come on in!" you would be illogical (and a little crazy). Are orthodox Christians claiming that the Trinity is both simultaneously existent and non-existent? Of course not. We are saying that one God is made up of three persons. Illogicality has nothing to do with the Trinity; the Trinity is actually quite logical. Whether or not Jehovah's Witnesses find the Trinity rational is another story, but it is certainly not illogical. "Inconceivable to the human mind" may be a better way to describe the Trinity.

A fourth argument that Witnesses may use is the mathematical impossibility of the Trinity. The argument goes that one thing cannot be three things yet exist uniformly as only one. God cannot be three beings (Father, Son, and Holy Spirit) yet uniformly exist as only one god. The problem with this argument is two-fold: a misunderstanding of the Trinity and a misunderstanding of simple mathematics.

First, the Trinity is often times better described as what it is not as opposed to what it is. God the Father is not God the Son, God the Son is not God the Holy Spirit, and God the Holy Spirit is not God the Father (see *Figure 3.4*). Practically speaking, although Jesus is God, the Father was not crucified on the cross. Just as well, although the Holy Spirit is God, the Son does not bestow spiritual gifts to Christians. Once this is understood, it may be easier to comprehend the three-fold role that God plays in three persons.

Figure 3.4

Second, the Trinity is indeed mathematically possible. 1 x 1 x 1 = 1. Problem solved. Granted, this explanation may be viewed as a tactless diversion from the real issue at hand – the idea that nothing in nature exists that is trinitarian in concept, not even in mathematics. If God is triune in nature and God created the universe, then surly something should exist that shares three distinct properties yet exists as one entity. Nature, in fact, is full of trinitarian concepts.

Here's where a quick demonstration-experiment may help them understand. If you have a Jehovah's Witness over for dinner, ask them for a couple minutes while you whip something up in your kitchen – something that exists in nature as three substances yet as only one at the same time. Then, go to your stove. Boil some water, make sure it is steaming, pour it in a bowl, and then put some ice in the bowl. Immediately show them what you've got. They should see that there are separate things existing all at the same time (water, steam, and ice) yet they are made of the same thing (H_2O). Voilà, a trinitarian concept in nature (though not a *perfect* representation of the Trinity).

THE GOSPEL IN DIALOGUE WITH JEHOVAH'S WITNESSES

It should go without saying that talking about the gospel in dialogue with Jehovah's Witnesses will orbit the person of Jesus, especially his divinity and sonship. The work of Jesus' atonement can only be rightly understood in light of his person. It is one thing for God to create a being to take away the sins of the world; it is a whole other thing for God to be the one who takes away the sins of the world. Sometimes, simply taking the time to thoroughly explain a theological concept like the Trinity will be enough to make the conversation comfortable in talking about faith.

Granted, it may be rare to speak candidly about faith with a Jehovah's Witness. The organization fiercely protects its members from external influence, which severely limits their interaction with people from other faiths. In fact, Jehovah's Witnesses are warned that those outside of their faith group are dangerous, diluted, and delirious; so delirious, in fact, that *Watchtower* magazine has recently referred to non-Jehovah's Witnesses (and apostates) as mentally unstable or ill.

> Suppose that a doctor told you to avoid contact with someone who is infected with a contagious, deadly disease. You would know what the doctor means, and you would strictly heed his warning. Well, apostates are "mentally diseased," and they seek to infect others with their disloyal teachings. Jehovah, the Great Physician, tells us to avoid contact with them.[307]

This is another important aspect to understand when dialoguing – leaving the Jehovah's Witness faith group is a monumental challenge. Should a member decide to speak with a 'mentally diseased' Christian and leave the organization, they may face a lifetime of ostracization from their friends, family, and community. Jehovah's Witness congregations are typically taught to disassociate themselves from fellow members who are caught studying Jesus outside of the organization's purview.

According to one report, thirty-thousand Jehovah's Witnesses are shunned annually for various reasons to include questioning or promoting foreign theology.[308] Therefore, Jehovah's Witnesses have a lot at stake for leaving the faith should they choose to do so. We must be sensitive to the fact that we are not merely talking about interesting theological facts, but if they cease being a Jehovah's Witness they run the risk of leaving behind family,

---

[307] "Will You Heed Jehovah's Clear Warnings?" *The Watchtower*, July 15, 2011, 16.
[308] Public Broadcasting Station (PBS), "Myths & Realities,"
http://www.pbs.org/independentlens/knocking/myths.html (accessed January 9, 2012).

friends, and community. If we are serious about articulating the gospel in a manner that may lead a Jehovah's Witness away from their faith community, are we equally serious to provide them support?

Aside from being shunned, many Jehovah's Witnesses are taught that blasphemy of the Holy Spirit, which can come from rejecting any aspect of their theology, results in immediate and eternal separation from God without the chance of redemption. Other such blasphemy can include speaking critically of the Watchtower Society, involving oneself in the political arena, or even donating blood. This eternal punishment for blasphemy against the Holy Spirit transcends the faith group itself and, according to its theology, also applies to non-Witnesses. Consequently, those dialoguing about the gospel with Jehovah's Witnesses may be viewed as having blasphemed the Holy Spirit depending on whether or not a member changes their worldview as a result.

If you are known in your neighborhood for dialoguing with Jehovah's Witnesses on theology, it is possible that the leadership of the local Kingdom Hall might warn their missionaries of any potential trouble you may cause, intentional or non. Thus, if we want to build relationship of dialoguing about the gospel with Jehovah's Witnesses, it would be smart to do so by first fostering friendships and relationships. If anything, every time a Jehovah's Witness missionary comes knocking on the door we should probably steer clear of that lecture in New Testament Greek.

Door-to-door proselytism, or "publishing," is going to be the most common way of meeting with Jehovah's Witnesses in your neighborhood. If you haven't noticed already most Kingdom Halls are strategically built in neighborhood communities. This makes their door-to-door proselytism a much smoother process. If they come to your home and ask to share their message with you, be polite and have a listen. Afterward, ask them if they would like to come over another time to discuss what they believe with you – most will never decline such an invitation.

When they do come over, stay focused on discussing their beliefs about the Trinity and, most importantly, the person and work of Jesus Christ. Obviously, the two greatest disagreements you will have with them are the nature of God and the nature of Jesus. Yet, as we've seen, this is a very important topic to discuss, especially with regard to the gospel. We can understand one another more and, better, the gospel can be articulated well if we concentrate on those two topics.

Before starting a conversation, first clarify terminology. Explain that when orthodox Christians say Jesus, we mean the Son of God who is God and who came into human history to redeem the fallen state of humanity. This is very different from a created angel being who was sent by God to redeem and have full community with only 144,000 select few. If we don't define terminology right off the bat, dialoguing about the gospel could prove difficult.

Another important thing to keep in mind is that, like most rival worldviews, Jehovah's Witnesses believe in a grace-works hybrid salvation. They remain active in their process of salvation through door-to-door proselytism as well as tithes to remain in good standing with the organization. Naturally, this can become a heavy yoke to bear for those who realize that good works alone will not get them to God. Here is where dialogue about the gospel is helpful. Communicate that Jesus gives us a yoke that is easy and a burden that is light.[309] We don't work to get to God, we work because of God. Salvation isn't something we gain by ourselves, we need Jesus.[310] Inquire about how they view their own salvation, whether good works can merit the attention and love of Jehovah in addition to his grace.

If they admit that they believe their works will fall short, tell them that there is liberation from their grace-works hybrid salvation as found in the Jesus of scripture. Remember, if there are two states of being in a grace-works hybrid theology (those who do and think they succeed and those who do and feel they are failing), then there is going to be two types of strategies to approaching them. People who believe their works are earning their salvation need to be warned that they can't.[311] However, those who realize their works can't get them to God need to be comforted in God's grace.

Ultimately, they both need to hear that Jesus has already done the work for them and that they just need to have faith that this is true. "There is therefore now no condemnation for those who are in Christ Jesus. For the law of the Spirit of life has set you free in Christ Jesus from the law of sin and death."[312] Ask

---

[309] Matt. 11:30
[310] Eph. 2:8–9
[311] Gal. 3:10–11
[312] Rom. 8:1–2

them – when they die, whose works will they be claiming before God? Will they claim their door-to-door proselytism, their monthly tithes to the church, their good works for the organization, or will they claim the finished work of the uncreated Son of God, Jesus Christ, on the cross?

However, as we have seen, this conversation will stand or fall on their understanding of the nature of Jesus. If he is a created being, then of course they, as created beings as well, should feel competent enough to contribute to their salvation. But, if Jesus is God, then there is no way we can top the work of his life and the cross. A good way to get this discussion under way is to ask them a simple question; "Do you believe Jehovah has performed the greatest act of love for you?" Of course, without flinching, they'll answer positively.

However, according to Jehovah's Witness theology, only Michael the Archangel has performed the greatest act of love for us, but don't tell them that just yet. Instead, after they answer the question, read them John 15:13. "Greater love has no one than this, that someone lay down his life for his friends."[313] Don't worry, the NWT basically states the same thing. From John 15:13, tell them we can mutually understand that the greatest act of love is to sacrifice one's life for another. Then, ask the question again; "Do you believe Jehovah has performed the greatest act of love for you?" After they answer, ask them what Jesus was referring to in John 15:13. They'll most likely say that it was his death on the cross.

This is a problem for Jehovah's Witnesses since Jesus, a created being, has performed the greatest act of love – something Jehovah has not experienced. This means that Jehovah is incomplete of his own character since 1 John 4:8 states that God *is* love, and God himself, according to Witness theology, has not even experienced the greatest act of what he himself is. In other words, Jehovah has set a standard of love that he does not even qualify for. Jehovah exists in a lower standard of love than he set for himself.

It's crucial that we lead straight from this to the person of Jesus. Tell them that since God is a triune God, he *has* performed the greatest act of love for us through God the Son. While neither God the Father nor God the Holy Spirit

---

[313] John 15:13

were present and punished on the cross for our sins, God the Son was. Jesus is God in flesh, and he has laid down his life for a friend – you and me.[314]

Jesus considered us his friend and died for our sins even when he considered us his enemies.[315] The stinging question to then ask them is, "Why would I want to give up my God who performed the greatest act of love for me and trade him for the god of the Jehovah's Witnesses who is incapable of performing that greatest act of love?" The bottom line is this – if Jesus is not God, then he did something greater than what Jehovah can do. Not only that, but an archangel has outdone God. However, if Jesus *is* God, then God personally performed the greatest act of love for all of us.

In the end, Jehovah's Witnesses admirably defend the standards of God while discounting evidences that point to his triune nature and the divinity of Christ. And the tragic consequence of a poor understanding of Christ's nature is a poor understanding of Christ's work. Therefore, it is crucial to always bring the conversation back to the gospel when dialoguing with Witnesses. The Archangel Jesus of Jehovah's Witness is unique to our day and time, but is not a new idea. We can stand confidently on the shoulders of the apostles in contending that the God-Man Jesus came to do what only God could do through what only man ought.

---

[314] John 1:1,14; 15:13
[315] Eph. 2:4–5

CHAPTER FOUR

Islam & Silver Medal Jesus

" The Messiah, Jesus, the son of Mary, was but a messenger of Allah and His word...Allah is but one God, exalted is He above having a son... [Jesus] was no more than a Messenger; many were the Messengers that passed away before him."

QUR'AN (SURA AN-NISA' 4:171, AL-MA'IDAH 5:75)

The gymnasium was packed, loud, and chaotic just like every single pep rally I had ever been to before. It was a run-of-the-mill September day, and the football homecoming game was right around the corner.

As a member of the pep band, I was required to attend and participate in every single school-spirit event.

Situated about half way up the bleachers on a wooden platform among the rest of the band, I sat at the drum set and waited for the command from the director to kick off *Louie, Louie*. Or was it *Devil in a Blue Dress*? It doesn't really matter; they all sound the same when played by pep bands.

I locked eyes with the director, he raised his arms in the air, conducted the tempo with his hands, and we were off.

Nothing out of the ordinary that day. Nothing special to talk about when I got home. Just a regular old, boring pep rally giving the cheerleaders a chance to show off their new routine and affording the faculty yet another lame attempt at getting four thousand high school students excited about a football game we all knew was rigged.

I mean, it was the same opponent every single year, and they were terrible.

We had won 31–14 two years before and were expected to cream the same team again. I almost felt sorry for the neighboring rival school, but then again, I liked to win. And we did. 36–0.

Anyway, we played through a couple of severely outdated songs. Then, with the techno remix CD playing in the background, we watched while the cheerleaders flipped and cartwheeled around the gym floor to the thundering sound of applause.

No one ever clapped like that for me on drums. Then again, I wasn't that pretty.

As I was watching the cheerleading routine, I noticed a couple of police officers walk in the side door with some of the faculty members. They walked over to the principal who was sitting a few rows below me.

He stood up to greet them with a smile, but the cops looked less than enthused to deliver whatever message they had come to share.

About that time the cheerleading routine had ended with very little applause. Everyone was wondering the same thing I was – what in the world were those cops telling the principal?

Finally, after a brief conversation, he walked toward a microphone stand, tapped on it a few times, waited for the feedback screech to fade, and leaned into the microphone.

"Attention students, this will conclude our pep rally for the day. There has been an incident in New York City, which we are still receiving information about, but it appears that there has been an accident. A commercial aircraft has crashed into one of the World Trade Center towers."

That officially ended my run-of-the-mill day.

About five minutes after the announcement was made, we were all speculating as to what could have happened.

That's when I noticed my percussion instructor near one of the doorways, pointing at me and waving me over. I got up, pushed through the crowd, and managed to make it over to her without being questioned. We were supposed to stay put until the buses arrived to take us home.

"C'mon, I have the news on in the band room. I would feel terrible for the rest of my life if I didn't let a few of you watch this live." From her tone, something told me it was more than an airplane crash.

Those were the only words she said as we made our way through the halls into the band room. When I got there, both of the overhead TVs were displaying the same thing; one of the World Trade Center towers with a massive hole in its side billowing thick, black smoke.

I had never seen anything like it in my life.

There were about ten other students all huddled around the televisions. Most of them were already speculating as to what caused it: birds, engine malfunctions, computer failures.

There was one crazy kid who suggested that the pilot intentionally flew the plane into the tower. Before I could comment, another kid called him an idiot and moved the conversation along.

However, a few minutes later it would seem the crazy kid was right.

I watched the left side of the screen as a second airplane crashed into the second tower.

At first, I thought I was watching a replay of the first crash because it took the commentators a few moments to gather themselves and explain what had just happened. "Oh, my God! It appears as though a second plane has hit the other tower," one on-scene reporter frantically exclaimed.

My mind was blown. The rest of the day was a blur, saturated with doubts, questions, and fears of the unknown.

Why did those planes crash? Was it a coincidence? Who would do something like that?

We were released for the rest of the day as well as the day after.

When I came home, my parents were glued to the television screen. My dad told me that the government said it was Islamic terrorists who hijacked the airplanes and flew them into the towers.

Days to come would give birth to new vocabulary in the western world's everyday dictionary – jihad, Qur'ān, Sunni, Shi'ite, al-Qaida, mujahedeen.

Racial tensions between Arabs and everyone else heightened. Five days after the events of September 11th, an Arab man was shot point blank in the face with a shotgun in our neighboring city of Gary, Indiana.

The following day, a local Mosque was vandalized with spray-paint and Molotov cocktails.

The whole area was in an uproar over anyone associated with the Islamic faith, and I didn't even know what *Islam* meant.

For most of us, we didn't even know what a Muslim was, let alone what they believed. However, this didn't stop accusations that Islam was the root cause of these heinous crimes.

I needed to find out for myself if the faith was really a catalyst or just a scapegoat before I put my two cents in during arguments with friends.

Conservative radio shows blamed the Qur'ān while liberal ones told us we could not discriminate against Muslims and their beliefs. But what were their beliefs? What would make someone hijack a plane and kill thousands of innocent people? Was Islam really responsible for what happened?

ISLAM IN A NUTSHELL

Islam claims the exclusivity of salvation to their god Allah, who is the one and only true god of the universe. *Islam* means 'submission (to Allah)' and *Muslim* means 'one who submits.' As the world's fastest growing religion, there are over 1.5 billion Islamic followers, or Muslims, worldwide. This constitutes about twenty-five percent of the world's population. Islam began around 600CE under a man named Muhammad in modern-day Saudi Arabia after he had a series of visions. At the encouragement of his wife, Muhammad gathered a large following and declared himself a prophet. Eventually, his words were recorded into a collection called the Qur'ān. Muslims practice a heavily works-based salvation through obedience and conformity to Islamic holiness codes. The religion is generally broken up into three distinct groups: Sunni, Shi'ite, and Sufi. While they may differ on many things, all agree that Muhammad is the greatest prophet of Allah.

Allah, a single god, knows all things at all times and is ultimately wise. He has had a number of prophets to include Jesus Christ and the greatest prophet, Muhammad. Muslims believe that salvation may be obtained through strict adherence to the Five Pillars of Islam which are: the *Shahada*, Prayer (*Salat*), Fasting (*Sawm*), Alms-giving (*Zakāt*), and Pilgrimage (*Hajj*). The Shahada is a prayer which declares that "there is no true God except Allah and Muhammad is the Messenger of Allah," and is the closest sacrament Muslims have to baptism, the outward expression of conversion. Upon death, Allah will judge all people. If the faithful Muslim performed enough good works, they will go to one of the one hundred levels of heaven which are all still separate from the presence of Allah. Those who are not Muslim are banished to hell regardless of their good works in this life, including Jews and Christians.[316]

MUHAMMAD & THE BIRTH OF ISLAM

As stated earlier, the story of Islam starts with one man, Muhammad. He was born ca. 570CE to 'Abd Allah and Amina who both died when he was a young boy.[317] His grandfather raised him in the city of Mecca until he too passed away. As a young adult, Muhammad made a living as a marginalized shepherd in what is modern-day Saudi Arabia. His interest in religion seems to have started when he became bothered by the many different polytheistic religions that were popular in the Arabian Peninsula at the time. He believed that none of them were an accurate picture of God's character. Muhammad frequently sought solitude to fast and pray through his spiritual dilemma. On one such occasion, he decided to go into a cave to pray by himself. During his meditation, Muhammad claims an angel named Jibreel (Gabriel) appeared to him. Jibreel strangled Muhammad by the neck and commanded him, "Recite!" or "*Qur'ān!*"[318] Of course being surprised by this, Muhammad initially didn't know what the angel wanted him to recite. Jibreel did this a few more times. With each strangle, Muhammad told the angel that he would read, but Jibreel continued to choke him. Finally, Jibreel gave Muhammad what would become a revelation in the series of revelations found in the Qur'ān.

Muhammad was terrified of his experience in the cave and questioned whether he was possessed by a demon.[319] He spoke with his wealthy and affluent wife who convinced him that this was a sign he was divinely called by God to become a prophet. Muhammad believed her, took the title, and also won his first convert to Islam, his wife Khadija. A few more of Muhammad's family members followed suit – then a few more acquaintances. Soon he had a small band of followers, and with this new following, he began to preach. Muhammad reached back to his previous struggle with the spiritual climate of

---

[316] Sūra Al-Mā'idah 5:82, Sūra At-Tawbah 9:31–35
[317] Jonathan E. Brockopp, *The Cambridge Companion to Muhammad* (Cambridge: Cambridge University Press, 2010), 3–4.
[318] Ibid, 4.

the Arabian Peninsula for the focus of his preaching and became well known for campaigning against the polytheism he had despised so much. Instead of many gods, Muhammad emphatically taught that there was only one god whose name is Allah.

Now, to be fair to the polytheists, Muhammad's idea of Allah was not completely original. It is possible, some theorize, that Muhammad fabricated a monotheistic god, Allah, through the combined influence of Jews, Christians, and polytheists. While appreciating the idea from Jews and Christians that God is one, Muhammad may have borrowed the identity of the character of that god from polytheists. Of the many gods available to worship in Muhammad's time, he may have chosen Ilah, the South Arabian moon god.[320]

ILAH THE MOON GOD?

Some speculate (although, not convincing enough for many) that Muhammad incorporated Ilah, a lunar deity, into Allah's identity. As the theory goes, Allah was faithfully worshiped by the *Hanifs*, those who rejected paganism in order to follow the true religion of Abraham. In the Qur'ān, Muhammad exhorts his readers to be as devoted to Islam as the Hanifs who worshiped the God of Abraham in the midst of rampant polytheism.[321] This god of Abraham was, supposedly, Ilah the moon god.[322] They worshiped Ilah in pagan temples all throughout Arabia. The Hanifs viewed Ilah, the moon god, as higher than any of the other gods. In a world inundated in polytheism, this may have been like comparing Zeus to Poseidon. If they lived during ancient Greece, they would have no problem with a temple containing Zeus, Poseidon, and Athena. They would simply ask to be pointed to the Greek's version of the moon god and would be able to worship Ilah. Worship of the moon god, Ilah, would have been a prevalent and well-known religion by the time Muhammad began preaching. Thus, it is speculated, Muhammad conveniently borrowed Ilah (Allah) from the

---

[319] Ron Rhodes, *Reasoning from the Scriptures with Muslims* (Eugene, Oreg.: Harvest House Publishers, 2002), 65.
[320] Alfred Guillaume, *Islam* (London: Penguin Books, 1990), 7.
[321] Sūra Al-Rūm 30:30, *Muhsin Khan*
[322] Yoel Natan, *Moon-o-theism: Religion of a War and Moon God Prophet*, Vol. I (Morrisville, NC: Lulu Enterprises, Inc., 2006), 537.

Hanifs. Nevertheless, he could not completely subscribe to their view of the nature of god.

Where Muhammad departed with the Hanifs in his day was concerning their toleration of polytheism. Muhammad disagreed with the existence of other gods, something it seems that Hanifs may have tolerated. For Muhammad, if there was only one god it was Allah. Even though the Hanifs may have tolerated polytheism while worshiping the true god of Abraham, Muhammad did not. This is where strict Islamic monotheism comes into existence. By selecting Ilah as the only god and rejecting all other deities, Muhammad transformed Ilah worship into something it had never been before. Consequently, Muhammad never started a new religion. He simply consolidated Ilah worship by invalidating the other, lesser-known gods and imported the "one, true Abrahamic religion" narrative into Islam.[323]

Proponents of this theory see proof of Ilah's influence on Muhammad in the often-utilized crescent moon as Islam's unofficial icon. This icon is very closely associated with Islamic culture, even though most Muslims refuse to accept semi-official icons like the cross of Christianity or the Star of Dave in Judaism. For example, the flag of Turkey, an officially Muslim state, proudly displays the crescent moon. The top of minarets, which are towers used to call Muslims to prayer, are usually crowned with a crescent moon. All of these, it is speculated, are residue of Ilah worship. As interesting as this idea may sound, many others see no correlation between Ilah and Allah. They argue that the crescent moon represents nothing more than a reminder that Allah uses the moon to mark the times and seasons in relation to Ramadan.

MUHAMMAD'S REJECTION AT MECCA

Muhammad began to take his monotheistic message further into the city of Mecca now that he had a god to preach and a small following to preach to. It didn't take long for Muhammad to face rejection by the religious and political leaders of the city. By 622CE, Muhammad and his seventy-five followers were forced to flee Mecca to the city of Medina in the north because of political pressure. (This journey in reverse, from Medina to Mecca, is reenacted today by faithful Muslims as a pilgrimage called the *Hajj* and also marks the beginning of the Muslim calendar.) Muhammad was both welcomed and received as a prophet and leader upon their arrival in Medina; however, it was difficult for him to sustain his growing assembly since Medina was not a wealthy city.

His solution for their financial woes was simple – they would attack passing caravans and steal any goods they found. Muhammad's forces raided passing caravans near the vicinity of Medina and became a little richer each time. He justified these attacks as retribution for being exiled from Mecca since most of the caravans passing by Medina were crucial to the Meccan economy. This was his attempt to strangle Mecca economically, forcing them to repent and receive him as the leader he believed himself to be. The raids occurred frequently since Medina was situated along a main road in the Arabian Peninsula. Muhammad initially gave orders from Medina to his band of 300 men to carry out these attacks. He was essentially hands-off at first, but would eventually lead three of the raids in person.[324]

Naturally, this upset the citizens and political leadership of Mecca who were relying on the caravans to keep their city's economy ticking. The economic leader of Mecca, Abu Sufyan, ordered a small army of 1,300 men to stop Muhammad's followers at Medina.[325] This resulted in the Battle of Badr, the fourth major military conflict of Muhammad's forces at the time. Against all odds, Muhammad stood victorious over Abu Sufyan's forces even though he was outnumbered four to one. This made Muhammad extremely wealthy, popular, and powerful. Perhaps the greatest spoil of this battle was people, as an influx of converts poured into his sphere of influence. The popular opinion among Muhammad's new converts was that his god, Allah, acted as the source of victory over an army four times the size of his own. So people came, listened, and converted.

A few years later, Mecca retaliated for both the Battle of Badr and Muhammad's continued attacks on their caravans. This time Abu Sufyan brought with him an impressive 10,000-man army. Muhammad heard of the

---

[323] Ibid., 537.
[324] Michael Lee Lanning, *The Battle 100: The Stories Behind History's Most Influential Battles* (Naperville, Illi.: Sourcebooks, Inc., 2005), 74.
[325] Ibid.

size of Abu Sufyan's army but was only able to muster 3,000 men to match. He knew his military success might be short-lived without another victory, so he opted for wit over might. Muhammad ordered all 3,000 men to quickly dig a trench around Medina.[326] When Abu Sufyan's army arrived, the trench put the city walls out of his force's reach, and the attacking army had to lay siege to the city. This was something they were unprepared for and were only able to sustain the siege for three weeks. Eventually, the army ran out of supplies and morale and had to return to Mecca. Once more, Muhammad had miraculously defeated the military might of Mecca, resulting in even more converts joining his ranks.

JEWISH–MUSLIM RELATIONS IN MEDINA

Over time, Muhammad's theology slowly developed and expanded in Medina. In fact, a majority of the Qur'ān, or at least Qur'ānic teaching, was developed while Muhammad was in Medina. One of the more interesting developments in Islamic thought during this time centered on Jewish–Muslim relations. It may be surprising to learn that, given today's religious climate, Muhammad was initially amiable to the Jewish tribes living in Medina. In fact, he strongly desired religious union with the Jews. Muhammad envisioned one grand, unifying faith that encompassed all monotheistic faiths. He was so convicted by this idea that he borrowed heavily from Jewish theology and their religious calendar since he viewed Judaism as close to the original monotheistic faith. Accordingly, most of Islam's religious feasts and ceremonies are modeled after Jewish customs.

For example, the Muslim food preparation requirements met in *halal* are nearly identical to the Jewish *kosher*. Muslims don headwear called a *kufi* which models after the Jewish *kippah* (or *yamekah*). Muhammad instructed Muslims to pray five times a day (*Salat*) towards the holy Jewish city of Jerusalem.[327] (It would not be until after Muhammad's death that the *Qibla*, or *direction*, Muslims prayed changed to Mecca.) The Muslim day of rest *Yawm*

---

[326] Ibid.
[327] Stephen J. Shoemaker, *The Death of a Prophet: The End of Muhammad's Life and the Beginnings of Islam* (Philadelphia: University of Pennsylvania Press, 2012), 227.

Al-Sabt is related to the Jewish day of rest *Yom Shabat*, or Sabbath. On the 10th day of Murham, the first month on the Islamic calendar, Muslims celebrate the *Day of Ashura*, a fast to commemorate Muhammad's fasting. The origin of this Muslim holiday is closely related to the Jewish *Yom Kippur*, or *Day of Atonement*, which is celebrated shortly before the *Day of Ashura* on the 10th day of the seventh month of the Jewish calendar, *Tishrei*, and also involves fasting.[328] Perhaps the most famous of all Muslim religious holidays is *Ramadan*. Beginning in August, it is a 30-day fasting celebration that commemorates Muhammad's first revelations of the Qur'ān from Allah. *Ramadan* may owe its origins to a very similar Jewish holiday called *Shavuot*, or the Festival of Weeks. Celebrated around June, this holiday commemorates the day that the nation of Israel received the Torah from God at Mount Sinai.

Despite Muhammad's multiple attempts to syncretize Judaism with his newly-forming faith of Islam, the Jews remained adamant that they served and worshiped a different god from Muhammad. Consequently, the Jews wholly rejected Muhammad's authority. This, in turn, caused a scorned Muhammad to turn against them. Perhaps he may have been hurt by their rejection of his idea to share a common brotherhood of faith, unifying all people under one religious roof. He toiled to bring Muslims and Jews together under his prophetic authority, but they had rejected him. Even though he had drafted legislation that protected Jews by giving them legal right to aid and relief, still they denied his religious prophecy.[329] He acknowledged their customs and adopted them to his new religion, but regardless of this gesture, they did not recognize his authority. Whatever the case may be, Muhammad grew extremely antagonistic towards the Jewish tribes in Medina.

Having once celebrated the Jewish faith, Muhammad now withdrew his admiration and replaced it with anger. The idea of melding Judaism and Islam was put behind him. In a fierce polemic, which can be found in the Qur'ān, he estranged himself from the Jewish forefathers he had only recently venerated. In it, he demonstrated that the Jews had been disobedient to religious leadership in the past. "[The Jews] were covered with humiliation and poverty and returned with anger from Allah...because they [repeatedly] disbelieved in

---

[328] Francis E. Peters, *Muhammad and the Origins of Islam* (Albany, NY: State University of New York Press, 1994), 204.

the signs of Allah and killed the prophets without right. That was because they disobeyed and were [habitually] transgressing."[330] Now, Muhammad reasoned, the Jews were doing the same to him.

They denied the truth and must be punished. Muhammad's allegations against the Jews ranged from rejecting the authority of Moses, Jesus, and himself, to denying the truth of Allah's new revelation through the developing Qur'ān.[331] It was time they received their due punishment. In 627CE, Muhammad exiled multiple Jewish tribes from their homes into the surrounding desert. To ensure the Jewish population wouldn't later rebel against him, Muhammad ordered the execution of all the men from the Qurayza tribe while the remaining women and children were sold as slaves.[332] After these events, there was little objection from anyone to Muhammad's authority in Medina.

MUHAMMAD'S DEATH & THE SPREAD OF ISLAM

In 630CE, Muhammad's forces were finally strong enough to take on Mecca. After a brief skirmish and finding little resistance, Muhammad was accepted as their new religious and political leader. His birthplace had finally become the center of his growing empire as more and more leaders in the area, fearing him, eventually gave over their leadership to him. Mecca was established as the "Holy City of Islam," and from it, Muhammad sent out emissaries to proselytize on behalf of his new religion.[333] Muhammad's campaigns solidified Islamic control of the entire Arabian Peninsula in less than twenty years as a result of Muhammad's military leadership. However, only two years after returning to his hometown, the rising Muslim world was shocked when Muhammad died in Mecca in 632CE. At his death, Muhammad boasted thousands of converts and twenty-three major battles to his leadership.

---

[329] Irving M. Zeitling, *The Historical Muhammad* (Cambridge: Polity Press, 2007), 126.
[330] Sūra Al-Baqarah 2:61, *Sahih International*
[331] Sūra Al-Baqarah 2:86–91
[332] Fred M. Donner, "The Historical Context," *The Cambridge Companion to the Qur'ān*, ed. Jane Dammen McAuliffe, (Cambridge: Cambridge University Press, 2006), 27.
[333] Michael Lee Lanning, *The Battle 100: The Stories Behind History's Most Influential Battles* (Naperville, Illi.: Sourcebooks, Inc., 2005), 74.

Fighting and conquest were not deterred by Muhammad's death. Disunity quickly arose among Muhammad's followers. It was not over the continued spread of Islam's influence, but who should be at the helm. There was stark division among Muslims over who would become *caliph* (leader of the Muslim community) as Muhammad's successor. This dispute was never resolved and has divided Muslims ever since. Those who favored Muhammad's cousin, Ali, became the Shi'ites; those who favored Muhammad's father-in-law, Abu Bakr, became the Sunnis. A series of civil wars amongst Muslims broke out, to include the major Battles of Bassorah and Siffin where an estimated 80,000–90,000 men lost their lives to this dispute.[334]

Nevertheless, the Muslim conquest, or *Fatah* (opening), of the Middle East continued to occur for roughly one hundred years.[335] During this time, Islam spread as far west as the Iberian Peninsula, as far south as modern-day Yemen, as far east as modern-day Pakistan, and as far north as modern-day France. In 732CE on the one hundredth anniversary of Muhammad's death, Frankish forces defeated the invading Muslim army at the Battle of Tours in modern-day France. This battle was a watershed for Muslim expansion as their northern borders of influence would never again be pushed as far as modern-day Spain in the west and modern-day Croatia in the east.

The *Fatah* paints a violent picture of Islam's beginnings. Consequently, some Muslim apologists maintain that the *Fatah* was strictly a spiritual conquest in an attempt to downplay Islam's violent birth. They argue that the *Fatah* was solely accomplished through extremely persuasive Islamic missions work, which only testifies to the truthfulness of Muhammad was solely accomplished through message. However, this is highly improbable. Historical records do not corroborate this narrative, and the Qur'ān itself seems to imply a combination of Islamic missions work and military conquest; "Slay the idolaters wherever you find them. Arrest them, besiege them, and lie in ambush everywhere for them. If they repent and take to prayer and render the alms levy, allow them to go their way. Allah is forgiving and merciful."[336]

---

[334] Various sources as battle casualties during this time period are almost impossible to accurately calculate.
[335] This conquest included all of the modern–day Arabian Peninsula, Jordan, Israel, Palestine, Egypt, Yemen, Iraq, Iran, Afghanistan, Pakistan, Syria, half of Turkey, and Algeria.
[336] Sūra At-Tawbah 9:5, *N. J. Dawood*

ISLAM & MUSLIM SCRIPTURES

Now that we know the background behind Islam, what do Muslims believe as far as scriptures are concerned? First, let's examine their scriptures. It might surprise some to learn that most Muslims believe certain portions of the Bible to be sacred and true. In fact, many Muslims consider the Torah (*Tawrat*), Gospels (*Injil*) and the Psalms (*Zabur*) as part of their scriptures. In addition to these, however, they include the Qur'ān and the *hadīths* which are collections of narrations originating from the words and deeds of Muhammad. Muslims are taught that additional revelation was required from Allah because men had corrupted any scripture written prior to the Qur'ān. For example, the Gospels in the New Testament would have been uncompromised if it weren't for Paul. Accordingly, many Muslims believe that Jews and Christians have altered scripture over time to suit their own beliefs. As we will examine, the same can equally be said of Islam.

In order to undo the damage men had done to Allah's will in writing, Muhammad was given the Qur'ān. The Qur'ān is by far the most sacred and correct text to Muslims. It is the absolute highest written authority in Islam. The Qur'ān describes itself as "a transcript of the eternal book...sublime, full of wisdom."[337] To most Muslims, it is flawless in content, design, and logic.[338] Furthermore, the Qur'ān actually affirms the previously mentioned portions of the Bible by explaining them through a Qur'ānic hermeneutic. As the Qur'ān itself claims, "it was not [possible] for this Qur'ān to be produced by other than Allah, but [it is] a confirmation of what was before it and a detailed explanation of the [Bible]."[339]

To its credit, the Qur'ān stands unequalled in medieval Arabic literature in terms of literary and linguistic achievement; without it, Arabic may not have been the *lingua franca* in most of the modern Middle East. Since the Qur'ān was originally written in Arabic, and given the difficulty in transliterating Arabic into English, there are many different Anglicized forms of the title *Qur'ān*; i.e., Qur'an, Koran, Qur'ān, Curan, Alcoran, al-Qur'ān, Alkoran, etc. They all mean the same thing, but *Qur'ān* is the most popular choice.

---

[337] Sūra Az-Zukhruf 43:3–4, *N. J. Dawood*
[338] Sūra An-Nisa' 4:82
[339] Sūra Yunus 10:37, *Sahih International*

It is divided into 114 chapters (*Sūra*) in non-chronological order. All different lengths, each Sūra becomes increasingly shorter as the reader moves through the book. When referencing a Sūra, it is common to first identify the passage by name followed by the chapter number and verse. For example, one would not reference the verse quoted above as Qur'ān 43:3–4, but rather Sūra Az-Zukhruf 43:3–4. This is similar to quoting John 3:16 over Bible 3:16, although the Qur'ān is not divided into different books as is the Bible. Rather, the Qur'ān is one continuous volume attributed to the same author.

The Qur'ān is believed to have been orally dictated by Muhammad to some of his educated followers since Muhammad, himself, was illiterate. However, the Qur'ān didn't exist in textual form until sometime between 600–630CE.[340] This should raise immediate suspicion of the trustworthiness of the original text since its author died before seeing the completed work. In fact, canonization of the Qur'ān did not begin until at least twenty years after his death and would not officially finish until the third caliphate (*leader*), 'Uthmān, commissioned the task.[341] Muhammad would most likely not recognize the arrangement or edition of the Qur'ān in its present form were he to see it today. Of course, the same argument could be made about the New Testament; however, as a whole, the New Testament is comprised of letters that traveled throughout the Roman Empire while the apostles were alive, and were not a direct dictation from God to one man alone.

The Qur'ān, as mentioned before, is one man's revelation from Allah. It is relatively small, just about the size of the Gospels. To Muslims, the Qur'ān is the final revelation from Allah until the end of time. The Qur'ān is where Islamic society derives almost all of its theology, sociology, philosophy, and judiciary theory. To say the Qur'ān has an influence on the Muslim worldview and theology would be an understatement. It is not uncommon when entering a Muslim's house to see the Qur'ān placed atop the bookshelf as the highest book in the house, above all other knowledge because it is a direct revelation from Allah. In the minds of most Muslims, the Qur'ān is "beyond doubt from the Lord of the Universe" and should be treated as such.[342]

---

[340] Harald Motzki, "Alternative accounts of the Qur'āns formation," *The Cambridge Companion to the Qur'ān*, ed. Jane Dammen McAuliffe, (Cambridge: Cambridge University Press, 2006), 59.
[341] Ibid., 45.
[342] Sūra Yunus 10:37

While the Qur'ān to Muslims is a fundamentally perfect revelation without error, the work is somewhat shrouded in mystery, leaving scholars to scratch their heads in concern for its formation and the timeline surrounding it. Religious scholar Jonathan Brockopp summarizes the dilemma:

> To some Western scholars, the relationship between the Qur'ān and Muhammad seems too convenient, as if stories of the Prophet's life were designed to explain differences found in the Qur'ān. For the Meccan period, the problem is complicated by the fact that the Qur'ān is the only writing we possess that derives from that period ... Muhammad's doubts in his early mission (as described in the Qur'ān) were hard to understand given the almost-unbelievable expansion of Islam after his death. Although some histories dutifully record the Prophet's despair, others gloss over those weak moments in favor of a more triumphant picture, one that better fits with his ultimate success.[343]

Aside from discrepancies in the timeline of Muhammad's life, what does the Qur'ān teach? This is, after all, the primary reason we should examine the text. And as with any truth claim, ultimately it does not matter who says it or how it is said; what matters is what is said. Does the Qur'ān teach truth? Is it truly a reflection of God's character and will? Before answering these questions, it is wise to being with surface-level aspects of the Qur'ān that have made their way into popular culture. Prior to dialoguing with Muslims, we should take care not to bring with us caricatures of Islamic theology, as this will lessen our trustworthiness in presenting truth. For this reason, we'll examine the Qur'ān's treatment of women, the fabled reward of women in the afterlife, and further Muslim relations with Christians and Jews. Afterwards, the theology of Islam as derived from the Qur'ān will be surveyed.

ISLAM & MUSLIM SCRIPTURES: WOMEN

The issue of women in the Qur'ān is perhaps one of the most notorious among Islamic ideas. Many in the Western world see images of Islamic women on

---

[343] Jonathan E. Brockopp, *The Cambridge Companion to Muhammad* (Cambridge: Cambridge University Press, 2010), 5–6.

television covered from head to toe in black garbs called abayas and hijabs and wonder to themselves why these women wear something which seems extremely alien to them.[344] Because abayas and hijabs are so drastically foreign to Western fashion and are frequently associated with misogyny, full Muslim garbs can often cause controversy. In Europe, for example, legislation is moving in various countries to outlaw burkas – an enveloping Islamic garb worn by some Muslim women to cover their entire body while outside.[345] But why do Muslim women wear these garbs in the first place?

In short, abayas, hijabs, and burkas are worn by Muslim women to hide their bodies from being seen by Muslim men – and all men for that matter. The theory behind this idea goes that if a man cannot see a woman's face, thighs, legs, etc., he will not lust after her. Thus, covering a woman makes it easier for a Muslim man to not offend Allah while also retaining the decency of Muslim women. It is considered indecent in some Muslim countries for a woman to expose anything other than her feet and hands because her body may unintentionally catch a few straying eyes. Essentially, in this mindset Muslim men do not own their sin, opting instead to blame women for causing them to stumble – not unlike Adam's blaming of Eve for his sin in Genesis 3:12.

While this may seem strange to Westerners, it is not uncommon to find Muslim women who prefer their cultural garb over the more revealing fashion found in many non-Islamic cultures. Citing decency and civility, Muslim women believe wearing this apparel is a moral step up from the way Western women dress. Therefore, to some Muslim women wearing abayas, hijabs, and burkas is more of a cultural issue than a religious one. There are, however, instances that render this statement only true in part.

Some women do not want to be subject to a dress code yet are finding themselves with no other choice but to conform. This is when the issue of Muslim women's apparel leaves the sphere of culture and enters the realm of misogyny. While the issue of what to wear is not necessarily a dangerous one, it does reflect a broader mindset among Muslim men of how they are to treat women. Finding the source of their overbearingness towards women is not a difficult task. The Qur'ān supports misogyny, depending on its interpretation,

---

[344] Abayas cover a woman's body while hijabs cover their head.

which despite the best attempts of watering the doctrine down cannot deny that women are second-class citizens in Qur'ānic teaching.

It may surprise some to learn there is actually a Sūra in the Qur'ān titled *The Women*. In it, *Sūra An-Nisā'* (The Women) gives practical advice to Muslim men on the treatment and social standing of women. To be sure, men are reminded in this Sūra that women are of equal human dignity; however, they are not of equal social standing.[346] For example, we read in Sūra An-Nisā' 4:11 that women are worth one half the value of a man.[347] Elsewhere, Sūra An-Nisā' 4:3 teaches that men may partake in polygamy.[348] Further still, Sūra An-Nisā' 4:34 instructs men to take charge of women in all social aspects be it family, community, or politics.[349]

Verses like these reveal that the intended audience of the Qur'ān is men, not women. It is, at times, difficult to see how women may gleam benefiting encouragement or empowering inspiration from the Qur'ān, short of the wholesale removal of misogynistic verses such as the ones found in Sūra An-Nisā'.[350] This may be a foreign concept to Christians since it is clear that the Bible was written for every man and woman without regard to their status in equality. Men and women were both endowed with the creator's image and, consequently, both have equal intrinsic value.[351]

The low view of women in Islamic theology has led to another, more sinister grievance. According to the Qur'ān, it is acceptable to Allah for men to beat their wives and deny her relations because of a man's inalienable right to govern over her. Sūra An-Nisā' 4:34 states, "but those wives from whom you fear arrogance – first advise them; then if they persist, forsake them in bed; and finally, strike them."[352] This verse alone should cause extreme

---

[345] Bruce Crumley, "France Moves Closer to Banning Burqa," *TIME Magazine*, http://www.time.com/time/world/article/0,8599,1983871,00.html (accessed January 9, 2012).

[346] Sūra An-Nisā' 4:25

[347] According to inheritance, what is an equal share for men is that of two women. See Sūra An-Nisā' 4:11.

[348] Sūra An-Nisā' 4:3

[349] Sūra An-Nisā' 4:34

[350] Of course, the argument may be made that other verses within Sūra An-Nisā' can be used in support of the positive treatment of women taught in the Qur'ān, such as 4:4 which encourages Muslim men to give lavish wedding gifts to their wives. However, just one verse later, women are referred to as property. It would seem for every step forward in the positive treatment of women in the Qur'ān, there are two steps backward lurking around the corner.

[351] Gen. 1:27

[352] Sūra An-Nisā' 4:34, *Sahih International*

concern for the welfare of women within Islamic culture. And while many countries in the world have made domestic violence a serious offense, there are many more where laws drawn from the Qur'ān (Sharia law) are the *lex terrae*. In short, while the Qur'ān may teach a high view of a woman's intrinsic value, it elsewhere denies women social liberties enjoyed by men and oftentimes places women in dangerous situations.

ISLAM & MUSLIM SCRIPTURES: HOURIS (VIRGINS)

Another controversial topic in Islamic theology is men receiving virgins in the afterlife. As the notorious idea goes, when a Muslim man dies he is rewarded with seventy-two or forty virgin women as an incentive for sacrificial acts of martyrdom. This is perhaps one of the most infamous notions concerning women in Islamic theology. The idea finds its origin, at least in part, in the piecing together of a few Qur'ānic verses.

- **Sūra Ar-Rahmān 55:56** "Therein are bashful virgins whom neither man nor jinnee (angels) will have touched before."[353]
- **Sūra Al-Wāqi'ah 56:35** "We created the houris and made them virgins, loving companions for those on the right hand."[354]
- **Sūra An-Naba' 78:31** "As for the righteous, they shall surely triumph. Theirs shall be gardens and vineyards, and high-bosomed maidens for companions."

From these verses, and other references to the *houris* found in the hadīths, the idea of being rewarded with virgin women was born.[355]

Some Muslims scholars have elaborated on the Qur'ān's description of these women, which lends credibility to the idea that the *houris* were created for a purpose different from that of women in general. To these Muslim scholars

---

[353] *Jinnee* is the Arabic word for *angel*. You may already be familiar with the term *genie* or phrase *genie in a bottle*.
[354] "Those on the right hand" is a poetic reference to saved Muslims. Those on the left hand would be damned.
[355] Brian R. Farmer, *Understanding Radical Islam: Medieval Ideology in the Twenty-First Century* (New York: Peter Lang Publishing, 2008), 55.

the *houris* are "perfect" in the sense that they are equal in age, stature, and figure.[356] They are also exempt from certain bodily functions that, in my opinion, may have to do with ancient cleanliness codes.[357] In other words, the *houris* are the "ideal women" so far as a seventh century male perspective is concerned. It is highly possible that Muhammad and other early Muslims leaders viewed them as a gift or incentive in exchange for obedience from younger men.

As an aside, if you are a woman and offended by reading this, you have every reason to be so. At times, according to one's interpretation, the Qur'ān teaches ideas that endorse misogyny, which has acted as a springboard from which demeaning actions and policies against women have been justified in certain instances. Now, if you are a man and not offended by reading this, then you should probably repent. Seriously. Go. Do it now.

This being the case, we must attempt to avoid a Western, reductive perception of women in Muslim culture. This is especially true if we consider "misogyny" and "Arab" as practically synonymous. Misogyny isn't simply an "Arab issue" or a "Muslim issue," and is by no means unique to Islam. It is an "everyone issue" that must be met head on no matter what religious context it is discovered. Granted, the Qur'ān makes this particularly challenging within Islam due to its clear instruction on the treatment of women in certain instances. This is not, however, license to cast all Muslims in the light of misogyny; rather, it is a caution of what may come in certain instances.

An interesting question to ask is whether or not an equivalent to the houris exists for Muslim women. Some have proposed that, under specific circumstances, women do not receive sensual gratification in the after life but are instead gifted with free salvation ticket, so to speak, which is applicable to anyone they chose. Tragically, according to some extremist interpretations, this only becomes available to Muslim women who are facing death by an "honor killing" due to sullying her family's reputation. They are given the choice between an "honor killing" and martyrdom, where the latter is complimented with salvation for herself and one other.[358] Most would opt for a martyr's death as

---

[356] Muhammad Saed Abdul-Rahman, *The Meaning and Explanation of the Glorious Qur'an*, Vol. 10, 2nd ed. (London: MSA Publications, Ltd., 2009), 373.
[357] Anat Berko, *The Path to Paradise* (Westport, Conn.: Greenwood Publishing Group, Inc., 2007), 166.
[358] Faegheh Shirazi, *Muslim Women in War and Crisis: Representation and Reality* (Austin, Tex.: University of Texas Press, 2010), 3.

a last effort for community or family approval in this life and the next. This highlights the general difference between men and women in Islamic theology. There is a distinct advantage of being male within Islam despite the intrinsic value of both genders before Allah.

THE GREATER JIHAD: A SPIRITUAL STRUGGLE

When considering the relationship between Muslims and other worldviews, specifically Jews and Christians, many will immediately jump to war, strife, and violence. There isn't really a relationship; murder and terrorism mar parts of Western civilization, Israel, Palestine, Egypt, Nigeria, and other countries where these three worldviews clash. The past decade has only reinforced our immediate response to Muslim relations with Jews and Christians. In fact, the first thought that may have popped into your head after seeing Muslims, Jews, and Christians in the same sentence is disagreement, strife, turmoil, or war. This is the unfortunate association made by most who live in Western civilization, particularly North Americans. When we think about the relationship between Muslims, Jews, and Christians, it is usually negative. This, in turn, affects the way we evangelize to Muslims. Christians often engage in reactive apologetics with Muslims because of poor Muslim–Christian relations.

Granted, the last decade witnessed a rise in attention to Islam from the West due to violence and war. New words appeared in popular American vocabulary seemingly overnight – fatwa, mujahidin, jihad. And perhaps this word, *jihad*, more than any other post-9/11 imported Arabic word describes the relationship between Muslims, the Qur'ān, Jews, and Christians. But what does jihad mean? The answer to that question is surprisingly difficult. There seems to be a non-consensus of what jihad means, even to Muslims; however, there is general agreement of the existence of two types of jihad – the greater jihad and the lesser jihad.[359]

The greater jihad is compulsory for every Muslim to participate in. In fact, it is considered by many Muslims to be the Sixth Pillar of Islam since it is

---

[359] John Bowker, *What Muslims Believe* (Oxford: Oneworld, 1995), 79.

ultimately the inner struggle for purity and salvation.[360] The greater jihad is a never-ending work performed by Muslims to prove themselves pure and self-controlled before Allah so that they may be worthy of his love. Since all humanity is sinful, this never-ending work is a 'struggle' or a 'fight.' As Christians, we know this struggle for self-control is impossible to achieve short of the grace and mercy of God; therefore, Muslims are forever locked in an inner battle for purity. In this instance, the greater jihad is basically fighting for Islam to rule over one's entire being. From every thought to every action, the greater jihad struggles to tame the flesh.

The greater jihad has, in the past decade, been presented as the only proper definition of jihad for all Muslims everywhere. Proponents of this view of jihad are usually Muslims who are desperately trying to rebrand Islam as a peaceful religion in response to what they feel was an unfortunate reaction to Islam when the West met Islamofascism face-to-face in 2001. To them, all of jihad entails "striving or exerting [oneself] to the utmost against something disapproved."[361] This definition fits perfectly with the greater jihad but completely misrepresents the lesser jihad. The greater jihad is most assuredly the personal struggle every Muslim will face throughout their life in order to maintain their faith; however, the lesser jihad is physical war against anything Allah would disapprove of with regard to economics, politics, ethics, culture, and religion.

THE LESSER JIHAD: A PHYSICAL STRUGGLE

The lesser jihad is what the West recognizes as terrorism or violence in the name of Islam. Muslims who practice the lesser jihad are called "jihadists" or "mujahidin." They are, by far, the smallest crowd in the Muslim population, but yield the loudest voice and strongest actions. Why jihadists practice the lesser jihad is completely linked to Islam's foundations, and the history of Islam is key to understanding why jihadists fight for Islamic supremacy. The lesser jihad was born out of the rejection of Muhammad as Allah's prophet by

---

[360] Ninian Smart, *The World's Religions*, 2d ed. (Cambridge: Cambridge University Press, 1998), 300.
[361] Zahid Aziz, *Islam, Peace and Tolerance* (Wembley, United Kingdom: Ahmadiyya Anjuman Lahore Publications, U.K., 2007), 41.

the polytheists, Jews, and Christians of Mecca and its surrounding communities during his lifetime. He fought for the authority of Islam to reign supreme during his lifetime; when he died, the lesser jihad was solidified forever as one of his last wishes to his followers. Muhammad desired for them to run non-Muslims out of the Arabian Peninsula and away from Muslim lands unless they paid homage to Muslim authorities.[362] This reflects his aspirations of seeing the known world united under the authority of one religion, worldview, economy, culture, and government.

To fulfill this vision, Islam has been wrought with a continual struggle for Islamic supremacy from its inception, a struggle that continues to this day. Because Islam is not the universally recognized worldview and religion, jihadists have returned to violence to finish Muhammad's and, ultimately, Allah's desire. The lesser jihad is justifiable and forgivable violence in the minds of jihadists not only because of Muhammad's legacy but also because the Qur'ān expressly pardons it. This is especially true with regard to martyrdom for a jihadi cause.[363] In the minds of jihadists, they are following Muhammad's example when they cast aside patient proselytizing for deplorable violence.

Early on in his career as Allah's greatest prophet, Muhammad first attempted to convert Jews and Christians by proselytism and even held a favorable view of some Christians as people who were upright, restraining from sin, and doers of good works.[364] In fact, non-Muslims were actually allowed to practice their religions so long as they recognized Muhammad's authority and paid him homage, or *jizya*.[365] Fighting only began sporadically between Muhammad's followers and local city-states, mainly as self-defense or retaliation for assaults by Muhammad's followers on trade caravans.[366] These caravan raids were essentially strategic and economic actions with no religious influence. Muhammad was determined to bolster his religious leadership through proselytizing and political leadership through aggression and retaliation.

---

[362] Muhammad's expulsion order that only Muslims to be left on the Arabian Peninsula: Ishaq, *Sirat*, p. 689; Koelle, *Mohammedanism*, section ii: 19, p. 231; *Sahih Bukhari*, vol. 4, bk. 52, no. 288; vol. e, bk. 53, no. 393; vol. 5, bk. 59, no. 716; *Sahih Muslim*, bk. 019, no. 4366; and *Malik's Muwatta*, bk. 45, no. 5.18.
[363] Sūra 'Āli 'Imrān 3:157
[364] Sūra 'Āli 'Imrān 3:113–115
[365] Sūra At-Tawbah 9:29, *N. J. Dawood*

Eventually, after repeated failure to convince Christians and Jews to join his ranks, Muhammad added religious defamation to the list of justifiable reasons for fighting. The Qur'ān recounts that Allah's patience wore thin with the "stiff-necked" people, "those worst of the creatures," and commanded that they be counted as combatants until they repented.[367] They were, after all, becoming a hindrance to the spread of Allah's word and warning of the End. While the "people of the book" and polytheists were at one time tolerable, they had since become a vexation. Now, absent a formal treaty or a refusal to pay *jizya*, non-Muslims could be subject to attack for their resistance. This comes in spite of Allah's previous declaration, "that whoever killed a human being...shall be deemed as having killed all mankind."[368] Allah's policy with relating to non-Muslims seems to have drastically changed at this time. Such progressive revelation makes the Qur'ān a difficult text to follow along, but provides us with a clear picture of the religion's evolution.[369]

As one might guess, deliberately telling the world that it must convert or face death is not necessarily the best P.R. strategy. Consequently, Islam is in a continual uphill battle to present itself as a religion that promotes peace due to its history of violence in the Qur'ān. One strategy used is to deny the concept of jihad altogether, emphasizing the greater jihad as the only true definition for the term. When this topic is brought up with a Muslim apologist, they might first argue that the concept of jihad as a "holy war" doesn't even appear in the Qur'ān. This is not entirely true since many Qur'ānic verses speak of "striving (jihad) in the path of Allah," a phrase meant as a physical struggle, or the lesser jihad.[370] A second argument points out the difference between the words *jihad* (struggle) and *qital* (warring). According to this argument, *jihad* in the Qur'ān should be interpreted spiritually whereas *qital* may be understood as physical violence.[371] This lessens the amount of violent references in the Qur'ān from over 40 (jihad) to only a handful (qital).

---

[366] Ninian Smart, *The World's Religions*, 2d ed. (Cambridge: Cambridge University Press, 1998), 298.
[367] Sūra Yā-Sīn 36:8; Sūra At-Tawbah 9:29; Sūra Al-Bayyinah 98:6
[368] Sūra Al-Mā'idah 5:32
[369] Tom Greggs, *New Perspectives for Evangelical Theology: Engaging with God, Scripture and the World* (Oxon, United Kingdom: Routledge, 2010), 188.
[370] Reuven Firestone, "Jihad," *Medieval Islamic Civilization: An Encyclopedia*, Vol. 1, ed. Josef W. Meri (New York: Taylor & Francis Group, LLC., 2006), 419.
[371] Ibid.

Again, this argument falls short of accounting for the concept of the lesser jihad throughout the entirety of the Qur'ān. Here are just some of the verses that teach the concept of lesser jihad regardless of the word choice;

Sūra Aṣ-Ṣaf 61:4 "Allah loves those who fight for his cause in ranks as firm as a mighty edifice."

Sūra Al-Baqarah 2:190 "Fight for the sake of Allah those that fight against you, but do not attack them first."

Sūra Al-Baqarah 2:191 "Slay them wherever you find them. Drive them out of the places from which they drove you."

Sūra At-Tawbah 9:38 "Believers, why is it that when you are told; 'March in the cause of Allah,' you linger slothfully in the land? Are you content with this life in preference to the life to come? If you do not go to war, Allah will punish you sternly, and will replace you by other men."

Sūra Al-Baqarah 2:193 "Fight against them until idolatry is no more and Allah's religion reigns supreme."

Sūra Al- Anfāl 8:12 "Allah revealed His will to the angels, saying: 'I shall be with you. Give courage to the believers. I shall cast terror into the hearts of the infidels. Strike off their heads, strike off the very tips of their fingers!'"

Furthermore, many references to the concept of jihad exist in the hadīths. In fact, one chapter in the hadīths is titled "Fighting for the Cause of Allah."[372] So, it is fair to say that jihadists are able to create the concept of the lesser jihad based on what the Qur'ān teaches, regardless of whether or not they are justified in doing so.

THE END TIMES & JIHAD

Given that the driving force behind jihad seems to be Islamic dominance, why do some Muslims believe that Islam needs to be the worldwide dominant religion? Unlike Christianity (and scripture) which teaches that Christians do not hold the responsibility of bringing the entire world under Christian rule, a Muslim can be lead to truly believe it is their responsibility to bring the world under the authority of Islam. Part of this drive for world Islamization may stem from their view of the end times. According to some Islamic eschatology, the world must be under complete Islamic control before the end of the world may occur. In this popular view, Jerusalem is the setting for the initial phase of the apocalypse, which only exacerbates the delicate socio–political situation in modern Israel.[373]

During this *Qiyamah* (the Muslim end times), a time known only by Allah, Jesus will physically return to earth with the *Mahdi* (the twelfth Imam) and will end all wars, ushering in an era of peace.[374] This messianic era of peace will come after Jesus kills *ad-Dajjal*, the antichrist figure in Islam, and defeats his followers.[375] The followers of ad-Dajjal include polytheists, pagans, atheists, Jews, and Christians. To be clear, according to most Islamic scholars Jesus will return to kill all the Christians. A little strange, I know, but we must remember that to Muslims Jesus is a great prophet in a line of many whom Allah sent to reveal his character and will.

Christians will certainly not suffer alone from the wrath of Jesus as Jews and any other non-Muslims will be included. However, as some Muslims believe, the worldwide annihilation of non-Muslims and, consequently, the ushering of the messianic era with Jesus will not occur until the world is under Muslim control. Thus, with mounting impatience some Muslims have turned to jihad to speed the process up, but for most Muslims, this is admittedly sometime in the far future.

Eschatology aside and regardless of whether or not the world has accepted Islam as their worldview, Muslims are called by Allah to be the driving force behind global politics, economy, and cultural influence. If this does not happen, the world will forever be out of balance without fully submitting to the tenets of Islam. Thus, in the minds of some Muslims the global financial crisis of 2008 was due, in large part, to banks not adopting Islamic business practices and political leaders not adhering to Islamic leadership techniques. Without Islam as the reigning worldview, the world will never function as it should. In this aspect,

---

[372] *Sahih Bukhari*, Vol. 4, Book 52
[373] M. A. Muqtedar Khan, *Jihad for Jerusalem: Identity and Strategy in International Relations* (Westport, Conn.: Greenwood Publishing Group, Inc., 2004), 114.
[374] Charles Upton, *Legends of the End: Prophecies of the End Times, Antichrist, Apocalypse, and Messiah from Eight Religious Traditions* (Hillsdale, NY: Sophia Perennis, 2004), 39.
[375] Gustave Edmund Grunebaum and Gustave Edmund Von Grunebaum, *Medieval Islam: A Study in Cultural Orientation*, 2nd ed. (Chicago: University of Chicago Press, 1958), 194.

Islam is extremely theocratic; in the minds of extremist jihadists, it can be founded by violence and terrorism.

ISLAMIC JIHAD AND CHRISTIAN CRUSADES

A third argument used to counter accusations that Islam is an abettor of violence is usually the opposite accusation – Christians can also be violent. Besides, was it not the Christians who sparked the Crusades, Thirty Years War, and the Spanish Inquisitions? Aren't today's Christians bombing abortion clinics and assassinating abortion doctors? Yes. A resounding "yes" should be our answer. We should never try to minimize violence in Christian history, as this will only build a case against ourselves and against Jesus. When the accusation of Christianity's violent history (and to some extent, modern events) is raised, the answer is always yes. But here's the important part to emphasize – the reason and justification of violence in Christianity is completely different from that of Islam.

When Christians commit violence under the banner of Jesus Christ, they are directly violating what he commanded Christians to do – namely not to commit violence under the banner of his name.[376] When jihadist Muslims commit violence in Allah's name, they believe they are fulfilling what Muhammad and, ultimately, Allah commands of them.[377] The difference is staggering. Yes, there is violence in Christian history, but according to Jesus himself, there shouldn't be. Christians who commit violence in the name of Jesus are in deep, deep sin. From Pope Urban II who launched the First Crusade in 1096 to Scott Roeder who murdered abortionist Dr. George Tiller in 2009, any violence committed in Jesus' name is horrendously sinful and exceptionally damaging to how the world views him. The same cannot be said of Muhammad who declared violence in the name of Allah as a justifiable and noble act in certain situations.[378]

This brings up *the* question many in the western world are contemplating about Islam – is it a religion of peace? Considering everything

---

[376] Matt. 26:51–54; Luke 22:49–51; John 18:10–11; Eph. 6:12
[377] Sūra Aṣ-Ṣaf 61:4; Al-Baqarah 2:190-193; At-Tawbah 9:38; Al-'Anfāl 8:12
[378] Sūra 'Āli 'Imrān 3:157

mentioned so far it would be very easy to believe that Islam is not a religion of peace; however, for every verse in the Qur'ān we find that commands violence, a Muslim will find an equal amount of verses commanding peace. Many Christians and Muslims get into shouting matches over whether Islam is a religion of peace or violence based on the sheer volume of violent and peaceful passages found in the Qur'ān. As if to believe that by loading both sides of a proverbial scale, Islam will be definitively classified as a peaceful or violent religion based on the amount of peaceful or violent verses alone.

Be careful not to get caught up in this. Arguing over whether or not Islam is a religion of violence or peace should not be the goal of Christians who are serious about engaging Muslims with the gospel. We should focus on understanding Muhammad as a violent man while leaving room for his followers to be peaceful. If not, we risk broad stroking an entire class of people and furthering the divide between us. Remember, if we claim that Islam is a religion of violence, the same could be said about Christianity, regardless of whether or not the violence is justifiable by the Qur'ān or Bible respectively. It is the leaders and texts of those two worldviews that must be examined for violence, not the followers and history.

In case the violence in Christianity's history does come up, it is good to iron out our response before entering this topic of discussion. The important thing to explain initially is that all Christians are taught to pray for peace and are called to be peacemakers, but not everyone who calls themselves Christians are actually Christians.[379] Case in point – the Crusades. The leaders of the Crusades were liars, murderers, and far from being Christians. This includes the popes who called for the Crusades. They were greedy to the core, and most of them used Christians as pawns in their ruthless land-grab conquests. Thanks to them, Christian history drips wet with innocent blood. But at the end of the day, they were either Christians in deep sin or not Christians at all.

It is equally important to remember that our job is not to be apologists for Christian history but rather the history that birthed Christianity. We are apologists for the historic events of Jesus' life, death, resurrection, and message. With our own history in mind and should the topic arise, violence in

---

[379] Isa. 26:3; Matt. 5:9

Islam should not be our primary focus. It shouldn't even be a secondary focus. Our focus should be on the fact that Islamic theology teaches that Jesus plays second fiddle to Muhammad. It teaches that Jesus came to announce the coming kingdom of Islam, not the arrival of the kingdom of God. Islam teaches that Jesus was sent to proclaim the coming of Muhammad, not to proclaim the fulfillment of the Messiah in his person and work. This should be our driving factor to dialogue with Muslims, not the fact that jihadist Muslims kill other people because they believe they're doing Allah's will. Focusing on anything other than Jesus would be a clear case of reactive apologetics. Never forget this – it's always about Jesus.

THE THEOLOGY OF THE QUR'AN

The theology of the Qur'ān is not terribly difficult to define because it teaches clear principles and theological concepts. According to the Qur'ān, Allah is the only god and is only one person.[380] This is different from Christianity in that it rejects the concept of the Trinity. Consequently, Muslims view the Trinity as polytheism. While God is one God in three persons, Allah is one god in one person. The spirit of Allah is not a person of Allah but an extension of his will. Likewise, Allah does not have a son. It's literally just Allah. In fact, to equate anything to the person of Allah is tantamount to heresy and has a specific name, the sin of *širk*.

It is interesting to note, however, that a trinitarian concept does indeed exist within Islamic theology. With Allah as the obvious candidate for the Father figure in this Islamic trinity, Muslims hold the Qur'ān up to a divine standard as the immutable word of god, thereby creating a type of extension of Allah on earth. As the late Dr. Ninian Smart, widely considered the father of modern religious studies, describes:

> It is easy to think of the Qur'an simply as a book and to say
> that the Muslims have faith in the words of a holy book. But
> this does not convey the centrality and power of the Qur'an in
> Muslim eyes. If you were to look for a rough equivalent to the

---

[380] Sūra Al-Mulk 67:1–3; 112:1

Christian Incarnation (the divine nature of Jesus) in Muslim piety, it would be the Qur'an.[381]

Christians understand that Jesus is the immutable word of God as discussed in the opening words in the Gospel of John.[382] Therefore, in some ways, the Qur'ān is to Muslims as Jesus is to Christians in so far as reverence, revelation, and knowledge of salvation are concerned.[383] Likewise, jinnees (angels) are viewed as a higher creation than humans and are the beings that see to the introduction and completion of Allah's will. Again, a correlation can be drawn with the Holy Spirit who introduces the sinner to Christ and makes God's will known to us. While Muslims will most likely never admit to a trinitarian concept in their faith, it nonetheless exists as a caricature of the true, trinitarian Godhead and originates from the biblical truth of God's triune existence. While this is an interesting idea to ponder, Islam does depart from representing God's character in more radical ways than the Trinity.

According to the Qur'ān, Allah is sovereign over his creation to the point that he created sin.[384] Allah's will is so pervasive in the universe that nothing is done without his cause, purpose, or will. This may not seem so different from the Christian understanding of God's sovereignty over creation, but Islam takes it a step further. From every good action performed to every criminal act, from every star's creation to every petal that falls from a flower, Allah not only designed and purposed those actions to occur – he was the one behind them.

This poses an obvious philosophical challenge – if Allah is all good and completely sovereign over his creation to the point that he created sin, does it stand to reason that Allah is not all good? Trying to wrestle with this problem of evil, or theodicy, Muhammad concluded that Allah must have created sin. Since everything Allah does is good, then it is not a far leap to imagine that sin created by Allah must be a good thing. This, of course, presents a serious challenge to Islamic theology. Typically, Muslim apologists have responded to this problem

---

[381] Ninian Smart, *The World's Religions*, 2d ed. (Cambridge: Cambridge University Press, 1998), 289.
[382] John 1:1–14
[383] This analogy could be further teased out since Muslims believe the Qur'ān provides them with salvation (because of the words found within its pages), that it is directly given from god, that god is a part of the Qur'ān, and that it deserves our utmost respect.
[384] Sūra Al-Falaq 113:1–2

by reminding us that the motivations behind Allah's actions are well beyond the scope of human understanding.[385] Orthodox Christianity teaches that God is all-good and all-loving, and by allowing for humanity's free will in the Garden, he allowed for the possibility of our rebellion. However, God did not create sin but rather he created beings with the possibility of them sinning.

Believing that Allah created evil has Islam to the idea of fatalism, which is demonstrated throughout the Qur'ān. Sūra An-Nisā' 4:78–79 declares; "When they are blessed with good fortune, they say 'This is from Allah.' But when evil befalls them, they say 'It was your fault.' Say to them 'All is from Allah.'" Notice the Qur'ān says *all* is from Allah, both fortune and evil. No matter what happens in your life, it was Allah behind the scenes.

To follow fatalism to its logical conclusion, a Muslim's salvation depends entirely on Allah's will, and there is no way they can possibly be sure that Allah has chosen them.[386] The Qur'ān states in four different places that Allah is the one who either guides people to himself for salvation or away for damnation.[387] This fatalistic view of god means that everything down to every minute detail was preplanned, for better or for worse, for righteousness or for evil, and cannot be unaltered.

Did you fall and scrape your knee? Allah willed it. Did you win a million dollars? Allah willed it. Did you drop your pen outside? Allah willed it. Did your grass turn brown? Allah willed it. Is there sin in the world? Allah not only willed it, he created it. Are you damned to hell for all eternity? Allah was the one who guided you into sin and pushed you there.

It must be stated that this concept of fatalism is not foreign to Christianity. There is a philosophy of sovereignty in Christianity called *hyper-Calvinism* (or *high Calvinism*) that is just as incorrect as fatalism in Islam. Hyper-Calvinism shouldn't be confused with Calvinism, often associated with Reformed Theology. Reformed Theology teaches that we were all destined for eternal separation from God because we all live under the curse of Adam (original sin), but God in his sovereignty elects some for salvation.

---

[385] Umar F. Abd-Allah, "Theological dimensions of Islamic Law," *The Cambridge Companion to Classical Islamic Theology*, ed. Tim Winter (Cambridge: Cambridge University Press, 2008), 249.
[386] Sūra An-Nisā' 4:49
[387] Sūra Ar-Ra'd 13:27; Sūra 'Ibrahim 14:4; Sūra An-Nahl 16:93; Sūra Al-Muddaththir 74:31

God does not righteously or maliciously plan out every step we take to end in either salvation or damnation. If we are saved, it's because of God's grace and mercy in the life and work of Jesus.[388] If we are not, it is because of our own sin.[389] God's judgment is not predetermined but is his just reaction to our rebellion. We are not puppets on a string but rather passengers on a flight with a firm destination and are now free to move about the cabin. *ding* Reformed Theology has less to do with every single, minute detail of everyday life and more to do with overall redemption.

Hyper-Calvinism, however, teaches that God made a conscious decision of who would go to heaven and hell before creating humanity. Every single action in our lives is accounted for or against our pre-determined outcome that is ultimately controlled by God. This hyper-Calvinistic concept is very similar to Islamic fatalism. Allah has already made up his mind about the eternal destiny for all of humanity, and there is nothing anyone can do about it.[390] One can only work hard as an obedient and dedicated Muslim, hopeful that Allah puts you on the heaven list. It's like buying a lottery ticket in hopes that you'll win. Of course, you'll have zero chance of winning if you don't buy the ticket in the first place (do not submit to Allah), but the overall odds of you actually winning are fairly slim. This is because Allah requires two wills to be aligned for salvation – the Muslim's will (and works) and Allah's own will to love them eternally.

But Allah's love is not something he dispenses freely; rather, it is given in response to a Muslim's unwavering devotion to him. Sūra 'Āli 'Imrān 3:31 states this clearly; "If you should love Allah, then follow me, [so] Allah will love you and forgive you your sins."[391] Allah never freely loves any of his creation without his creation first loving and obeying him. Furthermore, Allah only loves those who consistently love him; "Allah loves those who rely [upon Him]...and Allah loves the steadfast."[392] An ancient Islamic Imam summarized these verses well when he remarked, "[Allah's love] issues from the effect of

---

[388] Eph. 2:4–9; Rom. 5:15–16

[389] 2 Thess. 1:8–9; Rom. 5:12–14

[390] Ninian Smart, *The World's Religions*, 2d ed. (Cambridge: Cambridge University Press, 1998), 295.

[391] Sūra 'Āli 'Imrān 3:31, *Sahih International*

[392] Sūra 'Āli 'Imrān 3:159, 146, *Sahih International*

the blessing of obeying Muhammad."[393] This view of God is a completely foreign concept to scripture which emphatically declares that he loves us through Jesus regardless of our love for him; "But God, being rich in mercy, because of the great love with which he loved us, even when we were dead in our trespasses, made us alive together in Christ."[394]

There is no love from Allah absent our obedience to him. Even if you practice enough penance and perform enough good works, there is still the possibility that Allah has not predetermined your salvation from eternal punishment, thus rendering your entire life's devotion moot. The whole point of penance and works is to escape the inevitability of sin in one's life, but if Allah does not will you into heaven, then your lifetime of penance and works was for naught. The inevitability to sin is due in large part to the sinful world Muslims live in. In fact, at one point in a Muslim's life they were completely sinless before Allah. This means that Islam denies original sin.[395]

ISLAMIC CONCEPT OF SIN

Original sin is the fallen, sinful, rebellious condition humanity finds itself in even before a person is born. Because Adam, acting as our representative to God, sinned and rebelled against God, his sin is transferred to us through his lineage because we can all trace our ancestry back to him.[396] We are born into sin even before we have the conscious ability to choose between right and wrong.[397] The Qur'ān, however, teaches that Adam and Eve begged for forgiveness after they sinned and Allah granted it to them.[398] From this variation of the biblical account Muslims are taught that humanity is born in the morally neutral condition of *Al-Fitrah*, or a natural state of submission to

---

[393] Shahzad Bashir, "Muhammad in Sufi eyes: prophetic legitimacy in medieval Iran and Central Asia," *The Cambridge Companion to Muhammad*, ed. Jonathan E. Brockopp (Cambridge: Cambridge University Press, 2010), 222.
[394] Eph. 2:4–5
[395] Cyril Glassé and Huston Smith, *The New Encyclopedia of Islam*, reprinted ed. (Walnut Creek, Cali.: AltaMira Press, 2001), 431.
[396] Rom. 5:12–21; 1 Cor. 15:22
[397] Ps. 51:5
[398] Sūra Al-'A'rāf 7:25

Allah.[399] Nevertheless, over time humans become sinful and require continual repentance and works in order to be restored to *Al-Fitrah* and to salvation.

As an aside, it is interesting to note the intersection of Mormon and Islamic theology in the idea of *Al-Fitrah* and its relation to humanity's expulsion from Eden. According to both rival worldviews, the fall of humanity was not a universally evil event with lasting consequences on the human race; rather, it was a time for humanity's liberation from limited knowledge and ability. It has already been demonstrated that Mormonism teaches that the fall delivered humanity from ignorance and non-existence.[400] Similarly, Islam teaches that Adam's isolated sin allowed for humanity to leave its infantile state in Eden. Islamic theologian Shabbir Akhtar concisely describes this concept;

> Islam, by contrast, sees the Fall as simply one powerful and contained manifestation of evil - more accurately, disobedience to God's will - that has no larger implications for human nature in general or even for Adam's nature in particular...Indeed, Muslims view Adam's expulsion from Eden as the occasion for the rise of man.[401]

Both Islam and Mormonism draw the same conclusion when teaching that humanity is born morally neutral and was liberated from its previous state in Eden. Again, we see two rival worldviews with more similarities between each other than with orthodox Christianity.

Given that humanity is born in a morally neutral condition while the world is morally corrupted, all humans will sin at some point in their lives. Most Muslims believe this to occur sometime during their teenage years. The time preceding a human's first sinful act is usually described as the age of accountability. During the teenage years, a human is no longer able to accidentally sin but now controls his or her own moral destiny. Furthermore, when Muslims begin to experience sin in their teenage years, the sin does not originate from within the individual. Rather, they fall into sin because of external influence. The reason people sin is because Allah has intentionally

---

[399] Sūra Ar-Rum 30:30
[400] "Adam fell that men might be; and men are, that they might have joy." 2 Nephi 2:25
[401] Shabbir Akhtar, *A faith for all seasons: Islam and the challenge of the modern world* (Lanham, Mary.: Ivan R. Dee Publisher, 1991), 155.

created every human being to be susceptible to temptation.[402] Unlike Christianity, which teaches that sin originates from within the individual, Islam teaches that sin always originates from external influences.[403] A Muslim's environment influences them to sin. Were it not for a morally corrupt environment, a Muslim could ostensibly live their entire life without sinning. Sin is never the fault of the individual but is the result of a sinful environment. In other words, the devil made them do it.

This may provide an explanation as to why many Muslims believe that all of culture must be under the auspices of Islam. If all external influences are under the influence of Islam, then there will be no external causes for humans to sin. Government, art, culture, music, film, theatre, fashion, etc. should all fall under Islam, so they do not cause a person to sin. If they are not, these aspects of human life present opportunities and temptation to sin. Sin never originates from within the individual – it always originates from the actions of others or the environment they find themselves in. Thus, the orthodox Christian concept of sin is completely foreign to Islam.

It should go without saying that this is a severely dangerous doctrine to believe, and it completely opposes the gospel. It shifts the responsibility and ownership of sin away from the individual and onto an external source, which is the very same thing Adam did in the Garden when God asked him to account for his sin. Instead of owning his own sin, Adam blamed his wife for giving him the fruit and then blamed God for giving him his wife![404] Blaming external sources for our own sin ultimately leads to blaming God for our own rebellion against him.

As dangerous as it is, the denial of original sin is nothing new, even to Christianity. Something similar to this Islamic belief in Christianity is Pelagianism. During the fourth century, a British monk named Pelagius taught that Adam's sin set a bad example for his offspring, but his sinful actions carried absolutely no consequences for humanity.[405] To Pelagius, people are born in a morally neutral condition before God – they haven't sinned but

[402] Sūra An-Nisa' 4:28
[403] Hammudah 'Abd al-'Ati, *Islam in Focus*, 4th ed. trans. Al-Falah (Cairo: Al-Falah Foundation for Translation, Publication & Distribution, 1424/2003), 68.
[404] Gen. 3:9–12
[405] Millard J. Erickson, *Christian Theology* 2nd ed. (Grand Rapids, Mich.: Baker Books, 1998), 649.

haven't done anything good either. It is only when people sin do they need forgiveness from God to return to their morally neutral condition and favor with God. Sound familiar? Pelagius was rightly condemned as a heretic in 418CE at the Council of Carthage, and Pelagianism was subsequently discounted as unbiblical.

The biblical view of our moral status before God is that of complete depravity. There is no way around it; even before we're born, we are already sinful. It may sound like a bleak situation to be in, but it only serves to magnify the extreme lengths God went through with his son to get us back. We are all born into sin because of Adam's fall. As Paul explains, "just as sin came into the world through one man, and death through sin, and so death spread to all men because all sinned."[406] One psalmist puts our condition this way; "Behold, I was brought forth in iniquity, and in sin did my mother conceive me."[407] Paul further explains that, "all have sinned and fall short of the glory of God."[408]

And just in case we are confused by the timing (perhaps we are born in a morally neutral condition and inevitably sin later in life), Paul tells us, citing the example of Jacob and Esau, that "though they were not yet born and had done nothing either good or bad – in order that God's purpose of election might continue, not because of works but because of him who calls – [Rebekah] was told, The older will serve the younger. As it is written, 'Jacob I loved but Esau I hated.'"[409]

There is no way of getting around it – because of Adam's sin we are all born with slates full of sin even before we make a conscious choice to sin. And we see the effects of this in everyday life. For example, if we are all born in a morally neutral condition, then why do we strain to teach our children to behave well and not sin? Why is it harder for a toddler to understand how to share but acting selfishly comes naturally to them? It's because sin is inherent to us all. If we believe we may return to an original state of sinlessness without external aid from God, then we only fool ourselves into believing cancer patients do not require treatment but need only to will or work themself into

---

[406] Rom. 5:12
[407] Ps. 51:5
[408] Rom. 3:23
[409] Rom. 9:11–13. Or, Jacob I am *committed to* but Esau I am *uncommitted.*

good health. Our sin issue is that deep. Perhaps the biggest problem with believing that humans are born in a morally neutral condition is that we believe we can return to that state on our own without the cross.

It is important to discuss and explain original sin with Muslims since it is such a foreign concept to many of them. The power of the cross of Jesus cannot come into full focus without the realization that we are completely powerless to contribute to our own salvation due to our perpetually rebellious state. Since Muslims are taught that the Psalms are inspired, discuss the meaning of Psalm 51:5 with them. "Behold, I was brought forth in iniquity, and in sin did my mother conceive me." What does it mean to be "brought forth in iniquity?" Why do our mothers conceive us in sin if we are born in a morally neutral condition?

Stress to them that this verse teaches that all humans are born into sin – they do not simply fall into sin years after their birth. From the day of conception every human being is subject to sin from within themselves and not simply from their environment. Sin permeates us from our first moment of existence. This is why we do not need to teach toddlers what is wrong. Instead, they need to learn what is right. If we were born in a morally neutral condition, why are humans naturally inclined to sinfulness over righteousness? Furthermore, can the tenets of Islam allow us to overcome complete depravity? Can Allah forgive us for not only sins we have committed, but also sins of omission (not doing what we were supposed to do)?

THE QUR'AN & THE CRUCIFIXION

Perhaps the greatest difference between the Christian and Islamic understanding of sin is the Christian and Islamic understanding of sin's solution. If a Muslim held to the biblical concept of original sin, that they need a greater work than they could ever produce for God's love and salvation, perhaps we could point to the crucifixion event in Jesus' life as that greater work. Most Muslims do not believe in Jesus' crucifixion. The Qur'ān teaches that Jesus was never crucified but was instead substituted with a criminal for a staged crucifixion.[410]

Sūra An-Nisā' 4:157 explains the Islamic view of the crucifixion;

And [for] their saying, "Indeed, we have killed the Messiah, Jesus, the son of Mary, the messenger of Allah." And they did not kill him, nor did they crucify him; but [another] was made to resemble him to them. And indeed, those who differ over it are in doubt about it. They have no knowledge of it except the following of assumption. And they did not kill him, for certain.[411]

This verse has led many Muslims to completely deny Jesus' crucifixion. In fact, the thought that a prophet of Allah (as they believe Jesus was) would be killed in such a defamatory way is appalling to many Muslims. For this reason, Muslims deny a historical fact that even many atheists will readily acknowledge. The popular theory goes that instead of dying on the cross Roman authorities replaced Jesus on the cross with Judas or another criminal.[412] Jesus was allowed to live out his life in isolation for fear of the Jewish leadership's retaliation of the trickery and would later ascend into heaven by the power of Allah. This hypothesis not only flies in the face of biblical evidence for Jesus' crucifixion but also extra-biblical evidence as well.

When arguing for the historical event of the crucifixion with Muslims it may be more persuading to argue from extra–biblical sources at first. These sources are in no way tied to the theology and cannot be accused of bias towards the Christian worldview. This may take a little research on our part, but it is not hard to find. The vast majority of scholars associated with neither Christian nor Islamic theology believe that based on the evidence the crucifixion event was indeed a historical fact.[413] Two thousand years ago, Roman authorities crucified a man by the name of Jesus. It is an event

[410]Daniel A. Madigan, "Themes and topics," *The Cambridge Companion to the Qur'ān*, ed. Jane Dammen McAuliffe, (Cambridge: Cambridge University Press, 2006), 89.
[411] Sūra An-Nisā' 4:157, *Sahih International*
[412] Norman L. Geisler and Abdul Saleeb, *Answering Islam: The Crescent in Light of the Cross*, 2nd ed. (Grand Rapids, Mich.: Baker Books, 2002), 67.
[413] Christopher M. Tuckett, "Sources and methods," *The Cambridge Companion to Jesus*, ed. Markus Bockmuehl (Cambridge: Cambridge University Press, 2001), 123–124.

recorded by Roman and Jewish historians aside from the New Testament authors. Here are a few examples of these extra-biblical sources.

- "On the eve of the Passover Yeshu was hanged…since nothing was brought forward in his favor, he was hanged on the eve of the Passover." (Talmud, *b.Sanhedrin* 43a)

- "'Ulla said: 'And do you suppose that for [Yeshu of Nazareth] there was any right of appeal? Was a beguiler, and the Merciful One hath said: Thou shalt not spare neither shalt thou conceal him.' It was otherwise with Yeshu, or he was near to the civil authorities." (*The Amoa* Ulla)

- "Christ … was executed at the hands of the procurator Pontius Pilate." (Cornelius Tacitus, *Annals* xv. 44)

- "(Christ was) the man who was crucified in Palestine because he introduced this new initiation rite to the world." (*Peregrinus* 11, Trans. Harmon 1913–67)

- "Pilate…had condemned [Christ] to the cross…" (Flavius Josephus, *Antiquities* xviii. 33)

- "Christus, the founder of the name, was put to death by Pontius Pilate." (Cornelius Tacitus, *Annals* xv. 40)

The Qur'ān and, consequently, Muhammad do not stand the scrutiny of such a wide array of historical analysis. The crucifixion of Jesus is a historical fact that must be established when dialoguing with Muslims. The entire message of the atonement stands or falls on the willingness of a Muslim to accept the crucifixion (and, in turn, resurrection) of Jesus. Thankfully, the majority of evidence is against Qur'ānic teaching. This is an issue Muslims must wrestle with considering the Qur'ān's fallacious accusation. It may just be the first aspect of Islam a Muslim rejects, and what a better starting point for dialogue than the truth of the cross of Christ?

THE QUR'AN & ARABIC HERITAGE

It may surprise some to learn that the Qur'ān contains an Adam and Eve narrative, altered slightly to fit Islamic theology. (This seems to be a common occurrence with rival worldviews, as Mormonism has its own rendition of the creation narrative as well.) Remember, Islam accepts much of the Old Testament. Most Muslims will have no contention with the Bible from the Garden of Eden up until Abraham. After this, however, sharp disagreement occurs between the Qur'ān and the Bible. One such disagreement is the source of many issues concerning salvation, ethnic heritage, and divine rights to land.

Arabic Muslims trace their heritage, or at least their spiritual heritage, back to two people we're already familiar with, Ishmael and Abraham, or *Isma'il* and *Ibrahim*.[414] The equation of the Qur'ānic *Ibrahim* and the biblical Abraham as the same person worshiping the same god is a major contributor to the idea that Islam is one of the three "Abrahamic faiths," with Judaism and Christianity being the other two. The claim is that all three faiths are simply branches from the same root. Of course, most Christians, as well as most Muslims, would disagree. The Bible teaches that only one thread of God's work in salvation spans from Abraham to Jesus. In a similar manner, the Qur'ān explicitly teaches that Islam is the true faith founded by Abraham and not a faith stemming from Judaism or Christianity, despite Islam being the youngest of the three.[415]

Furthermore, Islam teaches that Abraham is the father of not only a faith, but also the entire Arab ethnicity. Surprisingly, the Qur'ān does not mention much about this ethnic Arabic lineage tied back to Ishmael and Abraham, despite popular Islamic teaching to the contrary. It mentions that Abraham and Ishmael built the *Ka'aba* (the house) and dedicated it, and elsewhere it equates Ishmael to a prophet chosen by God to fulfill the promises of Abraham.[416] However, as far as the Abraham-Ishmael link to the Arab ethnicity is concerned, the Qur'ān is relatively quiet on the matter.

---

[414] Walid A. Saleh, "The Arabian Context of Muhammad's Life," *The Cambridge Companion to Muhammad*, ed. Jonathan E. Brockopp (Cambridge: Cambridge University Press, 2010), 31.
[415] Sūra Al-Baqarah 2:136
[416] Sūra Al-Baqarah 2:127

From sources outside of the Qur'ān, mainly the hadīths, Muslims are taught: that Ishmael and Abraham built the *Ka'aba* in Mecca and settled there after its construction,[417] that Ishmael was the father of their ethnicity,[418] and was the direct forefather of Muhammad.[419] There are more references outside of the Qur'ān for the Arabic lineage to Abraham through Ishmael than inside. The oldest surviving biography of Muhammad, compiled by Muhammad Ibn Ishaq and edited by Abu Mohammed Abd el Malik Ibn Hisham, opens with a twenty-nine generation lineage from Muhammad back to Abraham, thus "proving" to Arabic Muslims that Muhammad was indeed the direct descendant and, subsequently, the descendant of promise from Abraham.[420]

As an aside, this lineage should be looked at with suspicion considering the brevity of the list itself. If Abraham lived between 2000—1500BCE and Muhammad was born ca. 570CE, this would mean that each of the men in Muhammad's lineage would have to have lived on average 71–88 years. While this is not impossible, it seems highly improbable considering the average life span of a male in Rome was between 25–30 years.[421] This number would only slightly increase by Muhammad's day, but it would not be until the 1990s that men could expect to live to 72 years old.[422]

THE PROMISE OF ABRAHAM

So, why Ishmael? What is so important about him that Muhammad would want his lineage and faith traced back to this one man? The answer begins with Ishmael's father, Abram (later called Abraham). According to scripture, when God decided to advance his promise of the coming Messiah he chose Abram and his wife Sarai (later called Sarah). At that point in time they had no

---

[417] Phyllis Trible and Letty M. Russell, "Unto the Thousandth Generation," *Hagar, Sarah, and their Children: Jewish, Christian, and Muslim Perspectives*, eds. Phyllis Trible and Letty M. Russell (Louisville, Kent.: Westminster John Knox Press, 2006), 9.
[418] Ibid.
[419] Ibid., 194.
[420] Jonathan P. Berkey, *The Formation of Islam: Religion and Society in the Near East, 600–1800* (Cambridge: Cambridge University Press, 2004), 66.
[421] Sarunas Milisauskas, *European Prehistory: A Survey* (New York: Kluwer Academic, 2002), 366.
[422] Kevin Kinsella and Cynthia A. Taeuber, *An Aging World II* (Darby, Penn.: Diana Publishing Co., 1993), 21.

children. God made a promise to Abram that he would be the father of a great nation and that all the families of the earth would be blessed because of him.

> Now the Lord said to Abram, "Go from your country and your kindred and your father's house to the land that I will show you. And I will make of you a great nation, and I will bless you and make your name great, so that you will be a blessing. I will bless those who bless you, and him who dishonors you I will curse, and in you all the families of the earth shall be blessed."[423]

This was an amazing promise God made to Abram. He would become the patriarch of a great nation who would both inherit the blessing of land and, in turn, bless all the families of the earth; a promise that would be repeated numerous times throughout his life and would ultimately be fulfilled in Jesus.[424] However, first things first. Obviously, in order to become the father of a great nation, Abram needed to become a father. This meant that God would give Abram and Sarai a son despite her barrenness.[425]

So, with their faith in God's promise, they waited with joyful anticipation for pregnancy. And waited... and waited. Years passed until Abram finally decided to bring his impatient concern before God who, in turn, reminded Abram of his promises. Abram believed God, and his faith in God's promise was counted as righteousness.[426] (Conversely, the Qur'ān teaches that Abraham's works justified him before God.[427]) So Abram waited some more. Unfortunately, Abram and Sarai's impatience got the better of them. Sarai convinced Abram (who didn't offer much objection) to sleep with their servant Hagar, an Egyptian woman they brought out of Egypt with them years before.[428]

Sarai's plan worked – Hagar became pregnant with Abram's child. In time, Sarai became discontented with the plan, to say the least. Perhaps Hagar flaunted her pregnancy to Sarai, or maybe Sarai's jealously of Hagar's fertility finally got to her. Whatever the case, Sarai forced Hagar into exile.[429]

---

[423] Gen. 12:1–3
[424] Gen 12:1–7; 13:14–17; 15:5–21; 17:2–8; 18:18; 22:17–18; 24:7; Gal. 3:7–9
[425] Gen. 17:17
[426] Gen. 15:2
[427] Sūra Al-Baqarah 2:124
[428] Gen. 16:1–2
[429] Gen. 16:6

However, an angel stopped Hagar as she was journeying. The angel had a simple yet challenging message for her;

> "Return to your mistress and submit to her. Behold, you are pregnant and shall bear a son. You shall call his name Ishmael, because the LORD has listened to your affliction. He shall be a wild donkey of a man, his hand against everyone and everyone's hand against him, and he shall dwell over against all his kinsmen."[430]

Not the best of news, but at least she got to go home. A few months later, Hagar gave birth to Ishmael.

With the arrival of Ishmael, Abram finally had a son. He figured that the promised nation could finally begin. Abram didn't see a way around Sarai's barrenness, and Abram requested that God would alter his plans now that he technically had a son. During prayer, Abram, whose name had since changed to Abraham, pleaded with God, "Oh that Ishmael might live before you!"[431] Abraham pleaded with God that Ishmael would be the child of promise. Perhaps Abraham simply wanted to move on with God's promise, as his wife (now named Sarah) was no doubt wrought with concern over her infertility. The emotional strain on his family up until that point must have been severe. They had waited and waited, and they finally had a son even though the situation wasn't ideal. If God would simply let go of the previous agreement and make do with what was already there, Abraham wouldn't have to worry about his or his wife's inability to conceive a child. But does God agree?

> "No, but Sarah your wife shall bear you a son, and you shall call his name Isaac. I will establish my covenant with him as an everlasting covenant for his offspring after him. As for Ishmael, I have heard you; behold, I have blessed him and will make him fruitful and multiply him greatly. He shall father twelve princes, and I will make him into a great nation. But I will establish my covenant with Isaac, whom Sarah shall bear to you at this time next year."[432]

Abraham would have to wait some more.

---

[430] Gen. 16:9, 11
[431] Gen. 17:18
[432] Gen. 17:19–21

Eventually, God followed through on his promise for Sarah to bear a son. Abraham's second son arrived and was named Isaac. Finally, the promise of God would be fulfilled in this child. But, just as things were starting to look up for Abraham, God threw yet another curveball – he called Abraham to sacrifice Isaac. It was a strange request considering the language of the request itself; "Take your son, your *only* son Isaac, whom you love, and go to the land of Moriah, and offer him there as a burnt offering on one of the mountains of which I shall tell you."[433] Notice that God calls Isaac Abraham's only son. Unless God is terrible at math, he must have been getting at something deeper by calling Isaac Abraham's only son. Something spiritual. God called Isaac Abraham's only son because Isaac is the intended son through whom the promise God made Abraham would come to fruition. God knew Abraham had two sons, but in the context of his promise with Abraham, the only son who matters is Isaac. Thus, Isaac becomes the child of promise, not Ishmael.

With this in mind, Abraham followed God's command to sacrifice Isaac but was stopped only moments before by an angel.[434] This sacrifice was a foreshadowing of God sacrificing his only son for the atonement of all our sins. It was a prophetical action that illustrated God's promise by Abraham's faith in God. The promised "only son" of Abraham was being sacrificed to paint a picture of things to come when the only Son of God would face death on the cross. It was a beautiful portrayal of the fulfillment of the promise God made Abraham hundreds of years before it would culminate with Jesus at Golgotha.

Jews and Muslims, however, view this act as a test of Abraham's faith which was vindicated, and as a reward, he was granted the promise that grew into ethnic nations. Still many more Christians, Muslims, and Jews believe that with Abraham's promise comes the eternal claim to a certain plot of land along the Mediterranean Sea.[435] In Old Testament times, it was referred to as Canaan. In New Testament times, it was Palestine. Today, it is modern-day Israel, Gaza, and the West Bank. This means that the interpretation of Abraham's sacrifice could have a profound effect on the current geo-political situation in Israel, but we'll get back to that later.

---

[433] Gen. 22:2, emphasis added.
[434] Gen. 22:11

Unlike Christians and Jews who believe that Isaac was presented as a sacrifice to God, Muslims are taught that it was Ishmael who was presented as the sacrifice. Furthermore, the Qur'ān teaches that Abraham wasn't even a Hebrew – he was the first Muslim.[436] What is perhaps more perplexing in this confusion over which son Abraham was told to sacrifice is the surprising fact that the Qur'ān actually teaches that Isaac, not Ishmael, was the son offered for sacrifice despite the official Islamic position.

> And [Abraham] said, "Indeed, I will go to [where I am ordered by] my Lord; He will guide me..." And when he reached with him [the age of] exertion, he said, "O my son, indeed I have seen in a dream that I [must] sacrifice you, so see what you think." He said, "O my father, do as you are commanded. You will find me, if Allah wills, of the steadfast..." And [Allah] blessed him and Isaac. But among their descendants is the doer of good and the clearly unjust to himself.[437]

Regardless, if Ishmael was the child of promise, son of a righteous Muslim father, and all Arabs descend from Abraham through Ishmael, they are then privileged to salvation and the land promised to Abraham's descendants. However, if Isaac was the child of promise and all Jews descend from Abraham through Isaac, then they are privileged to salvation and the land of Israel. See how the interpretation of this narrative can be a bit tricky?

If Isaac is the only son of Abraham, then Ishmael and his descendants have no right to the land of Israel and no claim to the faith of Abraham that provides salvation. This is why the situation with Israel and Palestine remains at a stalemate. The theological debate surrounding this standoff is bigger than a piece of land. If the Palestinians lose the land, then by proxy they might not be the children of promise. Some Jews (and Christians) believe Israel is presently and eternally Jewish land because of Isaac. Muslims lay claim to Israel because of Ishmael. Both groups of people have been there for centuries, and for centuries they have been fighting over the issue. But the truth of the matter is this – both groups have missed the point entirely.

---

[435] Gen. 17:8
[436] Sūra 'Āli 'Imrān 3:65
[437] Sūra As-Sāffāt 37:99–113, *Sahih International*

PRIME MEDITERRANEAN–FRONT PROPERTY

Above all else, Abraham's promise was one of faith. It was a spiritual inheritance to salvation. God's promise to Abraham has more to do with a spiritual inheritance that is everlasting and less to do with a physical inheritance that passes away. We know this because God told Abraham that "all the families of the earth shall be blessed," not simply those belonging to his physical progeny.[438] The wrong understanding of this promise is that physical relation to Abraham guarantees both a physical (land) and spiritual (salvation) inheritance. It doesn't, the promise was ultimately meant for a spiritual inheritance, and it is fulfilled in Jesus.[439]

This was such a pervasive misunderstanding during the New Testament period that the disciples and apostles were constantly correcting peoples' understanding of the promise of Abraham. Many Jews believed that their salvation came from their physical relation to Abraham and with that also came the deed for their land. For example, when the religious leaders relied on their ancestry for salvation, John the Baptist said that God could make physical descendants out of rocks.[440] John basically told them that being a physical child of Abraham is about as useful as being a rock so far as salvation is concerned.

Later on, the religious leaders would again default to Abraham as their answer for why they were spiritually free and out from under bondage. Jesus told them that being Abraham's children is pointless without Abraham's work (his belief in God's promise).[441] Furthermore, Paul declares, "if you are Christ's, then you are Abraham's offspring, heirs according to the promise."[442] So how do we become Christ's so that we may become Abraham's offspring and heirs to the promise? Simple – faith in Jesus. Receiving the promise of Abraham for yourself "depends on faith, in order that the promise may rest on grace and be guaranteed to all his offspring."[443]

---

[438] Gen. 12:3
[439] Rom. 4:13–14, Gal. 3:16–18; 4:23–5:1, Eph. 1:10–14
[440] Matt. 3:9
[441] John 8:34–41
[442] Gal. 3:29
[443] Rom. 4:16

It is important to note that the New Testament writers rarely speak to the promise of Abraham as a promise of land. They are much more concerned with Abraham's promise as a spiritual inheritance, a guarantee that through faith in Jesus we are rescued from our sin and ushered into the everlasting kingdom of God. The ultimate purpose of the promise of Abraham was not meant for a physical deed of land that will perish but a spiritual inheritance of eternal life. Granted, God would use Abraham's descendants to establish a physical kingdom in a physical land, but this is not the central focus of the promise God made to Abraham. The central focus is Jesus.

Additionally, Abraham himself never received an inheritance of land, "not even a foot's length," but he did receive an inheritance of everlasting life.[444] When his descendants did inherit land, the physical kingdom they established was only meant to foreshadow the spiritual kingdom of God and, ultimately, a picture of heaven for all who have faith in Jesus. Furthermore, the promise of a physical inheritance always came with one caveat – obedience by Abraham's descendants, something they ultimately could not achieve.[445] God took the land away from the Israelites on multiple occasions, but he never withdrew his promise of the coming Messiah and eternal salvation for those who had the faith of Abraham.

Today, due to a misunderstanding of the promise of Abraham, the world is witness to an ongoing conflict between the Muslim and Jewish population, believing they both have a divine right to a strip of land in the Middle East. Let's assume for a moment that Abraham's promise has more to do with an eternal deed to physical land than it does to eternal salvation – who's right? Do the Jews deserve Israel, or do the Muslims? Should the modern state of Israel be broken up into two countries, Israel and Palestine? Should there only be one? This dilemma is not just reserved for Muslims and Jews. There are also many Christian organizations whose entire purpose is to support Jewish occupation and settlement of Israel, Gaza, and the West Bank. Contrarily, there are many Christian organizations that believe Israelis are unlawfully occupying the land and should leave. Which group is right? The answer, much

---

[444] Acts 7:5
[445] Deut. 6:10, 15, 18–19; 8:19–20; 9:5; 30:17–18, Lev. 20:22; Josh. 23:12–16, Jer. 18:1–10; 19:10–11

like the theological debate surrounding the stalemate between Israel and Palestine, is much bigger than land.

In light of sharing the gospel, we shouldn't be as concerned with who gets what land according to whoever's interpretation of Abraham's sacrifice. There are many Christians who sincerely believe that God's promises to Abraham include a literal state of Israel. Likewise, there are many sincere Christians who believe that Israel was destroyed a long time ago and God has, in a sense, moved on. But, if we have any hope of sharing the gospel with Muslims, then we should be more concerned with what the promise of Abraham and his sacrifice of Isaac really points to – God the Father offering his only Son Jesus for our sins.

God did not call Abraham to sacrifice his son in order to give his descendants the eternal deed to some prime Mediterranean–front property. That land will go away one day, only to be recreated when God's plan of salvation is wholly fulfilled.[446] God called Abraham to sacrifice his only son so that we could see his plan of salvation unfolding hundreds of years before Jesus was born. When dialoguing with a Muslim about the Muslim–Arabic lineage from Ishmael, we shouldn't spend too much time on the land debate. Instead, we should stress that this passage has more to do with spiritual inheritance than it does with physical inheritance. It paints a beautiful portrait of Jesus' sacrifice for us hundreds of years before it happened. We should always stress that the promise of Abraham is ultimately not about land – it's about Jesus.

Additionally, because of the differences in how Muslims understand Abraham, we should also emphasize that the Abraham of Christianity and Islam is not the same Abraham. The Abraham of Christianity sinned by going to Egypt, sinned by having Ishmael, was blessed by having Isaac, and lived righteously by faith.[447] The Abraham of Islam didn't sin by going to Egypt, didn't sin by having Ishmael, wasn't blessed by Isaac, and lived righteously by works.[448] These are two completely different people. Abraham is not Ibrahim. Islam, however, teaches that they are the same person. This perpetuates the widely misunderstood idea that Islam, Judaism, and Christianity are all simply

---

[446] Rev. 21:1–2
[447] Gen. 15:2

branches of faiths that stem from the same root, and that they are all equally legitimate. This is completely untrue. Islam is not an Abrahamic faith, it is an Ibrahimic faith.

ISLAM, CHRISTIANITY, & THE ABRAHAMS

How many times has it been said that Christianity and Islam worship the same God? The argument usually goes that the god of Christianity and the god of Islam are the same monotheistic deity. The only difference is that they are referred to by different names. After all, the word for 'god' in Arabic is 'allah.' If you were to pick up an Arabic translation of the Bible, God is referred to as Allah. Besides, the only thing separating Christianity and Islam is a disagreement about the importance of Jesus. They're essentially the same faith, but they do differ over Jesus... right?

If you've ever heard these arguments, what was your response? If we want to participate in gospel-centered dialogue with Muslims, we need to be prepared to refute the idea that the God of the Bible and Allah are the same god and that Christianity and Islam are essentially worshiping the same god. The truth is that they're not as will be demonstrated throughout this chapter. But the idea is so pervasive in the West, particularly in North America, that we as Christians need to have a response ready to refute it.

It doesn't help that many secular and religious leaders and organizations promote the misunderstanding that Islam and Christianity are sister faith systems which worship the same god. In 2001, just three months after the 9/11 attacks, *National Geographic Magazine* published an article entitled 'Abraham: Journey of Faith,' which seemed to be an attempt to answer the rise of questions over Islam in the immediate post-9/11 world. In it, they attempted to demonstrate how "Abraham's biblical trek through the Middle East kindled three major religions, whose past and present conflicts would surely sadden this patriarch of peace."[449] It is highly unlikely that the Abraham we read about in scripture would be surprised at the current conflicts. God warned Abraham that his offspring would not be given a land free from native

---

[448] Sūra Al-Baqarah 2:139
[449] Tad Szulc, "Journey of Faith," *National Geographic Magazine*, December 21, 2001.

inhabitants.[450] It is improbable, unlike what National Geographic suggests, that Abraham would be surprised his descendants rub shoulders with other people groups. Nevertheless, the overarching message of this article was a demonstration on how the three sister faiths from Abraham were essentially one and, through their bitter histories together, were disappointing their father.

Shortly before the *National Geographic Magazine* article, one guest on the popular Oprah Winfrey Show expressed their views about the relations between Christianity and Islam. "Islam and Christianity and Judaism, and all the world's religions share a common heritage. We come from the same root. And our prophets and the characters in our holy books are the same. In Islam, all the religions are permitted to exist in peace with these others until Judgment Day."[451] Again, popular culture yearns to meld Islam, Christianity, and Judaism into the same category so that they would see the value in theological ecumenism.

The last sentence of that quote betrays the misunderstanding of the guest's knowledge of Muhammad's position on idolaters and polytheists – should they reject Muhammad's message, they were to be shunned, disowned, or even terminated.[452] Allowing such misleading comments on a television show viewed by millions is not only irresponsible, it is dangerous. Of course, it cannot be said outright that *National Geographic Magazine,* Oprah's television program, and other organizations support or oppose this view of Islam's relation to Christianity.[453] However, a pervasive misunderstanding about the realities between Christianity and Islam is created when these organizations allow themselves to act as outlets through which misinformation is channeled.

So why are leaders in the media so misinformed about the differences between Christianity and Islam? I suppose this is where I tell you about the secret Muslim agenda in the liberal media to take over the world, that Muhammad is the third most popular boy's name in Belgium, that parts of London's skyline is littered with minarets, and that we should burn the Qur'ān

---

[450] Gen. 15:18–21
[451] Rod Dreher, "Islam According to Oprah: Is Oprah Winfrey a threat to national security?" *New York Post*, October 8, 2001.
[452] Sūra An-Nisā' 4:89, 5:51
[453] "The opinions expressed by the hosts, guests and callers to Oprah & Friends are strictly their own." www.oprah.com

to teach Muslims a lesson. What lesson exactly, I'm not sure, but... that'll teach them. Having lived both in Europe and the United States, I've heard the Muslim conspiracy theories enough to know that this issue goes beyond Christianity versus Islam. This issue is actually all about the person and work of Jesus.

There exists an agenda not to push Islam onto the world but to minimize the need for Jesus in salvation and to expand the broad term of "god" to include beings that aren't God. That is the real agenda. And it is working not because people are unwillingly misinformed and mistakenly confusing Jesus' role as humanity's savior. No. It is working because people are willingly ignorant about his person and work. Consequently, if one is willingly ignorant about Jesus, they are usually also willingly ignorant about the differences between the "Abrahams" of Christianity and Islam. Paul summarized this phenomenon well;

> But God's angry displeasure erupts as acts of human mistrust and wrongdoing and lying accumulate, as people try to put a shroud over truth. But the basic reality of God is plain enough. Open your eyes and there it is! [...] People knew God perfectly well, but when they didn't treat him like God, refusing to worship him, they trivialized themselves into silliness and confusion so that there was neither sense nor direction left in their lives. They pretended to know it all, but were illiterate regarding life. They traded the glory of God who holds the whole world in his hands for *cheap figurines* you can buy at any roadside stand (Romans 1:18–23, *The Message*, emphasis mine).[454]

Herein lies the point – cheap figurines. The way to minimize Jesus as savior is to turn him into a "cheap figurine." If you can have non-unique, "cheap figurine" Abraham, then you can have a non-unique, "cheap figurine" Jesus who can fit the mold of gracious savior to the Christians, heretical rabbi to the Jews, and silver-medal prophet to the Muslims. If Abraham can act as the root for different interpretations of God, then so can Jesus.

However, if the world had its way in making Jesus simply one man who is equally valid in multiple faiths, then how can his exclusive declaration of salvation be reconciled? Jesus repeatedly declared that he is the only means of salvation. He wouldn't have gotten an invitation onto Oprah's show by saying things like this:

- "Enter by the narrow gate. For the gate is wide and the way is easy that leads to destruction, and those who enter by it are many. For the gate is narrow and the way is hard that leads to life, and those who find it are few."[455]
- "I am the way, and the truth, and the life. No one comes to the Father except through me."[456]

Likewise, Peter wouldn't get the time of day from *National Geographic Magazine* if they heard his message at the Pentecost feast; "This Jesus is the stone that was rejected by you, the builders, which has become the cornerstone. And there is salvation in no one else, for there is no other name under heaven given among men by which we must be saved."[457] At the core of Christianity is the person and work of Jesus on the cross, in his death, and with his resurrection. It is inescapable to deny that Jesus sees no room for alternate interpretations of his person and work if one examines all the claims he made during his life.

In the context of Islam, this means that Jesus cannot simply be the second most important prophet from God. It is incompatible with the biblical account of his life. Jesus is not a second-rate prophet. We cannot be satisfied with a silver medal Jesus. He is either preeminent in our lives or he is not there at all, since Jesus allows no room for competing prophecy concerning God's plan of salvation. On the stage of divine authority, there is only one actor, one monologue, and one prophet deserving our adoration and applause. No one compares to Jesus; no one even comes close. In fact, when someone challenges this view, as with the case of Muhammad, a simple comparison of Jesus and the challenger will always clarify why Jesus can make the extravagant claim that he is the way, the truth, and the life.[458]

---

[454] Rom. 1:18–23. Eugene H. Peterson, *The Message Remix: The Bible in Contemporary Language* (Colorado Springs, Colo.: NavPress, 2006), 1644.
[455] Matt. 7:13–14
[456] John 14:6
[457] Acts 4:11–13
[458] John 14:6

JESUS & MUHAMMAD

What are the differences between Jesus and Muhammad? How does the prophet of Islam fare against the savior of Christianity? To begin, let's first look at their statuses as savior. According to Islam, Muhammad was not a savior. William Miller (1892—1993), a Presbyterian missionary to Iran, explained this well.

> Islam has no Savior. Mohammad is rarely called Savior. He is said to have brought God's laws to men, and they, by keeping those laws, must satisfy God's requirements and win His approval. Since many Muslims realize that they [fall short of Koranic standards] ... they recite extra prayers in addition to those required for each day, they make gifts to charity, and go on pilgrimages not only to Mecca, but also to other sacred shrines, in order to gain merit, and if possible, balance their account with God. But since God does not make known how the accounts of His stand, a Muslim facing death does not know whether he is to go to paradise or to hell. After all, the decision is made by the arbitrary will of God, and no one can predict what that decision will be ... and so the Muslim lives and dies, not sure of his final salvation.[459]

Muhammad does not function as a savior within Islam, which prevents Muslims from knowing their standing with Allah until their day of reconciling after death. Additionally, the Qur'ān states that Jesus is not a savior; "The Christians say the Messiah is the Son of God. Such are the words they utter with their mouths, by which they emulate the infidels of old. God confound them! How perverse they are!"[460]

While Muhammad does not claim to be a savior and further disparages the Christian's belief in Jesus as their savior throughout the Qur'ān, the Bible presents a different case. Concerning Jesus, John the Baptist publicly declared, "Behold, the Lamb of God, who takes away the sin of the world!"[461] Paul taught that "our citizenship is in heaven, and from it we await a Savior, the Lord Jesus Christ."[462] Likewise, Paul teaches that Jesus is the savior; we can rest assured that our salvation is not based on the arbitrary will of God but on his justification

---

[459] William Miller, *A Christian's Response to Islam* (Nutley, NJ: Presbyterian & Reformed, 1977), 82–83.
[460] Sūra At-Tawbah 9:30
[461] John 1:29

of us through our faith by his grace. This is because "we have been justified by faith, we have peace with God through our Lord Jesus Christ."[463] Muhammad is powerless in Islam to forgive sin and cannot communicate with a believer in Islam, except perhaps through the Qur'ān and hadīths. Jesus, however, is alive, making supplication for us, and is always available to us through prayer as our mediator to God.[464] This is a huge difference between the two. As the eternal savior, Jesus is alive. As a man, Muhammad is dead.

What about the morality of Jesus and Muhammad? What kind of man was Muhammad compared to Jesus morally? Simply put, there is no comparison to be made. In the Qur'ān, Muhammad confessed his imperfection, praying a simply hope for his own forgiveness; "And who I aspire that He will forgive me my sin on the Day of Recompense (Sūra Ash-Shu'arā 26:82)." During his life, Muhammad abetted the mistreatment of Jews, Christians, and anyone who would not accept his leadership.[465] He also called for the murdering of men and the slavery of woman and children while in Medina.[466] Muhammad was a polygamist who married a total of thirteen women.[467] Even if Muhammad would deny this list of moral failures, he most certainly recognized the fallibility of his own life.[468]

Jesus, unlike Muhammad, is morally perfect. He called for the death of no one and viewed all of humanity as intrinsically equal in worth. In fact, he taught through his own parables and actions that racism is contrary to the nature of God in spite of deep racial tensions between Jews and Samaritans.[469] There are many passages that attest to Jesus' sinless nature, but here are just a few.

- 1 John 3:5 – "in him there is no sin"
- 2 Corinthians 5:21 – "made him to be sin who knew no sin"
- 1 Peter 2:22 – "he committed no sin"

---

[462] Phil. 3:20
[463] Rom. 5:1
[464] 1 Tim. 2:5
[465] Sūra Al-Baqarah 2:190; Sūra At-Tawbah 9:5, 29; Sūra Al-Fath 48:16, 29; Sūra At-Tahrim 66:9
[466] Fred M. Donner, "The Historical Context," The Cambridge Companion to the Qur'an, ed. Jane Dammen McAuliffe, (Cambridge: Cambridge University Press, 2006), 27.
[467] W. Montgomery Watt, Muhammad: Prophet and Statesman, (Oxford: Oxford University Press, 1961), 102.
[468] Sūra Al-Qaṣaṣ 28:15-16, Sūra Ṣād 38:23-24, Sūra Aṣ-Ṣāffāt 37:139-148
[469] John 4:7–42; Luke 10:25–37

What's more is that Jesus lived a sinless life even though he was tempted in every way humans are. The author of Hebrews stated it well; "For we do not have a high priest who is unable to sympathize with our weaknesses, but one who in every respect has been tempted as we are, yet without sin."[470] Jesus was tempted yet lived a completely sinless life unlike Muhammad.

As an aside, if you bring up the fact that Jesus never demanded the death of anyone, a good Muslim apologist might quote Jesus in Luke 19:26–27; "But as for these enemies of mine, who did not want me to reign over them, bring them here and slaughter them before me." The important thing to remember is context, context, context. Jesus starts this passage by saying, "A nobleman went into a far country to receive for himself a kingdom." The verse before that states, "As they heard these things, he proceeded to tell a parable." It is painfully obvious that Jesus was telling a parable and not ordering the death of anyone. Ironically, just one verse before the parable sentence, Jesus says that the Son of Man came to seek and to save the lost, not to forcefully demand their allegiance.[471]

What about miracles? How do Muhammad and Jesus compare in recorded miracles? According to the Qur'ān, Muhammad did not perform a single miracle. The Qur'ān itself is said to be a miracle because Muhammad was illiterate, but this claim is very subjective. During the years following Muhammad's death, people started to wonder why Muhammad, the greatest prophet of god, had performed no miracles whereas Jesus performed many. This was a difficult objection to over come, but the solution was simple. Muhammad's followers began to retrofit his life with miracles, extremely bizarre miracles at that.

Some of those miracles include: Muhammad traveling invisibly, splitting the moon in two (it was later repaired of course), making trees greet him, throwing sleeping sand in his enemy's eyes, and ordering a sand storm for victory at Badr.[472] These miracles seem bizarre because there is no

---

[470] Heb. 4:15
[471] Luke 19:10
[472] Uri Rubin, "Muhammad's Message in Mecca: Warnings, Signs, and Miracles," *The Cambridge Companion to Muhammad*, ed. Jonathan E. Brockopp (Cambridge: Cambridge University Press, 2010), 43.

apparent value to them. What is the point of throwing sleeping sand into your enemy's eyes? Why split the moon in two?[473] To display Allah's power? Wouldn't splitting the moon have had adverse effects on the earth?

The recorded miracles of Jesus, on the other hand, were numerous, had apparent value to them, and should be accepted by Muslims. Here are just some of the miracles recorded of Jesus:

- Cast out demons (Matt. 8:28–32; 15:22–28)
- Healed lepers (Matt. 8:3; Luke 17:14)
- Healed diseases (Matt. 4:23, 24; Luke 6:17–19)
- Healed a paralytic (Mark 2:3–12)
- Raised the dead (Matt. 9:25; John 11:43–44)
- Restored sight to the blind (Matt. 9:27–30; John 9:1–7)
- Restored and cured deafness (Mark 7:32–35)
- Fed the multitude (Matt. 14:15–21; Matt. 15:32–38)
- Walked on water (Matt. 8:26–27)
- Healed the sick (Matt. 8:5–13; 9:22)

Compared to Muhammad, Jesus performed not just valuable miracles but also many, many more of them. It got to a point where the New Testament authors simply stopped recording them because they were so numerous. In fact, John wrote that, "there are also many other things that Jesus did. Were every one of them to be written, I suppose that the world itself could not contain the books that would be written."[474]

The more you compare the two, the more it becomes clear that Jesus performed far more recorded miracles than Muhammad ever did. In addition, Muslims actually believe and accept that Jesus did perform miracles. This is because they accept Jesus as a prophet and their source for his miracles is the Gospels. Consequently, if they accept that Jesus performed miracles then they must also accept that he performed many more than Muhammad. So, it

---

[473] Oddly enough, there are Muslim apologists who cite vague photographic evidence that the moon was actually split at one point in its history. Ibid., 59.

[474] John 21:25

deserves to be asked – if Muhammad is the greater prophet, why were all the miracles reserved for his forerunner almost six hundred years prior?

It seems strange that God allowed his second-string prophet to perform loads of divine miracles while reserving tree greetings and moon splitting for his number one guy. If comedy clubs worked like that, they'd be out of business pretty quick – imagine the main act opening for the rookie comedian. This may be something we can discuss with Muslims. If Muhammad was truly Allah's premier prophet, why does Jesus upstage him? Does it not make more sense that Jesus is the premier prophet by his works alone when compared to Muhammad?

Aside from morality and miracles, here are just a few more ways Muhammad compares to Jesus.

	Jesus	**Muhammad**
Prayer	Taught humility and intimacy[475]	Taught ritualistic sacrament[476]
Women	Taught men to love, treat fairly[477]	Taught men to beat disobedient ones[478]
Worship	Taught he is worthy of worship[479]	Taught not to worship Jesus[480]
Enemies	Taught to love and forgive[481]	Taught to seek out and destroy[482]
Slavery	Had no slaves[483]	Owned many slaves[484]
Last Words	Forgiveness[485]	Cursing[486]
Sin	Was sinless[487]	Was declared sinful[488]
Identity	Claimed he is the Son of God[489]	Taught Jesus was not the Son of God[490]
Patience	Is patient towards us[491]	Requires patience from us[492]

[475] Matt. 6:5–13
[476] Bukhari, Vol. 1 488 - Passing in front of someone praying negates that person's prayer, 489 - It is sinful to pass in front of a person praying, 660 - Raising prayer before an Imam results in Allah turning your face into that of a donkey, 685 - Should prayers rows be crooked, Allah will disfigure your face, 690 - Should prayers rows be crooked, Allah will not hear those prayers, 717 - Looking up during prayer results in blindness, 759 - Bowing imperfectly results in nullified prayer
[477] Jesus healed women, forgave women, and encouraged women all over the Gospels.
[478] "As those you fear may be rebellious admonish, banish them to their couches, and beat them." - Sūra An-Nisā' 4:34
[479] Matt. 8:2
[480] "If the Most Gracious had a son, I would be the first to worship him." – Sūra Az-Zukhruf 43:81
[481] Matt. 5:44, Luke 22:52; 23:34
[482] The massacre of 800 Jewish men (noted in Sūra Al-'Aḥzāb 33:26)
[483] Jesus had no slaves, rather he performed the acts of slaves to set an example (John 13:5). See also 1 Tim. 1:8–10
[484] Bukhari Vol. 5, # 541 and Vol. 7, # 344.
[485] Luke 23:34
[486] "May Allah curse the Jews and Christians for they built the places of worship at the graves of the prophets." Bukhari, Vol. 1, #427
[487] 1 John 3:5; 2 Cor. 5:21; Heb. 4:15; 1 Pet. 2:22
[488] "Therefore have patience; Allah's promise is surely true. Implore forgiveness for your sins, and celebrate the praise of your Lord evening and morning." Sūra Ghāfir 40:55
[489] John 5:18–27; 10:36; Matt. 26:63–64
[490] "Christ the son of Mary was no more than a messenger: many were the messengers that passed away before him." Sūra Al-Mā'idah 5:75
[491] 2 Pet. 3:9

Notice I have been writing Muhammad was and Jesus is. No, I'm not crazy. I understand Jesus lived and died many years ago. But, herein lies an important distinction between Christianity and Islam. Christianity's greatest prophet, Jesus, was not held down by death. Islam's greatest prophet, Muhammad, remains captive to death. Jesus sits enthroned next to God the Father acting as our High Priest and only mediator between God and us.[493] Muhammad, however, has finished his work forever. I am glad our only mediator can still actively teach his followers to pray, live, worship, and enter into communion with God. Muhammad, however, is not afforded this same privilege, but claims higher standing regardless. From an orthodox Christian perspective, Muhammad essentially took the gold medal off the neck of Jesus Christ and put it on himself.

Jesus is the gold medal savior and takes second place to no one. This is the challenge every Muslim must wrestle with when hearing the gospel – Jesus leaves no room to share the status of redeemer. Furthermore, Jesus claimed to be more than our redeemer alone. He revealed himself to be God.[494] Not only does this commit the highest sin in Islam (širk), equating something with Allah, but also directly challenges the Islamic idea that Jesus was simply a prophet in the line of many prophets. Since Muslims accept the biblical Gospels (Injil) as authoritative, we can dialogue from them in order to paint a picture of Jesus as the Son of Man, the messiah who was executed by religious and political leaders for claiming to be God.[495]

The Jesus of the Gospels cannot play second fiddle to Muhammad because Jesus claimed to be equal with God. Either Jesus was truly the Son of God, or he committed širk by equating himself with God. Jesus cannot simply be viewed as a mighty prophet because if he were only a man his claims to be God would have invalidated his integrity as one of God's many prophets. How long would a prophet last who did not just speak for God but actually claimed to be God? Essentially, if Jesus were simply a prophet as Muhammad taught, then he would have been a liar and a deceiver. We know this isn't true. His

---

[492] Sūra Ar-Ra'd 13:22
[493] 1 Tim. 2:5
[494] For example, John 8:58. The title "I am" is the same title God used to identify himself to Moses in the burning bush. See Exod. 3:14.
[495] Luke 22:66–71. The titles *Son of Man* and *Son of God* imply deity. Such a declaration, that one claims to be God, was punishable by death during Jesus' day. This is the reason for v. 71.

claims to deity were validated at his resurrection. Therefore, Jesus must either be wholly accepted or wholly rejected.

OVERCOMING PREJUDICE

Now that we know a bit about Islamic history and what Muslims believe, how do we utilize this information when sharing the gospel with Muslims? I think the better question might be how we shouldn't share Jesus with Muslims. It seems that with the rise of Islamofacism throughout the world Christians are reacting by denouncing Islam as an evil religion with wicked followers of a radical faith that incites the sincerely loyal to violence. The argument goes that if a Muslim desires to achieve the highest reward in the afterlife they must adhere to the lesser jihad by being faithful to Muhammad's commands for violence as written in the Qur'ān and hadīths.

As a result, Christians protest the growing influence of Islam by burning Qur'āns, picketing mosque construction sites, and demanding legislation to curb any Islamic influence in Western culture. These actions are subsequently understood by the Muslim world as offensive attacks on their culture, their faith, and their way of life. Inevitably, an effigy of some public figure catches fire in the Middle East, and we lose another American flag under the trampling of angry feet. Obviously, something is wrong with this picture. As Christians we are not reaching the Muslim world at all. It would seem we are very good at telling Muslims what we are against rather than what we are for, since many Christians are uncomfortable with the Islamic worldview in every aspect be it religious, cultural, or political. Expressing this uncomfortable tension with public displays of wholesale Islamic rejection is not working, although we act as if it is.

The issue is far more complex than what many Christians would like to believe. For example, let's examine the adage, "Islam is a religion of violence." Of course, from what we can see in Muhammad's life, the Qur'ān, and the hadīths, there is an obvious aspect of totalitarianism in Islam that should not be ignored. Sharia law, for example, is not compatible with a democratic, Western society. Consequently, the practice of Sharia law in the secular and public arena should be fiercely rejected; however, to broad stroke all Muslims as totalitarian terrorists and all mosques as jihadist training camps is dangerously irresponsible. The moment we lose focus of sharing Jesus with Muslims we are no longer apologists but agitators of a seriously sensitive, geo–political issue rooted further back into history than most of us can imagine. As Christians we have the responsibility of determining which is more important, convincing the world that Islam is wrong or convincing Muslims that Jesus is our salvation.

It seems that the Christian church as a whole, particularly in North America, has gotten this backwards. It is more popular (and easier) to stand in a pulpit and call Islam evil than it is to guide the church towards Muslim missions throughout the world. It is much easier to attack Muslims and blame them for the instability in the Middle East (and the world for that matter) than it is to patiently pray for the Muslim and Arabic people whom God loves. It is easier to burn a Qur'ān in public protest than to open its pages to study why Muslims believe what they believe in order to better serve them as messengers of the gospel. Frankly, it's laziness in the Great Commission to try preaching the gospel through publicity stunts rather than relationship, research, and prayer. The gospel is much, much bigger than the cultural collision of Islam and the West. It's much, much bigger than any actions Muslims and Christians have taken against each other in the past.

If you really trust what the gospel teaches, here is a hard truth to swallow – God loved the terrorists of 9/11 just as much as he loves you.[496] If we are Christians and this does not sit well with us, then we have no business sharing the gospel with Muslims. God's design for this world never included sectarianism, violence in his name, and the subsequent hate that inevitably follows. His design for the world never included death or violence, crusades or jihads, inquisitions or terrorist attacks, or hate returned with hate. And God's solution for these problems is not tit-for-tat "evangelism." It is love, mercy, grace, patience, kindness, goodness, self-control, and humility as demonstrated through the only one who can get us out of this mess we've gotten ourselves into – his name is Jesus.

If we truly want to see Muslims come to Jesus and be welcomed home in the kingdom of God, then there is deep–seeded prejudice that needs to be

---

[496] John 3:16; 2 Pet. 3:9

put aside. While it is true Islam can incite violence, sometimes we forget that Christianity can as well. We only need to look at our own history to realize there is blood on our hands, but we know the blood on our hands has been wiped off and cleansed through Jesus. Why can we not extend the same invitation to Muslims?

THE GOSPEL IN DIALOGUE WITH MUSLIMS

Sharing the gospel with Muslims can be difficult. Often times even the words and terms we use can make communicating truth difficult. Our "Christianese" can get in the way of presenting a Muslim with a clear picture of who Jesus is. Take, for example, the common biblical phrase "Son of God." While "Son of God" was originally a Jewish messianic term, it was fulfilled in Jesus and is now something Christians utilize as one of many descriptions of him. So, when we hear "Son of God," we think of Jesus as being the only begotten son of God. When Muslims hear that term, being unfamiliar with the theology behind it, they often believe it means the Father having sexual relations with Mary – something completely intolerable to them (and Christians as well).[497] Even if they understand that the term "Son of God" does not infer sexuality, equating Jesus with God is also scandalous since according to Islam nothing, not even the prophet Muhammad, may be stationed on the same plane as Allah (širk).

This is such a sensitive title for Jesus that many missionaries to Muslims have come to refer to Jesus as the 'beloved Son who originates from God.' It could be argued that this softer term implies that Jesus was created, and while this is a valid concern, we need to remember that apologetics must be done within context. In the Muslim context, some Christian terms such as "Son of God" are loaded with negative presuppositions on the part of Muslims. If we can still teach a Muslim that Jesus is divine and that he was sent from the Father to redeem humanity without using "Son of God," should we not hold off on such complicating terminology?

While this is a widely contested point, I believe we should put theology before terminology and truth before vocabulary. One day in the future, a

---

[497] It is also good to note that many Muslims are taught that the Trinity is God the Father, Jesus the Son, and Mary the Mother.

former Muslim may come to embrace terms like the "Son of God," but getting them to meet Jesus needs to happen first. So, if it helps, tell Muslims Jesus is from God, that he is God's beloved son, but that he is not a created being and has always existed. This will commit *širk* and make things difficult, but if we explain what we mean by "Son of God" prior to using the term, we might have an easier time in the long run.

Another difficulty faced when evangelizing to Muslims is the texts involved – the Bible and the Qur'ān. More often than not, Muslims are unfamiliar with the Bible as a whole. It may surprise some Muslims to learn that the Bible constitutes more than simply the first five books of the Old Testament (*Tawrat*), the Psalms (*Zabur*), and four Gospels (*Injil*).[498] They may need an explanation surrounding both the Old Testament and New Testament; why are there so many more books, how long did it take to write, and who wrote them? These are just a few questions that Christians need to prepare to answer.

Many Muslims who are familiar with the additional biblical content beyond the *Tawrat*, *Zabur*, and *Injil* are often taught that the Bible Christians use today was fabricated at the Council of Nicaea in 325CE and, therefore, cannot be trusted. They are taught that the only reason why the Bible contradicts the Qur'ān is because of the content added at this meeting. An explanation over what actually happened at the council may dispel some of the haze and mistrust Muslims have with the Bible. At any rate, these questions and more may arise before Muslims are comfortable dialoguing from a formerly mysterious book.

The Qur'ān itself can also make it difficult to evangelize to Muslims since most Muslims are taught not to trust translations of the Qur'ān in any other language than Arabic. This is especially problematic if one does not speak or read Arabic. Attempting to use an English translation of the Qur'ān may prove futile since most Muslims will not accept the text outside of its native Arabic. In fact, most Muslim scholars unanimously reject the authenticity of any translation of the Qur'ān from its native Arabic, some

---

[498] Sūra Al-Māʻidah 5:34, 46; Al-ʻAnbyāʼ 21:105

going so far as to reject it even being the Qur'ān.[499] Unfortunately, there is really no way around this issue. There are, however, two ways of softening their position towards dialoguing out of a translated Qur'ān.

The first is refusing to use a Bible translated into English. This sounds strange, but hear me out. If a Muslim refuses to dialogue in English, opting instead for an Arabic Qur'ān, then a Christian should likewise refuse to dialogue in English, opting instead for a Hebrew and Greek Bible. Then, when the Muslim uses proof texts from the English Bible to defend their position, simply request that he or she reproduce that text in the original language to verify the authenticity of the translation – just the opposite of what they would request of the Christian. Naturally, the conversation will go nowhere, but if the Muslim is seriously interested in dialoguing, they must concede to read from a common tongue.

The second way of softening their position is to accept the Arabic Qur'ān but ask them to suggest a translation. They may have a favorite English translation of the Qur'ān from which they study but cannot use when dialoguing with a Christian. This will open the door of possibility for biased or poor interpretations in favor of their positions, but it will also afford us the opportunity to really examine Qur'ānic passages to compare them with scripture. The deeper we dive into the Qur'ān with Muslims, the easier it will be to see the disagreements it has with the Bible. This is especially helpful with parts of the Bible they accept as inspired.

Finally, should we find ourselves without a conversation starter to encourage them to study the Bible and Qur'ān, try finding aspects of both which agree, regardless to what degree, and begin paving the way towards the gospel. For example, the Qur'ān affirms that Jesus is the Word of God.[500] This idea is originally found in the Gospel of John.[501] John also tells us that the Word of God is God himself who became a man. It may be a good idea to present Jesus as the Word of God throughout John's gospel. Demonstrate how Jesus is the living embodiment of God's will through his words and deeds. As a bonus, John's gospel highlights Jesus's role as a sacrifice inherited through

---

[499] Abbas Jaffer and Masuma Jaffer, *An Introduction to Qur'anic Sciences* (London: ICAS Press, 2009), 257.
[500] Sūra 'Āli 'Imrān 3:45; Sūra An-Nisā' 4:171
[501] John 1:1,14

the gift of faith alone, something they need to hear in a heavily works-based system of salvation.[502] End on the fact that this Word of God from the Qur'ān is Jesus. He takes us out of the futile cycle of works-based salvation and into community with God through faith alone and by his grace alone.

Hearing that salvation comes through faith and not works is something that needs to be stressed. Muslims, no matter the sect, have almost no comprehension of the gracious gift of faith offered through Jesus. Always keep in mind that Allah only pardons and offers salvation to those who first love him, continue to love him their entire life, and do enough good works.[503] Allah's love is only dispensed in response to the love and sustained obedience of his followers.[504] These characteristics are the exact opposite of God who loves sinners prior to sinners loving him.[505] Furthermore, the Qur'ān is full of verses about those whom Allah has no love for, whereas the Bible is filled with verses about those whom God does love.[506]

Muslims live their lives unsure of their eternal destiny. Their only hope is through the combination of strict adherence to the Five Pillars of Islam and the unpredictable compassion from Allah. The idea that the work of salvation was already accomplished for them on the cross is a completely foreign concept. It is so counterintuitive for Muslims to believe justification through faith alone that they may not come to grasp this reality until long after our encounters with them. Don't be discouraged. Rather, stay consistent with the message that Jesus accomplished all the righteousness (perfect deeds, thoughts, and being) needed to grant us entry into an eternal communion with God. He attributes that work to us; we only need to recognize our own inability to accomplish what he did for us and ask for his forgiveness.

At the end of the day, dialogue with Muslims will take a lot of work on our part. Muslims need to know that Muhammad and the Qur'ān cannot compare to the person and work of Jesus. As Christians living in Western society, we need to cast aside our prejudice towards the entirety of the Islamic worldview in order to debunk its myth of a silver-medal Jesus. Additionally,

---

[502] Sūra ʿĀli ʿImrān 3:57
[503] Sūra Al-Baqarah 2:195, 222; Sūra ʿAli ʿImran 3:134; Sūra Al-Maʾidah 5:13; Sūra At-Tawbah 9:4, 108; Sūra Al-Hujurat 49:9; Al-Mumtahanah 60:8; Sūra Al-Buruj 85:14
[504] Sūra ʿĀli ʿImrān 3:31, 76, 146, 159; Sūra Al-Maʾidah 5:42
[505] Rom. 5:8
[506] Sūra ʿAli ʿImran 3:32, 57; Hosea. 3:1; John 16:27; 2 Cor. 9:7; 1 John 4:7

there are many misconceptions about Jesus within the Islamic worldview that deserve clarification or refutation. Likewise, there are many misconceptions about Islam that we harbor, which would be best suited for the waste bin before sitting at the table with a Muslim. Once we are at that table, be sure to consistently stick to the person and work of Jesus. Not only will this offer both sides a time of sharpening and clarifying one another's beliefs, but it will see Jesus glorified from the silver medal that Muhammad placed around his neck.

CHAPTER FIVE

Scientology & Robot Jesus

"Writing for a penny a word is ridiculous. If a man really wants to make a million dollars, the best way would be to start his own religion." [507]

L. RON HUBBARD (1911—1986)

Walk through the streets of Amsterdam at night and you'll see things that would make Hugh Hefner blush.

It was in this city that I was pulled over by a police officer and issued a citation for not having a functional headlight attached to my bicycle at night on a street fitted with a marijuana café to my right and a brothel to my left.

It was in this city where I learned the word for '*crack*' in seven different languages as a shady, old man paced back-and-forth on a street corner, whispering the words for potential foreign customers.

It was in this city where my wife and I watched a drug deal happen six feet in front of us before turning our attention to a group of teenage boys haggling with a prostitute in the street over how much it would cost them for their friend lose his virginity.

It was in this city where I visited a beautiful, medieval cathedral, adjacent to the Singel Canal, whose first floor was renovated into a brothel. Men as young as sixteen wandered in packs from window to window, perusing women as if they were a commodity to be bartered or sold.

In this city, anything goes.

Yet for all its blatant darkness, Amsterdam is, by far, one of the most stunning cities in Europe. In autumn, the brown and red leaves perfectly match the colors of the tightly snug brick flats that line the canals. Rustic, white windowpanes are filled with the warm, flickering glow of fireplaces inside.

---

[507] Eugene H. Methvin, "Scientology: Anatomy of a Frightening Cult," *Reader's Digest*, May 1980.

Large, white light bulbs, the size of softballs, line the canal archways and reflect warmly off the water.

For a moment, the reflection of the lights wavers and disperses, interrupted by a small boat floating under the walkway. The boat is carrying a man and a woman enjoying a date night away from the kids – she's leaning comfortably into his arms as he stares off into the night. The boat's gondolier, a teenager juggling this part–time job with school, whistles a soft tune as he slowly ducts to avoid the oncoming bridge. A light breeze sways the trees back and forth, forcing them to surrender some of their leaves. A woman, tightly bundled, walks briskly along the canal with books under one arm and her coffee in the other.

Amsterdam is truly a beautiful city.

It was in Amsterdam where God purged my mind of religious pietism and made me realize that, despite all the sin and darkness the city offers, Jesus would have gone there.

But not only that, Jesus *needs* to be there. The people of Amsterdam are hungry. They are searching for something they cannot find in drugs, sex, college, or careers.

What they are looking for is their Creator, and their Creator is calling for them. But they aren't listening. It almost seems as if they can't.

There are distractions all around them – entertainment, sex, parties, careers, and religions.

In the midst of all these distractions to keeping them deaf to God, there are also groups keeping them confused.

One such group I found in Amsterdam is the Church of Scientology.

THE CHURCH OF SCIENTOLO ...WHAT?

One evening, while riding a bike down the streets of Amsterdam (don't worry, I fixed the headlight), a strange sign caught my attention.

Granted, strange signs are one-in-a-million in Amsterdam, but this one was different.

The sign was completely blue with a strange white cross in the middle and the word *Scientologykerk* written below.

With what little Dutch I know, I was immediately led to believe this was some type of science church.

"Only in Amsterdam," I remember thinking to myself.

I had never heard of such an organization – a church for science? Perhaps it was the Dutch version of Christian Science.

Whatever it was, I was determined to find out.

I parked my bike across the small cobblestone street and stared at the sign.

From across the street, I peered into the large window, which showcased what seemed to be a meeting place equipped with thirty or so chairs all positioned towards a pulpit decorated with the same strange cross I had seen on the blue sign. Over to the right of the meeting place were couches and a few tables.

It seemed like a very relaxed atmosphere – like a modern coffee shop you might find in downtown SoHo.

After a car had passed, I walked across the street and entered the building. There was a large desk at the front with a receptionist.

"Mag ik u helpen?" the man said.

My reaction was similar to what yours must have just been. I raised my eyebrows and made a broken smile – the international sign for, "I have no clue what you just said."

"English?" he asked.

I nodded.

"Ah, well then, welcome to the Church of Scientology! Do you have an appointment?" he asked warmly and inviting.

"No, I just saw your sign outside and thought I'd check your place out," I responded while scanning the interior, trying to understand what exactly made this a church.

"Well, what do you know about Scientology?"

My attention snapped back to him – now we were getting somewhere.

"Nothing at all, I literally just saw the blue sign from across the canal and decided to come in. So, is this a church? What denomination are you guys?"

He chuckled, "Well, we are a church, yes. However, we are not Christian like I believe you think we are." He must have gotten that question a lot because of the strange cross. "Christians come here, but we are not a Christian church."

"Then what's with the cross on your sign?"

He smiled endearingly and tilted his head as if a toddler just asked why puppies are so fluffy.

"You see, the cross was originally a sign of peace in ancient cultures; however, Christians sort of appropriated it and have been using it for their symbol since Roman times."

I instantly did not like this guy.

"I'm pretty sure the cross is an ancient form of torture and execution which is the exact opposite of peace. Christians use it because it reminds them of sacrifice and forgiveness, not necessarily peace."

He seemed to realize that he might have offended me. You see in Amsterdam, Christians are few and far between.

"Yes, of course, I see your point. Well, not to skip topics, but the Church of Scientology is actually for anyone, even Christians. We have many people from many faiths who all come together here and use the methods of Scientology to clear their minds, enhance their life, and become better people."

He reached under the counter and pulled out a book, "The church is based on the principles of the mind found in this book."

He handed me a thick book with the word *Dianetics* adorned across the top in cheesy, metallic gold written over the backdrop of an exploding volcano. Over 40,000 sold in the Netherlands, the silver sticker informed me.

"If you would like, you can give that book a read and perhaps set up an appointment with us?"

Realizing I might have unintentionally led him on, I politely responded, "I'm sorry. I'm just visiting Amsterdam. I actually live in Germany."

"Ah, well then," he replied, "perhaps you can read it on your own time and come back again later."

His response sounded strange to me. Why would he simply end the conversation without giving me the address or phone number to one of their German offices?

What I did not know at the time is that Scientology was deemed an illegal organization in Germany after the state investigated the church and found it, in their opinion, to be a hoax.

As he saw me to the door, the man thanked me for stopping by and told me to enjoy my new book. He shut the door behind me the moment I stepped into the street. It was a strange meeting, for sure.

However, the strangest part to me was why he would not give me contact information to any German offices. I put the book in my backpack, hopped on my bike, and went back to my hostel.

SCIENTOLOGY IN A NUT SHELL

Scientology is not an easy worldview to study.[508] The organization is shrouded in secrecy and would rather tell you what they believe than for you to discover for yourself. As with many worldviews, it is nearly impossible to understand Scientology today without understanding where it came from. Meaningful dialogue with Scientologists requires at least a short introduction to how the church formed, and this will allow us to view the developmental theology of Scientology during its formative years.

The Church of Scientology, or simply *Scientology*, was founded by American science fiction author Lafayette Ronald Hubbard in December 1953. The Church of Scientology is headquartered in California while it maintains a spiritual headquarters in Florida. The Church's current population remains unknown; however, Scientology leaders claim upwards of eight million adherents. It is estimated that this number is grossly inflated from around 25,000 to 75,000 total active members in the U.S. because the church considers membership as anyone who has ever had any affiliation with the church regardless of current activity or attendance.[509]

Pinpointing the theology of Scientology proves an impossible task since no standard doctrine or dogma exists. As the Scientologist in Amsterdam eluded, anyone from any stripe and creed is invited to participate in the church so long as they are applying the methods of Scientology to "enrich" their lives.

---

[508] Scientology, Dianetics, Hubbard, L. Ron Hubbard, LRH, Operating Thetan, OT, Theta, Thetan, Saint Hill Manor, E-meter, and Religious Technology Center are trademarks and service marks of the Religious Technology Center, Church of Scientology International.

[509] Fred A. Bernstein, "In Pasadena, a Model for Scientology's Growth Plan," *The New York Times*, http://www.nytimes.com/2010/11/10/business/10scientology.html (accessed October 30, 2011) and Mark Oppenheimer, "In the Clear: On Scientology," *The Nation*, http://www.thenation.com/article/164059/clear-scientology (accessed November 5, 2011).

Nonetheless, there are core beliefs nearly all Scientologists generally hold. Scientologists believe that all human beings are basically good in their morality and are also immortal and spiritual beings with existence spanning across many different lifetimes. Accordingly, reincarnation is a fundamental aspect of Scientology's worldview.

A human being consists of three parts – body, mind, and thetan. A thetan is essentially the immortal identity and personhood of an individual, that which what is commonly referred to as a soul. In order to achieve complete happiness, or what Scientologists may loosely consider salvation, humanity must accomplish perfection in eight dynamics of life. This is achieved through a process called auditing, which is performed by an official Scientology minister who conducts auditing via one-on-one interviews. During these initial interviews, if a person is found to have psychological, emotional, or "life" problems then the cure is found in spiritual technologies that Scientology can offer them – for a price.

Ultimately, there is no absolute right or wrong since all epistemic truths may be transcended by the teachings of Scientology. Belief in God or "The Infinity" is necessary in order to truly unlock one's potential, but it is not defined.[510] There is no god aside from what each individual determines god to be. This makes Scientology extremely inclusive of other religions. Scientologists come from all religious backgrounds by simply adding to their previously held notions of reality.

L. RON HUBBARD

Like all other rival worldviews, Scientology was born through the leadership and founding of one man. L. Ron Hubbard was born on March 13, 1911 in Nebraska. He was raised in a military family as his father served in the U.S. Navy. Hubbard's childhood was never spent in the same place for very long because of his father's vocation. This afforded him the opportunity of moving multiple times during his adolescence.[511] Hubbard would later claim that his

---

[510] Harriet S. Selverstone, *Encouraging and Supporting Student Inquiry: Researching Controversial Issues* (Westport, Conn.: Greenwood Publishing Group, Inc., 2007), 204.
[511] Russell Miller, *Bare-faced Messiah: The True Story of L. Ron Hubbard* (Toronto: Key Porter Books, 1987), 23.

many travels as a child allowed him to tour extensively throughout Asia, studying Far Eastern ideas and learning eastern mysticism from monks.[512]

Hubbard attempted to follow his dream of becoming an author by writing adventure tales, western novels, and science fiction stories upon graduating from George Washington University. He found some success writing pulp fiction in the 1930s for dime-store magazines in New York City, but he eventually hit a dead end. When this avenue closed, Hubbard gave screenwriting a shot, but this also led to disappointment. Hubbard kept his head up during this time of failure, and regardless of his shortcomings in authoring, he never let his dream go. It's important to note that Hubbard burned with a passion for authoring science fiction and adventure novels. This will become important later on.

By the late-1930s Hubbard was a penniless, failed, pulp fiction author. Now married to Margret "Polly" Grubb with a child on the way, he needed to make some changes in order to support himself and his new family.[513] Following his father's tradition into military service may not have been Hubbard's first choice, but the global atmosphere was changing. On December 7, 1941, the Japanese military attacked the U.S. at Pearl Harbor. Seven months later Hubbard was commissioned as an officer in the U.S. Naval Reserve. He seemed to have enjoyed his time in the Navy considering he would later regale guests at cocktail parties in Los Angeles with stories that portrayed himself as a war hero. Hubbard's actual career, however, was lackluster and displayed his incompetency as a commander and leader.

One such military account occurred on May 19, 1943 near Cape Lookout, Oregon. It was here that Hubbard engaged what he thought were Japanese submarines.[514] He was so convinced that he was battling the enemy on America's doorstep that he called in two Army blimps and a Coast Guard vessel as reinforcement. After sixty-eight hours of dropping depth charges to neutralize the threat, Hubbard reported to his superiors that the Japanese submarines had "definitely sunk, beyond doubt."[515] However, upon review, it was determined that Hubbard was depth charging nothing more than water.

---

[512] Ibid., 40.
[513] Timothy L. Hall, *American Religious Leaders* (New York: Facts on File, Inc., 2003), 175.
[514] L. Ron Hubbard, U.S.S. PC-815 Action Report (24 May 1943).
[515] Thomas S. Moulton, U.S.S. PC-815 Action Report (24 May 1943).

His ability to command didn't get any better. One month later, Hubbard ordered an impromptu gun exercise in Mexican waters.[516] This would be akin to Mexican troops crossing into Texas to test their new army tank firing capabilities. It was a severely unwise decision. After a short tour aboard a larger vessel where he was strictly supervised, Hubbard was relieved of his command. This is, of course, on Hubbard's official naval records, most of which are available on public domain. But these records contradict the Church of Scientology's vision of Hubbard as a natural leader. When faced with his Naval records, the Church of Scientology has often argued that a second naval record exists but was not released to the public due to Hubbard's dealings with high–level classified information and missions. To the Church, the public record of Hubbard's military service is a front to keep the truth of his heroism and leadership hidden.

Hubbard spent the years after his military service in Los Angeles without his wife, Polly, and their children. He lived on a meager military pension without any clear goals ahead of him, driven only by his burning desire for fame and fortune. His luck turned around after he met and moved in with scientist Jack Parson who took an immediate liking to Hubbard. The two shared a common interest in the occult and the teachings of Aleister Crowley. Crowley had established a form of occultism called *Thelema* after supposedly receiving supernatural knowledge from a spirit being named Lam. Crowley's teachings are summarized in his work *The Book of the Law*, which were disseminated through an occult organization called the Ordo Templi Orientis (OTO) during the time Hubbard and Parson were friends. Parson led the OTO branch in Los Angeles known as the Agape Lodge.

Hubbard's health took a turn for the worse soon after moving in with Parson. In 1945, Hubbard was admitted to a nearby hospital for treatment of chronic ulcers which had plagued him for quite some time. During his hospitalization, Hubbard claims to have performed extensive research of psychoanalysis. This is the first occurrence of Hubbard's theories on the human mind, something that would later become Scientology's infamous mental health "technology" of *dianetics*. Hubbard returned to Parson's estate

---

[516] Jon Atack, *A Piece of Blue Sky: Scientology, Dianetics, and L. Ron Hubbard Exposed* (New York: Kensington Publishing Corporation, 1990), 93.

upon his release from the hospital, and the two went into business together. At the time, Hubbard was dating a woman by the name of Sara Northrup whom he would eventually marry despite still being married to his first wife, Polly.[517]

Hubbard's and Parson's business began to fail after Hubbard relocated to Miami with Northrup in an attempt to expand the business, but without a clear set of goals. Parson grew tired of Hubbard's poor business decisions and flew to Florida to confront him. When he arrived, he discovered that Hubbard and Northrup had purchased yachts with business funds and were planning on sailing around the world. Hubbard parted ways with Parson after a short legal battle. In 1946, he bigamously married Sara Northrup, age twenty-two, and relocated to southern California.[518] The marriage would end shortly there after in 1951.[519] Sara filed for divorce citing "extreme cruelty," "great mental anguish," and "physical suffering" on the part of Hubbard.[520] She also described him as a paranoid schizophrenic.[521]

DIANETICS AS THERAPY

In 1949, the American Psychological Association (APA) received a letter from Hubbard concerning a new theory he had developed about the "science of mind."[522] He claimed to have developed a technology that could cure psychosomatic ills, such as advanced trauma, which was buried deep in each human's subconscious mind. Hubbard's research fell on deaf ears as the APA ultimately ignored him due to his lack of credentials and, frankly, the absurdity of the research. Through a new friend and editor named John Campbell, who earnestly believed in Hubbard's technology, his "science of mind" techniques gained popularity through various science fiction periodicals. By May of 1950, a publisher had picked up Hubbard's refined work entitled *Dianetics: The Modern Science of Mental Health.*

---

[517] Bent Corydon, *L. Ron Hubbard: Messiah or Madman?* (New York: Barricade Books, 1992), 219.
[518] Timothy L. Hall, *American Religious Leaders* (New York: Facts on File, Inc., 2003), 175.
[519] Ibid., 208.
[520] Sara Northrup Hubbard v. L. Ron Hubbard, D414408 (Sp. Ct. Cali. 1951).
[521] Ibid.
[522] Eugene V. Gallagher and W. Michael Ashcroft, *Introduction to New and Alternative Religions in America* (Westport, Conn.: Greenwood Press, 2006), 171.

"Dianetics," Hubbard explained in his soon-to-be bestseller, "is the science of mind."[523] Simpler than physics and chemistry, Hubbard claimed that dianetics was on a much higher "echelon of usefulness" than those other sciences.[524] Dianetics had the power to invariably cure any psychosomatic illness.[525] In a time when men were returning from (or to) war, dianetics offered hope that few had experienced in hospitals, churches, or psychologists' offices across the nation. In just two short months *Dianetics* was already being mentioned in major news outlets throughout the country. Hubbard had written a hit – finally, his dream was being realized.

Dianetics therapy spread like wildfire throughout homes across America for three simple reasons; it was easy, affordable, and personal. A person only needed to purchase Hubbard's book and enlist a trusted family member or friend to perform an "auditing" session on them. Within a few short sessions they could expect to rid themselves of *engrams*, the root of all our life problems. (*Engrams* are memories of traumatic events that are experienced earlier in life but persist in the mind's subconscious memory, or as Hubbard coined *reactive mind*). *Dianetics* was so popular that bookstores had difficulty keeping the pop psychology on their shelves despite the APA repeatedly denouncing Hubbard's work.

As with every fad, the steam soon ran out. People began to lose interest even though *Dianetics* research and training centers had been established across the country. Hubbard needed to rethink his crumbling and quick–lived *Dianetics* empire. What was causing it to fail? How could he revive his success? Ultimately, Hubbard decided that decentralized control of dianetics therapy caused its own downfall. He reasoned that since dianetics therapy allowed anyone to perform it outside of Hubbard's control, why should people attend seminars or buy more books? Hubbard felt that he had a million dollar idea but had given the copyright to everyone. He needed a way to stay on top and in control; so, he went back to the drawing board. It didn't take long for him to devise a plan. Soon, Hubbard would be back on top of his dianetics empire, and this time he would be the emperor.

---

[523] L. Ron Hubbard, *Dianetics: The Modern Science of Mental Health* (Los Angeles: Bridge Publications, Inc., 2007), i.
[524] Ibid.
[525] Ibid.

DIANETICS AS RELIGION

Reminiscing his pulp fiction days, Hubbard once quipped, "Writing for a penny a word is ridiculous. If a man really wants to make a million dollars, the best way would be to start his own religion."[526] This quote exposes Hubbard's new plan for the comeback of dianetics therapy. His desire to stay on top was insatiable, and perhaps this was the way to do it – start a new religion and make yourself the leader. With ample funds from his chart–busting *Dianetics*, it was time for him to take dianetics therapy to the next level. In 1952, Hubbard gathered all of his closest disciples together to reveal something new, something fresh, something ground breaking. In front of his most loyal followers, he unveiled what he believed was the next step in dianetics therapy – the "electropsychometer."

The device, which would later be referred to as an "E-meter," was used during auditing sessions and acted as a glorified lie detector. It was simply a small box connected to two metallic cylinders that read a person's physiological reactions to certain stimuli during auditing sessions. Hubbard's invention wowed his audience of followers. He explained that the E-meter would be used on *pre-clears* (non-Scientologists) during auditing sessions in a new field of science in which they were all now apart of – Scientology.

Dianetics had unlocked the secrets of the human mind; Scientology now sought to unlock the secrets of the human soul. One year later, Hubbard founded the Hubbard Association of Scientologists. He was once again rising to the top with Scientology, but unlike *Dianetics*, Hubbard was determined to keep control of his empire. In 1953, that empire officially solidified into a religious organization when Hubbard incorporated the *Church of Scientology of California* in Los Angeles, and with that the Church of Scientology was born.

Hubbard envisioned the Church of Scientology would mimic Christian denominations in many ways. Its organizational structure was similar to the Roman Catholic or Presbyterian church – a top down approach meant he would enjoy isolated control over the whole body. Tithing was also practiced and Hubbard received a cut from each smaller Scientology branch. These

---

[526] Eugene H. Methvin, "Scientology: Anatomy of a Frightening Cult," *Reader's Digest*, May 1980.

tithes flowed upward from the branches to the "Mother Church," the name given to the Los Angeles office.

The Church of Scientology even had a proselytism program. Those outside the church were known as pre-clears or people who had not reached a certain level in Scientology auditing called "Clear." Each local organization recruited pre-clears off the streets and into auditing sessions where Scientology auditors, or ministers, would offer Church of Scientology services to get rid of their engrams and move them towards a higher state of Clear. This was the church's ultimate goal, to rid the world of pre-clears. Each person needed to become a Clear in order for the world to become a better place. This was such a conviction to Hubbard that he later suggested that ostracizing pre-clears from the rest of the Clear population would raise the general social order. Quarantining those whom Scientology auditors deemed "antagonistic" towards the church would prove to make the world an even better place.[527]

Hubbard's new empire was growing just as fast as it had when *Dianetics* was first released. The church opened offices all over the country and soon considered going international. It seemed that the church's expansion was unstoppable; however, after a run–in with the U.S. government, the Church of Scientology hit its first speed bump. Hubbard had discovered that some government agencies were monitoring the Church of Scientology and its practices out of fear that the organization might be a fraud. The FBI called him in for questioning. After his meeting, Hubbard increasingly felt as if the U.S. government had joined forces with the APA and were out to get him. He had to get away from their ever–watching eyes.

SAINT HILL MANOR

Hubbard purchased a large estate in England and relocated the Church of Scientology's headquarters to Saint Hill Manor in 1959 to escape his would–be adversaries. At Saint Hill, Hubbard manically churned out work after work, researching and developing new Scientology techniques at an impressive rate. Many of the techniques and strategies the Church of Scientology uses today

---

[527] Janet Reitman, *Inside Scientology: The Story of America's Most Secretive Religion* (New York: Houghton Mifflin Harcourt Publishing Company, 2011), 49.

were developed at Saint Hill. His motivation was driven by the belief that his research would free humanity from all its ailments, and those around him were the first fruits of his work. By 1964, Hubbard had given thousands of lectures, solidified much of Scientology's auditing session techniques, and grew confident in his works and movement. So confident, in fact, that he granted an interview with a major newspaper after years of reluctance. The interview would later change the tide of Scientology forever.

Hubbard hoped that by giving an interview the world would see his new religion not as a hoax based on pseudoscience but as a legitimate faith grounded in real science. The interview was featured in the widely circulated *Saturday Evening Post* in 1964.[528] The article, which was published under the title "Have You Ever Been a Boo–Hoo?" by James Phelan, didn't paint Hubbard in the favorable, philanthropic light he had hoped for.[529] Instead, Phelan tore apart Hubbard's "strange new religion" by discrediting him within the first few sentences. Phelan revealed that Dr. L. Ron Hubbard's prestigious title was not a M.D. nor Ph.D. but was a fabricated *Doctor of Scientology* recognized only by those within the organization he founded himself. The article described Hubbard as an "old-time snake-oil peddler" who was narcissistic, naïve, and intentionally deceptive. It highlighted Hubbard's two failed marriages, an additional unaccredited Ph.D. to his "Sci.D." and his affinity for writing science fiction. The interviewer also joked that Hubbard's exaggerated predictions for the church's growth rate would result in eight billion members by March 1970.

The article was in no way flattering to Hubbard. Rather, it portrayed him as a lunatic who was misleading young people by presenting science fiction as truth. This enraged Hubbard. His contemporaries would later recall that

---

[528] James Phelan, "Have You Ever Been a Boo–Hoo?" *The Saturday Evening Post.* March 21, 1964.

[529] The title is a reference to Hubbard's theory that in previous existences, much of humanity was a pre-historic creature that secreted water from an organ. This is the explanation, Hubbard claimed, for why humans cry. Phelan writes: "The boo-hoo [...] was a clam-like animal that lived millions of years ago and used to pump sea water from its shell through its eyes. It marked the transition from life in the sea to life on land, and 'may be the missing link in the evolutionary chain.' Life on the beach was miserable for the boo-hoo; sometimes it would get stranded there, or even attacked by predatory birds. [...] According to Scientology, *you* may have been a boo-hoo, aeons ago. If you were, your personality has been affected by some of the awful things that happened to you as a clam on the beach at the dawn of time. When a Scientologist audits you, he may discover evidence of your life as a clam. He then processes this, which is called 'running the boo-hoo.' This makes you weep like a clam pumping sea water through its eyes, after which you feel better."

Hubbard was never the same after this interview.[530] He went from pleasant to perpetually angry and grew increasingly suspicious of the public eye. Part of his reaction to this interview was altering the way Scientology operated. He was no longer referred to as L. Ron Hubbard, but rather LRH – a stern, rigid moniker to match his new personality. Personal insult to Hubbard meant insult to the whole church as the two became synonymous in Hubbard's mind. His public rejection meant the church's public rejection. Something needed to change in order for the Church of Scientology and, ultimately, Hubbard to be taken seriously.

Two years after the interview, Hubbard forever altered the course of Scientology. He resigned as the executive director of the church and promoted himself to an even more powerful position. Hubbard was no longer acting as the head of the church but became the source of all revelatory knowledge itself, a position beyond the church's hierarchy. He essentially went from pope to savior. His first act was to write an authoritarian manifesto in which he declared himself to be the sole source of all Scientology knowledge. The document warned Scientologists that the entire future of humanity depended on their full dedication and attitude towards the church.

He called for tough and dedicated individuals to see past the social veneer of reality to assure the survival of Scientology. LRH criticized other organizations throughout history, claiming no group had ever accomplished anything it set out to do because their heart and soul were not completely devoted to their respective causes. All faiths, all religions, and all governments had failed to realize their goals because they had weak followers. LRH wanted tigers, not household cats.

To Hubbard, Scientology was not a game – it was serious business that required seriously devoted followers. The Church of Scientology had once lightly held the future of humanity in contempt, but no longer. They would fix it swiftly and with force, whether it wanted fixing or not. The new church was going to be different; focused instead of unfocused, disciplined instead of undisciplined, effective instead of ineffective. It would become a militaristic

---

[530] Janet Reitman, *Inside Scientology: The Story of America's Most Secretive Religion* (New York: Houghton Mifflin Harcourt Publishing Company, 2011), 59–63.

environment for the spreading of peace. To do so would require a new base of operations away from both the U.S. and the U.K.

Shortly after the release of the manifesto, Hubbard and his crew set sail for the African nation of Rhodesia in hopes of establishing a society (maybe even a country) based entirely on Scientology with him as its head of state.[531] When the Rhodesian government would not allow him continued entry, Hubbard decided the best option for the survival of Scientology (and himself) was freedom from the overbearing restrictions of all governments. The governments of the United States, Great Britain, Australia, and now Rhodesia were suspicious of Hubbard's motives and were creating a hostile environment for him to build his empire. So, he decided to relocate the church's research headquarters to a place where governments could not interfere, where he could research Scientology techniques and theology free from human authority – the ocean.

SCIENTOLOGY AT SEA

In 1966, Hubbard purchased three ships and set sail for North Africa from England. The fleet of Scientologists would spend the next ten years sailing from port to port while Hubbard developed some of the most controversial ideas in Scientology. It is also feasible to believe that Hubbard was provoked to set sail for distant lands out of a desire to remain secluded from the public eye after the embarrassing interview at Saint Hill. Reporters could not chase him down while at sea, and before the dawn of the internet, anonymity was almost guaranteed for those who chose the nautical life. Additionally, many Scientologists who sailed with Hubbard noted his desire to stay hidden away even from his own crew, not to be disturbed as he furiously researched and wrote the future of Scientology.[532]

The overarching association of this fleet was the Sea Organization, or Sea Org for short. Sea Org was more militaristic than the lackadaisical organizations on land. Members were subject to crisp uniforms, a rank

---

[531] Bent Corydon, *L. Ron Hubbard: Messiah or Madman?* (New York: Barricade Books, 1992), 45.
[532] Janet Reitman, *Inside Scientology: The Story of America's Most Secretive Religion* (New York: Houghton Mifflin Harcourt Publishing Company, 2011), 104.

structure, and a reward/punishment system.[533] Many of Scientology's members joined Sea Org because of its promise to bring about world peace, but they found themselves as part of a militaristic system they previously protested.[534] Hubbard was running more than a tight ship; he was creating a strict religion with defined boundaries, physical and mental demands, and unwavering faith in one charismatic leader. Sea Org quickly became the elite branch of the church, a status that has not changed to this day. In fact, once a Scientologist makes the decision to join, members of Sea Org sign a billion–year contract binding them to the organization in future lives when they reincarnate.[535] It is fair to say, Sea Org is not for the lukewarm Scientologist.

By 1967, Hubbard was the admiral of an entire Scientology fleet. Multiple ships followed his flagship, the *Apollo*, wherever LRH desired to travel. During this time, LRH seemed to become particularly fond of receiving inspiration for his research through the aid of alcohol and drugs. Writing home to his third wife, Mary Sue, Hubbard once admitted, "I'm drinking lots of rum and popping pinks and greys."[536] Aboard the *Apollo*, LRH spent most of his days in isolation researching and writing while the church on land continued to steadily grow.

The more he developed his ideas, the more he desired to market them and at a steep price as well. Some of these ideas included a type of product chain Hubbard referred to as "OT," short for Operating Thetan. Each OT was a different level at which a Scientologist could operate within a certain framework of existence. OT levels cost upwards of thousands of dollars in the 1970s and have only risen since. Scientologists were encouraged (even pressured) to get people off the streets, into the church, and climbing up the OT levels. What OT levels are, exactly, will be examined later in the chapter.

LRH's constant isolation inevitably began to change him. Although the interview at Saint Hill embittered Hubbard, he was still confident in his work and legacy. Nevertheless, his perspective and stability seemed to change after

---

[533] Hugh B. Urban, *The Church of Scientology: A History of a New Religion* (Princeton: Princeton University Press, 2011), 124.

[534] Janet Reitman, *Inside Scientology: The Story of America's Most Secretive Religion* (New York: Houghton Mifflin Harcourt Publishing Company, 2011), 58.

[535] Hugh B. Urban, *The Church of Scientology: A History of a New Religion* (Princeton: Princeton University Press, 2011), 125.

[536] Bent Corydon, *L. Ron Hubbard: Messiah or Madman?* (New York: Barricade Books, 1992), 59.

a few years at sea. He became increasingly paranoid, worse than he had been in the U.S. before relocating Scientology's headquarters to Saint Hill. Hubbard believed that the world was set against him. It was bent on suppressing his success and desired only to see Scientology fail. The world had already tried sending authorities after him and using the media to discredit him, but Hubbard had not quit.

Eventually, Hubbard hatched his most dangerous suspicion yet. He believed that the world would infiltrate the church itself, destroying it from the inside out. Hubbard became obsessed with this thought. At first, he retaliated against this imaginary confrontation by cleansing his own command structure. Members of any organization within the Church of Scientology, particularly those of Sea Org, were subject to random security checks, or Sec Checks, in which they were interrogated about their feelings towards LRH among other things.[537] Those found guilty during Sec Checks were immediately discharged from their duty. Hubbard had begun an inquisition.

Questions asked during Sec Checks were bizarre and reflected Hubbard's fascination with science fiction. They included inquiry into whether or not a person had enslaved a population, committed genocide, destroyed cultures and economies, stamped out religions, trapped thetans, or deprived people of hope. Interviewees were even asked if they had ever made a planet radioactive or if they had come to earth for evil purposes.[538]

Some questions prompted minuscule confessions of imperfections such as whether or not the interviewee had ever wasted time when they should not have. Sec Checks, with all their peculiar questions, had just enough 'normal' questions that would cause anyone to fail. For Scientologists who did fail, to include those who were found to have even minuscule negative thoughts towards LRH, punishment would follow.

Ultimately, Sec Checks brought about no security for Hubbard as his paranoia persisted. He needed to know more in order to put his worst fears to rest. He needed proof that the governments of the world were conspiring against him. As any good military commander knows, the only way to uncover

---

[537] Hugh B. Urban, "Fair Game: Secrecy, Security, and the Church of Scientology in Cold War America," *Journal of the American Academy of Religion* (June 2006): 374.
[538] Hubbard, L. Ron, HCO Bulletin of 19 JUNE 1961, *Sec Check Whole Track*

that sort of information is through precise and discreet operations. So Hubbard did just that – he ordered a precise and discreet operation.

OPERATION: SNOW WHITE

Operation: Snow White began as the Church of Scientology's infiltration into the U.S. government. Its purpose was to position key individuals in strategic places, keeping their ears to the ground and reporting anything they heard concerning Scientology back to Hubbard. The infiltration grew increasingly aggressive as the operation penetrated more and more facets of the government to include the FBI, CIA, and IRS. In fact, the operation became so aggressive that it went international. Snow White operatives were said to have infiltrated governments all over the world.[539] It was a huge success for LRH who was able to retrieve thousands of documents related to himself and the Church of Scientology.

The operation was eventually uncovered when, in 1976, Hubbard ordered two covert spies to infiltrate the U.S. Courthouse in Washington, D.C. Their mission was to enter the office of an assistant to the U.S. attorney's office who was currently investigating Scientology and copy any information they could find pertaining to the investigation. Later, one of the covert spies confessed his involvement with this mission to the FBI and fully cooperated with the impending investigation that ultimately shut down Operation: Snow White. In 1977, the FBI raided Scientology buildings in Los Angeles and Washington, D.C. to find tens of thousands of documents, all incriminating evidence which unveiled Hubbard's paranoia. The mastermind behind the operation would never be linked to it since his wife, Mary Sue, took the fall for coordinating and heading up the largest case of domestic espionage in U.S. history.[540]

After Operation: Snow White, Hubbard would spend the rest of his life in extreme isolation in the California desert at a secret location known only as "W" to Scientologists and the public alike. By the last six years of his life, he

---

[539] "Mystery of the Vanished Ruler," *TIME Magazine*, January 31, 1983, 54–56.
[540] Janet Reitman, *Inside Scientology: The Story of America's Most Secretive Religion* (New York: Houghton Mifflin Harcourt Publishing Company, 2011), 114.

had mastered hiding. Government officials, press agents, and even family members all searched for Hubbard in vain. He communicated to the outside world only through his personal aids. These members were Hubbard's eyes and ears, carrying out his will to those in the church. LRH took a particular liking to one aid, David Miscavige.

Miscavige had been with Sea Org when Hubbard was aboard the *Apollo* and had served the Church of Scientology faithfully since his sixteenth birthday. He was Hubbard's bulldog, his go–to man to get things done. When Hubbard died alone in 1986 at the age of seventy-four, Miscavige was the one to make the somber announcement to his fellow Scientologists. At twenty-five years of age, Miscavige became the new face of Scientology and has served in that capacity ever since.

WHAT DO SCIENTOLOGISTS BELIEVE?

To pinpoint the exact beliefs of Scientologists would be impossible. Remember, anyone from any theological background is welcomed into the organization. It is entirely possible to be a Buddhist, agnostic, or Muslim practicing Scientology so long as one accepts certain core beliefs taught by the church. Eventually, Scientologists who are working their way through Hubbard's spiritual technology will usually adopt a more unified worldview from one authoritative source as opposed to borrowing from multiple worldviews. This one authoritative source, Hubbard, is the spring from which much of the Scientology worldview flows.

Many Scientologists believe that everything they are taught through the church comes from the mind and pen of L. Ron Hubbard. In actuality, Hubbard generously borrowed from other minds such as psychologist Sigmund Freud and occultist Aleister Crowley. In fact, it is not too far a stretch to view Scientology as a mixture of those two men's life works. Freud's early work highlighted his theory of the two types of human memory, the *conscious* and *subconscious mind.* Hubbard simply rebranded this idea into *analytical* and *reactive minds,* respectively.

From Crowley's work, Hubbard drew upon his use of esoteric knowledge, from which one could gain their differing levels of understanding depending on the amount of time one spends studying. According to Crowley, the more one studies his school of esoteric thought, *Thelema*, the more they advance their spiritual maturity and understanding. Likewise, the more one studies Hubbard's school of thought, *Dianetics*, the more they advance their spiritual maturity and understanding. Hubbard also borrowed heavily from Crowley's *Book of the Law* which summarizes human morality in absolutes; "Do what thou wilt shall be the whole of the law."[541] Thus, Scientology is, at least initially, very tolerant of other worldviews.

At the core of Scientology's worldview is moral absolutism, the quest for one's personal truth. Each member must find what is true for him or her, and this is usually accomplished through the process of moving from the state of pre-Clear to Clear. The higher a Scientologist moves up the Operating Thetan (OT) levels, the closer they are to discovering who they truly are and what their truth really is; however, there is a big problem with this idea. Moral absolutism is generally subject to an individual's own feelings and is absent from any objective standard of truth. The old adage "what's true for me is true for me and what's true for you is true for you" begins to break down when taken to the logical extreme.

For example, what if the belief that all Scientologists were toads was true for me? Would that be true for all Scientologists? Perhaps all Scientologists who are toads would agree, but what of the human Scientologists? Truth is not subjective; rather, it is objective and sustained by the objective mind of God. Ironically, moral absolutism doesn't even fit within the framework of Scientology itself, as we will soon discover. In fact, Scientology makes truth claims about the origins of humanity that contradicts other worldviews whose adherents may be Scientologists themselves.

IDEAS UNIQUE TO SCIENTOLOGY

It is important to understand beliefs unique to Scientology before having a dialogue in the attempt to share the person and work of Jesus with a Scientologist. In relation to moral absolutism, most Scientologists generally

---

[541] Aleister Crowley, *The Book of the Law*, reissue ed. (Newburyport, Mass.: Samuel Weiser, 1987), 23.

believe that all of humanity is basically good and able to attain god–like 'being' and abilities. Dianetics therapy acts as an enabler to return humanity to their basically good state of being, regardless of their worldview. Therefore, Scientology could be described as an applied religious philosophy with techniques for improving social life, self-esteem, work productivity, etc. Until a Scientologist graduates from the state of pre-Clear, their worldview can remain as in tact as the moment they entered a Church of Scientology mission. Scientology only compliments their worldview with techniques to rid themselves of those pesky *engrams*.

Scientology also teaches that humans are more than a physical body that lives once and vanishes forever. Humans are immortal, spiritual beings with literally infinite capabilities. Death is looked at as the shedding of one body and donning of another in an infinite cycle of reincarnation. This is best demonstrated in David Miscavige's eulogy for L. Ron Hubbard in 1986 when he described Hubbard's passing this way; "The body [Hubbard] had used to facilitate his existence in this [...] universe had ceased to be useful, and in fact had become an impediment to the work he now must do outside of its confines."[542] To Scientologists, the essence of L. Ron Hubbard progressed beyond the bounds of his physical body, but Hubbard still exists in a spiritual form.

Because a human's thetan(s), or soul, forgets the previous life, Scientology allows humans to draw on past knowledge and experiences from previous lives through dianetics therapy. In essence, dianetics therapy "reminds" our souls of our past knowledge and unlocks thousands of lifetimes of collected experiences. To do this, one must rid themselves of the memories of repressive, oftentimes unconscious, previous life trauma (*engrams*) through auditing provided by the Church of Scientology. In fact, all psychosomatic issues in the human race can be traced back to previous life traumas that lie dormant in what LRH identified as the *reactive mind*, borrowing from Freud's *subconscious mind*.

Humans are beings with thousands and thousands of lifetimes worth of experiences that have simply been forgotten along with both good and bad

---

[542] Elisabeth Arweck, "Hubbard, L. Ron (*b. 1911; d. 1986*)," *Encyclopedia of New Religious Movements*, ed. Peter B. Clarke (Oxon, United Kingdom: Routledge, 2006), 284.

memories, which can serve to either aid or torment us. Inside every human being exists a never–ending fountain of knowledge and power that we must learn how to tap into and harness. Within each person is the power to create and destroy worlds; however, we have been suppressed into believing we are simple, lowly mortal beings with but one powerless life to live.

Scientology presents its spiritual technology as the only way out of this cyclical trap, and when applied correctly and perfectly in accordance to the writings of Hubbard, humanity can achieve a level of understanding and power that can only come from the experience gained over thousands of lifetimes.

SPIRITUAL TECHNOLOGY: HOW IT WORKS

Practicing the spiritual technology of Scientology begins with a process called *auditing*. As previously alluded to, auditing occurs with a pre-Clear's first official visit to a branch or mission of the Church of Scientology. It is a free clinical meeting with church representatives. Individuals engage in one-on-one counseling sessions with an approved Scientology auditor. Pre-Clears are taken to a private room where they sit at a table across from the approved Scientology auditor.

The pre-Clear is given two metal tubes attached by wire to the E-meter. The auditor then asks the pre-Clear a series of questions while the E-meter reads the physiological responses of the person being questioned, somewhat like a lie detector session. The auditor is looking for responses to potential *engrams* such as previous life trauma, fears, or psychological issues. Once the auditing session is complete, the auditor should be able to identify traumatic events in the pre-Clear's preexistence based on the findings of the E-meter.

This preexistent trauma is then presented to the pre-Clear as the source of most (if not all) of their problems in this life. Normally, these problems take the form of depression or a vague, melancholy state devoid of purpose or meaning. Most people finding themselves in auditing sessions at the Church of Scientology are looking for answers spurred on by feelings of loneliness or loss, so the Church takes advantage of those who need guidance and truth spoken into their lives. Associating the pre-Clear's unhappiness in this life with unfortunate events in their previous lives opens the auditor up to offering them the solution that worked for the auditor and countless other Scientologists before them.

Inevitably, the auditor will tell them the solution is not found in a church, hospital, or psychologist's office; rather, it is found in more auditing sessions through the Church of Scientology. This is the only way to further identify other preexistent trauma in hopes of ridding the pre-Clear of all their *engrams*. Thus, according to the Church of Scientology, the only way to cure the pre-Clear's depression or unhappy state of being is the Church of Scientology. Unlike the first auditing session, the advanced sessions are not free and by no means inexpensive. The auditing sessions also delve deeper into the privacy of the pre-Clear.

Sec Checks may be used in between a pre-Clear's initial auditing and their first level of OT auditing sessions. Although the Church of Scientology officially abandoned Sec Checks in 1968, allegations have been brought forward that the practice still remains under the guise of "Integrity Processing" or "Confessional Auditing," serving as a milestone in climbing the OT ladder of auditing.[543] Unfortunately, for aspiring Scientologists there is nothing confessional about the process. *Confessional* implies voluntary admission of private information. Conversely, Sec Checks are mandatory if the pre-Clear wishes for the Church of Scientology to clear them.

During a Sec Check, the pre-Clear is asked a series of questions regarding their life sins, wrong doings, and embarrassing secrets. At this point, they are told that the E-meter is a flawless, physiological detector – if they lie, the E-meter will detect it. The pre-Clear is also promised confidentiality; however, the allegations brought up against Sec Checks have been initiated from former Scientologists who discovered that the church was collecting Sec Check information for the purpose of blackmailing dissenters.[544] As the allegations go, Sec Checks delve deep into the pre-Clear's life and intentionally draw out pertinent details of their current or past character flaws for use in the church's gain.

---

[543]Hugh B. Urban, "Fair Game: Secrecy, Security, and the Church of Scientology in Cold War America," *Journal of the American Academy of Religion* (June 2006): 374.
Susan Raine, "Surveillance in New Religious Movements: Scientology as a Case Study," *Religious Studies and Theology* Vol 28, No 1 (London: Equinox Publishing, 2009), 63–94.
[544] Laura Ann DeCrescenzo v. Church of Scientology International, BC411018 (Sp. Ct. Cali. 2009).

THE ORIGINAL O.T.

The pre-Clear may officially graduate to become classified as a Clear after climbing through different pre-Clear grades of orientation in Scientology. This momentous (and expensive) feat is followed by another classification ladder to climb consisting of fifteen levels referred to as "Operating Thetan."[545] A *thetan* is the essence of a person or what one might refer to as a soul. Thus, if one can control their *thetan*, they will be able to *operate* as they were meant to from the moment they were born. The ultimate goal of a Scientologist is to achieve the highest Operating Thetan level of "Cleared Theta Clear."[546] An Operating Thetan, or OT, is a Clear who can operate separate from the physical body and at differing levels of abilities with differing levels of esoteric knowledge.

One such ability, out of body experiences, is possible through *exteriorization* that may be learned through self-auditing sessions.[547] (In fact, higher OT level Scientologists cannot progress through certain self-auditing sessions without the ability to perform exteriorization.) By this stage in climbing the OT ladder, Scientologists have mastered the concept of exteriorization as proof that humans are eternal, spiritual beings. How else could a material–only body exercise its will apart from the body? From this logic, Scientologists believe they maintain the ability to control their 'thetan–being' free from the body.

Among many things, OT level auditing is the practice of spiritual disciplines through esoteric knowledge at its finest. Scientologists of lower OT levels are forbidden from knowing higher–level information, since they must first progress through the ranks in order to learn the hidden secrets of Scientology. (Not only are lower–level Scientologists and outsiders forbidden from knowing higher–level OT information, Hubbard once claimed that it is

---

[545] Many allegations of fraud have been brought against the Church of Scientology in public court for the exuberant costs of pre-Clear and OT auditing. By one estimate, to simply become Clear (about 1/3 of the entire Scientology program to Total Clear) it will cost a member $128,000. http://www.sweenytod.com/cos/pricelist.html (Accessed Oct 25th, 2011).

[546] L. Ron Hubbard, *Scientology 8-8008: How to Increase Your Spiritual Ability from Zero to Infinity* (Los Angeles: Bridge Publications, 2007), 207. Note: At the OT level of "Cleared Theta Clear" the Scientologist should have the ability to psychically move matter, control others from a distance, and create his or her own universe.

[547] Michael P. Pattinson v. Church of Scientology International, et al., CV-98-3958 CAS (SHx).

dangerous to one's health knowing such information without first following the proper procedures.[548]) In a similar manner to the early Christian heresy of the Gnostics, Scientology speaks and teaches through a special form and code that is only decipherable through their own instruction. The promised benefit is a type of salvation – the highest state of Operating Thetan.

The problem with studying esoteric knowledge is that it's, well, esoteric. We cannot access it from the outside, which makes it very difficult to study for evangelism purposes. By its very definition, even if we wanted to, we could not examine it with the intention of comparing biblical knowledge (or any knowledge for that matter) with that of Scientology's teachings. Lucky for us in this case, we have the internet.

Much to the dismay of the church's executive leadership, Scientology was dealt a devastating blow in 2008 when thousands of pages of OT information were leaked to the public via the internet, making them accessible to anyone through a simple search engine request. The result of the leak was an overwhelming public opinion that the Church of Scientology tyrannically presides over a cult following by abusing its members and suppressing its critics through legal action. As activist Julian Assange, point man for the leak, noted months afterward, Scientology is, "not only an abusive cult, but [it also] aids and abets a general climate of western media self-censorship, due to the fear of litigation costs."[549]

Many of these leaked documents show OT levels as nothing more than inward reflection and self-counseling sessions with an added twist of dianetics therapy. There is very little difference between the desired results of both eastern meditation and Scientology auditing. Both promise salvation through secret knowledge, contemplation on that knowledge, and inward meditation in general. For the most part, OT levels are simply the combination of eastern meditation and secret knowledge. Nevertheless, while there are many OT levels that simply build on previous spiritual technology, one OT level stands

---

[548] Michael Browne, "Should Germany Stop Worrying and Love the Octopus? Freedom of Religion and the Church of Scientology in Germany and the United States," *Indiana International & Comparative Law Review* (Indiana University: Trustees of Indiana University). 9 Ind. Int'l & Comp. L. Rev. 155, 1998.
[549] Andrew Fowler, *The Most Dangerous Man in the World* (Carlton, Australia: Melbourne University Press, 2011), 81.

out above the rest with regard to esoteric knowledge – strange, bizarre, esoteric knowledge.

Operating Thetan III has in recent years been a major point of criticism for the Church of Scientology. To some, it is a laughable idea as popularized in the hit television series *South Park*. To others, it is the indisputable sign pointing to the obvious conclusion that L. Ron Hubbard was a science fiction writer who became a religious leader and nothing more. The truth may be a mix of both opinions, but one can only make that determination from studying the OT levels for themselves. However, since exposure to higher–level Operating Thetan information can be detrimental to one's health as Hubbard warned, it's my opinion that it should not be discussed in this book for our own safety.

...just kidding. Here's OT III.

THE ADVENTURES OF EVIL GALACTIC OVERLORD XENU

Around 5 million years ago there existed a galactic federation of planets which represented 76 member worlds.[550] Coincidentally, these 76 planets all rotate around stars visible from earth. The federation was booming, and peace reigned throughout this part of the galaxy thanks to economic and political accord. However, despite its economic success, the galactic federation began to experience issues with overcrowding on all 76 planets. Each planet buckled under the weight of 178–250 billion inhabitants. Something needed to be done, so the head of the galactic federation devised a solution.

The answer would become far more sinister than any of the galactic federation citizens could ever imagine. A majority of the citizens were to be murdered, and their thetan (soul) subjected to "mass implanting," a process by which the thetans would be reeducated in order for them to forget everything they had witnessed. This would remove them from their home planets and physical bodies forever, thus curbing the overpopulation problem. To achieve this, the government lured them into a trap by mandating a new tax to be paid in person. None of the citizens ever saw it coming.

---

[550] This section is the interpretation of OTIII through the author's understanding and is not meant to reflect an exact recount of this information. Exact accounts of OTIII have been leaked into the public domain.

Having captured the target number of victims, the leader of the galactic federation forced the chosen "mass implanting" thetans to be relocated to the planet *Teegeeack*, a planetary body we contemporaneously refer to as "earth." This planet would serve as the perfect location to imprison the victims. He would implant dreadful memories and experiences into the thetans through mass implanting, strip them of their bodily existence, and impassively depart the planet while the remnants of a once flourishing galactic federation wandered aimlessly in a foreign desert of despair for all eternity.

Just when injustice seemed to reign supreme, there were murmurings of avenging this atrocity among some in positions of leadership who objected to the ruthless overlord. These brave few persuaded enough evil renegades to side with their cause. Soon, they had enough conspirators to seek revenge for this galactic injustice. But it was too late – the plan was already in motion, and the prisoners were being transported to Teegeeack. Nonetheless, a rebellion was brewing while the despot was away at Teegeeack. His people knew this malicious dictator as simply *Xenu*.

Xenu. The name should send shivers down the spine of everyone who reads these words since, in our previous lives, we all experienced the merciless actions that Xenu inflicted on billions of innocent people. He cruelly terminated their lives by transporting them to one of two locations on Teegeeack – those assigned to the Pacific region were transported to Hawaii and those assigned to the Atlantic region were transported to Las Palmas. Xenu then ordered every captive being to be situated at the base of volcanoes and blown up with H-Bombs.

When the thetans arose from their dead bodies, Xenu captured them in devices specifically designed to trap them. Each thetan was then transported to mass implant facilities where they were forced to watch hours upon hours of endless 3D film about a fictitious reality – religion, culture, economy, philosophy, art, and music were replayed over and over again until it was permanently implanted into the thetans. Most notable among these fictitious realities was the existence of God, the form of God in the physical person of Jesus Christ, and his death, burial, and resurrection.

Upon their release from the processing centers, the thetans began to combine into larger thetans until each mega–thetan consisted of a few hundred thousand individual thetans. These mega–thetans wandered Teegeeack until finding bodies they could inhabit. The mega–thetans would find new bodily existence in a peculiar mammal, the Neanderthal. Due to the possession of the mega–thetans, the process of evolution for these Neanderthals was quickened, and they eventually evolved into modern humans.

As for Xenu, he paid for his crimes. When he returned to his home planet, he was met by a valiant remnant of the galactic federation in rebellion against him. They rose against their evil oppressor and toppled his iron–fisted reign. The rebel alliance captured and incarcerated Xenu after a six-year military campaign. Ironically, his prison would be in a mountain. An electronic device bound him there, which is not unlike the way he destroyed all those innocent lives. With mountains he destroyed billions of lives, and by a mountain he remains a prisoner to this day.

Because of this one being, all of our problems may find their origin. Xenu created the idea of war and hate in the human soul. Xenu created the idea of socio–economic upheaval through associating money with power. Xenu even created the controversial figure Jesus Christ, who would mislead millions and millions of people into believing that they were fallen beings in desperate need of a savior.

Hubbard clarified this when he stated his undoubted belief in a Christ figure, explaining the reason that this Christ figure existed is because of the assistance he was given due to an implant.[551] This fictional character is nothing more than a delusion. In fact, the man who claimed to be Jesus two millennia ago was simply a human so susceptible to the implant of the Jesus idea that he became programmed to believe he was Jesus. He was simply a robot Jesus.

SCIENTOLOGY AND THE DANGEROUS APPEAL

Dianetics, Xenu, engrams, Teegeeack, the Galactic Federation, auditing; this all sounds like the stuff science fiction is made of. Why would anyone believe it? That may be a great question, but nonetheless we are faced with the Church of Scientology as a real and powerfully influential worldview. What is it that attracts people to Scientology? Aside from Scientology borrowing from

---

[551] L. Ron Hubbard, Philadelphia Doctorate Courses, Lecture 24 (1952).

eastern meditation and its surface–level tolerance of all people, what makes Scientology so attractive is esoteric knowledge.

Human beings have an insatiable appetite for privileged knowledge previously withheld from them. There is no greater feeling for self-worth and self-esteem than knowing information others do not. Think about it. Be honest for a moment, don't we feel great when telling someone for the first time that we're engaged, we're pregnant, we won a major award, we got a new job, etc.? We love knowing something others don't; while this is not necessarily a bad thing, our nature usually prefers the negative aspect of withholding or dispensing information intentionally for our own selfish benefit. This, of course, is the appeal of gossip.

If information is power, then esoteric knowledge is preeminence. Throughout the ages various religious, political, and social leaders have employed secret knowledge to affirm their place of authority. Knowing something others do not, especially when it is believed that the secret knowledge ushers a person into a better state of being, is immensely satisfying. It wields the ability to define a person simply by what they know instead of what they have done. As the old playground taunt goes, "I know something you don't know!"

This is nothing new as the desire to learn secret knowledge has been a weakness of humanity from the beginning. Case in point: the first sin of Adam.

> Now the serpent was more crafty than any other beast of the field that the LORD God had made. He said to the woman, "Did God actually say, 'You shall not eat of any tree in the garden?' And the woman said to the serpent, "We may eat of the fruit of the trees in the garden, but God said, 'You shall not eat of the fruit of the tree that is in the midst of the garden, neither shall you touch it, lest you die.'" But the serpent said to the woman, "You will not surely die. For God knows that when you eat of it your eyes will be opened, and you will be like God, knowing good and evil."[552]

Note that the reward for Adam and Eve's rebellion was the promise of "knowing good and evil." This was information previously withheld from them. It was esoteric knowledge they had been missing out on until know. The enemy presented the knowledge of good and evil as hidden knowledge that would unlock powers formerly unknown to them.

Moreover, they selfishly disobeyed the will of God by pursuing their own will to receive the hidden knowledge. This was selfish because they believed they could do a better job of progressing their lives than God. Ultimately, it was their selfish action outside the will of God, the idea that they did not need him to progress in any measure, which was sinful.[553] They ceased to worship God and started worshiping themselves. Sadly, as with most people today, our first parents surrendered to the lie that secret knowledge would act as a better god than the Creator and sustainer of all knowledge.

At the end of the day, there is nothing new about the appeal of Scientology. The church has simply redeployed the same technique from the Garden that promised divinity, or the ability to become godlike, through esoteric knowledge as well as their own actions such as auditing. The serpent's formula (esoteric knowledge + selfish action = divinity) is the same formula Scientology employs (OT knowledge + auditing = Cleared Theta Clear). The primary difference between the Garden and the Church of Scientology temptation is the end result.

While both promise a higher state of being, as the serpent promised the knowledge of God and Scientology promises the knowledge of countless lifetimes, Adam was starting from a different place than all potential Scientologists and was hoping for a different result. This is because Adam had walked with God, whereas people today are far from him. Adam knew God, but people today rarely have even a concept of him. Adam wanted to be co-equal in knowledge with God, but because people today have never known God they want to usurp him. Thus, Scientology begins its enticement by teaching that every person is a potentially perfect being awaiting the call or challenge to return to a state of perfection.

To be fair, there is a bit of truth to this idea. We were created in God's image and will one day exist in a state of perfection in Christ. This is not accomplished through something we know (esoteric knowledge) but through something he did (life, death, burial, resurrection). Unlike what Scientology

---

[552] Gen. 3:1–5
[553] Gen. 3:14, "Because you have *done this…*"

teaches, the only way to truly obtain perfection is through Jesus. We lack the ability in and of ourselves to accomplish anything beyond ethical or moral discipline which, even then, inevitably fails from time to time.

POISON IN A MEDICINE BOTTLE

Scientology continues its enticement by teaching potential and new members that they do not need God to achieve a state of divinity because they themselves are "god" or god–like. The highest level of OT, Cleared Theta Clear, comes with the ability to psychically manipulate space and time, control others from a distance, and create a universe by one's own power.[554] One of the easiest ways to manipulate someone into denying God is convincing them that they are god, that they are the source of salvation, and that they can achieve a state of salvation on their own. This is the dual–aspect approach of Scientology's appeal: (1) teach people they do not need God and already have individual power from within because (2) they themselves are a god.

Above any doctrine of Scientology, this is one deserving of our upmost attention, as it is perhaps the most pervasive and influential teaching of the church and subtly broadcasted through its celebrity outlet. As Christians, we understand that we are not God and we can never become God. In the Gospels, Jesus reiterates this truth by identifying what he considered as the most important command of God; "Hear, O Israel: The Lord our God, the Lord is one. And you shall love the Lord your God with all your heart and with all your soul and with all your mind and with all your strength."[555] This demands our entire posture of worship and negates any selfish, sinful desire of ever becoming the focus of worship.

The key to understanding depression, sadness, anxiety, and sin is not through the idea that humans are gods trapped in mortal bodies. This dangerous idea actually accomplishes the exact opposite of what it sets out to accomplish. Believing we are gods logically concludes with our selfish demand for worship. If we look to worship ourselves and not God, then we

---

[554] L. Ron Hubbard, *Scientology 8-8008: How to Increase Your Spiritual Ability from Zero to Infinity* (Los Angeles: Bridge Publications, 2007), 207.
[555] Mark 12:29–30

continue the downward spiral of tapping into the wrong source for healing and salvation. This is because we make really terrible gods.

In fact, if you think about it, this is how terrible we are at being gods – we can actually be tricked into believing that the same being that stumbled into depression, sadness, worries, and sin can pull us out. It's just as absurd to imagine a lifeguard saving themself from drowning or a paramedic reviving themself from cardiac arrest. This is because all sin issues are not actually problems with sin; rather, they're problems with worship.

All sin issues start out as worship issues.[556] This is why the first commandment is to have no other gods besides God.[557] If humans do not worship God, they will inevitably worship something or someone else since we were all designed to incessantly worship. It is not a matter of *if* we will worship but *what* or *whom* we will worship. Scientology proposes we worship ourselves as a god; through the acknowledgement and understanding of our own deity, we may discover the source of infinite power and wisdom within ourselves.

This leads down a rabbit hole of disappointment and destruction, as we are not sources of power and wisdom. Instead, we were designed to be recipients and vessels of God's gracious gifts through his love and grace. We cannot act as both the source and recipient of what every human being deeply desires, a restored and sustained relationship with the creator God. Human beings are bankrupt to fulfill themselves in joy and grace. We stand in desperate need of something from outside ourselves, not from within.

The moment we realize we are not God but we were created to worship God, we begin to see the effects of sin on the world and in ourselves. We start to realize our own impotency to lift ourselves above the fallenness of this world. And just the opposite is true. The moment we believe we are gods deserving of worship, we are blinded to the effects of sin in the world and invent all sorts of ideas of fixing the world and ourselves. These ideas inevitably lead to anything and everything besides worshiping God, following the Holy Spirit, and sharing Jesus, who is the only cure for what ails the

---

[556] Mark Driscoll and Gerry Breshears, *Doctrine: What Christians Should Believe* (Wheaton, Illi.: Crossway Books, 2010), 346.
[557] Exod. 20:3

human soul. This is the dangerous appeal to Scientology – poison in a medicine bottle.

THE GOSPEL IN DIALOGUE WITH SCIENTOLOGISTS

Getting the opportunity to share the gospel with Scientologists may be few and far between since they are a very rare breed. The Church of Scientology has fewer members than officially reported, which means our encounters with them may be limited. While the Church of Scientology reports membership in the millions, these figures include one–time visitors, supporters of the church, and lapsed members. A more conservative estimate of active Scientologists is somewhere between 25,000 and 75,000 in the U.S.[558] According to these numbers, a conservative estimation reveals that the Southern Baptist Convention is about 166 times the size of the entire Church of Scientology in the U.S.[559] So, this begs the question – why bother learning about such a small group?

What Scientology lacks in size it makes up for in influence. This is because the church is extraordinarily popular and influential in Hollywood celebrity circles. Celebrities are given (whether deserved or not) a substantial amount of influence on the big screen, television, and through other outlets such as social media. Tom Cruise, John Travolta, Nancy Cartwright, Beck, Jason Lee, Katie Holmes, Kirstie Alley, and Lisa Marie Presley are just among a few of the many celebrity Scientologists who are active members at the time of this book's writing. Among other perks, these celebrities are privileged to meet and fellowship at the Celebrity Centre International in Los Angeles, a clear acknowledgement of their high status in this culture. They are glorified within the Church of Scientology for one, obvious reason – they wield influence.

Thus, despite Scientology's meager population they have astonishing influence over Western culture. The power of Scientology is not in numbers, but in influence. Because Scientology has perhaps the closest direct influence

---

[558] Fred A. Bernstein, "In Pasadena, a Model for Scientology's Growth Plan," *The New York Times*, http://www.nytimes.com/2010/11/10/business/10scientology.html (accessed October 30, 2011)
[559] Executive Committee of the Southern Baptist Convention, *Annual of the 2007 Southern Baptist Convention: 150th Session, 162nd Year.* (San Antonio, Texas: 2007), 110.

to Hollywood celebrity culture, more so than most other religions, Christians wishing to share Jesus with Scientologists or those influenced by Scientology need to adopt the best method of doing so.

So, what is the best method? First, it's best not to dwell on the oddities of Scientology. Scientologists have not enjoyed positive limelight in the past few decades; their worldview, particularly that of OT III, is often the butt of many jokes. Remember, Scientologists invest immense amounts of personal wealth and resources for information the public may consider absurd. It isn't absurd to them. Beginning a conversation with Xenu and Teegeack is not the best idea. In fact, it may be perceived as antagonistic. It is far better to steer clear of ridicule or deconstructing their sci-fi–laden beliefs in favor of sticking to the perception Scientology has of the person and work of Jesus, especially his love and redemptive grace.

In fact, Jesus is the best place to start. Because most Scientologists' first exposure to Scientology is through *Dianetics*, it may be fruitful to give them a copy of the New Testament and ask them to read it with the same open mind with which they read *Dianetics*. Ask them to pay particular attention to the life and words of Jesus throughout the Gospels; encourage them specifically to read the Gospel of John since it contains much of Jesus' sayings. This might spark rich conversation considering Scientologists live in a world of teachings and sayings. They are very comfortable reading and processing the written words of one man, so asking them to do the same with Jesus may be interesting for them. Invite them to write down any differences they see between what Jesus and LRH taught and arrange to discuss these differences over coffee or dinner.

During these discussions, don't be surprised if vocabulary presents a communication issue. Scientologists will most likely be unfamiliar with terms such as *salvation* or *atonement* when discussing salvation. Depending on the Scientologist we are sharing Jesus with, they may have never heard words or concepts we use in everyday speech. Likewise, they will use terms we may be unfamiliar with such as *theta* for soul, *affinity* for love, *dynamic* for aspiration, *somatic* for pain or fallenness, etc. For this reason, we must strive to find a common vocabulary from which to dialogue.

When possible, we should substitute terms they may be more familiar with; however, always remember to define those terms at the outset. Try to contextualize where appropriate but stand ground when it is necessary. For example, after explaining what we mean by certain Scientology terminology, it may be beneficial to tell a Scientologist that God's *affinity* for humanity was so great that he sent his only son to overcome our *somatic* state of being and reunite us with him. However, we must correct the Scientology belief that we eternally exist as *thetans*. Rather, our being consists of one, unified soul. This is why it is so important to define, and regularly redefine, terms being used during dialogue.

Eventually these terms should be replaced, as they will carry with them resonances of Scientology if they leave the Church. Initially using terms from Scientology may be helpful explaining the gospel, but in the long run they may be harmful. Nevertheless, finding common ground aides us in the conversation, and finding such ground within the teachings of Scientology itself may provide the best opportunity to verify some aspects of their worldview as true. Which, to be fair, some aspects of Scientology are true. The conclusions of that truth are the issue at hand.

The problem with Dianetics and Scientology is not their observations but the conclusions of those observations. LRH eloquently wrote that humans experience various forms of pain in their lives because they have not reached their full potential. "[Mankind's] ethical and moral standards are high, his ability to seek and experience pleasure is great. His personality is heightened and he is creative and constructive."[560] Hubbard is exactly right – this is the way God designed all humans; as image bearers of God who are ethical, moral, revelers in righteous pleasure, and immensely creative among other traits. Where Scientology gets it wrong is in Hubbard's conclusion that returning to this state of perfection will serve to better *ourselves*, unlock *our* potential, and return us to *our* godlike eminence. We can be perfect worshipers of ourselves.

Christianity likewise desires to return humanity to a state not unlike what Hubbard describes but for very different reasons. We desire to reach our maximum potential of eternal glory so that we may worship and praise the God who created us and restored us. We owe it all to God and nothing to

---

[560] L. Ron Hubbard, *Dianetics: The Modern Science of Mental Health* (Los Angeles: Bridge Publications, Inc., 2007), 208.

ourselves.[561] To contextualize this in terms of Scientology, God created us in the state of Clear free from any engrams. He did this not so we could maximize our godlike potential but that we may worship God freely, fully, and faithfully. Adam was a Clear, but he chose to sin. He was subjected to the residue of sin, a type of engram. Ever since our expulsion from the garden, humans have been trying to become Clear again through our own methods and means with Scientology among them. God, on the other hand, has been saving us through faith in him and his works.[562]

Stress this to Scientologists – God has made the way to salvation for us; we don't have to climb the ladder of esoteric knowledge. The gospel, unlike Hubbard's works, is free information that proclaims Jesus as our savior from our own fallenness through faith alone, absent of any work we could ever do to add to our own salvation. Scientologists have been paying and working to hear a message of salvation for as long as they have been searching. They need to know that the robot Jesus of their faith is nowhere near the truth of who he really is. We need to introduce Scientologists to the savior Jesus who freely provides life–giving information, grace, love, and mercy to those who simply ask. They need to know that savior Jesus wants nothing more for us than to be free from the chains of bondage and works.

---

[561] Eph. 2:8–9
[562] Eph. 2:4–5

CHAPTER SIX

The Gospel & Savior Jesus

"I am the way, and the truth, and the life.
No one comes to the Father except through me."

JESUS OF NAZARETH, JOHN 14:6

Last year, my brother and I went on a pilgrimage to Santiago de Compostela in Spain. No, this isn't 1148CE nor were we trying to work off some venial sins. We just thought it would be something fun to do together. We weren't looking for anything paradigm shifting to occur as far as our spiritual lives were concerned. Instead, having not spent that much time together in many years, we just wanted to hang out with each other and get to know one another better. But, as is usual with God, I walked away from that week on *el camino* with more than I had anticipated. He challenged me to sharpen my understanding of the gospel and savior Jesus, something I'm not sure I'll ever finish in this lifetime.

It started when my brother and I met a guy who was doing the pilgrimage solo for spiritual reasons, somewhat of an ironic rarity on a once flourishing spiritual superhighway of the Roman Catholic Church. He was Catholic and was very interested in Catholic missions and evangelism. So, naturally, we struck up a few conversations on mission strategies and evangelism. Sometime during our discussion, I voiced my opinion that I hadn't seen much by way of missions or evangelism from Rome.

"I'm not sure the Catholic Church is doing the best they can to spread the gospel," I said, afraid I might have unintentionally offended him. But, he knew my tone was genuine. "Well," he responded with a smile, "it depends on what you mean by 'gospel.' As a Catholic, I am persuaded to believe that wherever the church is, the gospel is there as well. In that instance, the gospel hasn't stopped being spread by the Catholic Church; rather, people have just stopped caring about it. So, instead of trying to spread the gospel, we need to work on making it relevant to today's audience so that they will care."

This was a very curious definition of 'gospel,' one I hadn't heard before. According to him, the gospel is dispensed through the brick-and-mortar institution of the Roman Catholic Church. Where the Church is, there the gospel also resides. The two are inseparable. Accordingly, the gospel is primarily present wherever the church is. Jesus established an institution with the responsibility of dispensing the message of his love. Therefore, the gospel is dependent on the survivability of a religious institution.

This conversation brought to mind many other definitions of the gospel I had heard throughout the year. Months before we embarked on the pilgrimage, I recall reading articles from evangelical magazines, books, and journals about new Christian movements forming on the premise that the church should *be* the gospel rather than *preach* the gospel. This idea has sparked a movement of Christian missions across North America with terms like *missional, holistic,* and *organic* used to describe the church. This movement is known, more or less, as the emerging church movement. One influential emerging author and theologian visited Cambridge while my wife and I lived there. He was touring the U.K. for a new book release that was causing quite a stir among evangelicals. We decided to go in part because of the controversy that surrounded this author at the time.

During his talk, he summarized the gospel as the message that God's love will eventually win over all sin, evil, and tyranny regardless of humanity's participation. As he explained, the gospel is not something found in a brick-and-mortar institution but something lived in the lives of Christians (and others whether they know it or not). The gospel is action rather than message, although the gospel includes the message of God's love.

After hearing him speak, we walked outside of the building to head home when we heard a shouting voice echoing off the building walls. We walked towards the sound to find a crowd of people surrounding a street preacher on a soapbox – literally. He held signs and passed out leaflets about how the author we had just heard was going to hell for preaching false doctrine and espousing a false gospel. We were all sinners, the man declared, and needed the gospel as the cure for our rebellion towards God. However, never once did he explain what he meant by the gospel.

The street preacher reminded me of an email exchange I had with a notorious church a few years back. At the time, the congregation was a bit unknown, but they were up-and-coming as one of the most readily identified hate–groups in America. The congregation became notorious for picketing U.S. soldiers' funerals, protesting all manner of government and private events, being particularly unfriendly towards homosexuals, and always displaying hateful, gaudy signs that were obviously designed by a 4th grader with access to Microsoft Publisher 97™.

During the exchange, I asked why they had decided to protest public and private events in such an outlandish manner under the banner of Jesus. They replied that to understand God, one must understand how much he hates humanity. According to this group, the gospel is the message that God is infuriated with humanity and wants nothing more than to destroy them unless, of course, one was to join their church. In that case, you're good to go. But, ultimately, the gospel is a declaration that humanity is sinful and will experience God's wrath unless they repent and join the ranks of their congregation. Oh, and they also addressed me as "Kyle-Most-Vile." So, you know, that was nice.

This all got me thinking, especially during my time on the pilgrimage – what is the gospel? I know what it is in essence, Jesus' message of salvation. But there are so many definitions of the gospel, I think it would be wise for every follower of Jesus to step back, take a breath, and ask ourselves, "What do I believe the gospel is?" This is particularly true within the context of this book. Without a firm grasp of the gospel, how can we share Jesus with members of rival worldviews? Besides, if the gospel is truly a message Jesus wants us to deliver to the world, shouldn't it be something we have a firm grasp of?

WHAT THE GOSPEL ISN'T

I think it's always wise to first understand what something is *not* before understanding what something *is*. People can create many different ideas and interpretations of something to a point where it's almost unrecognizable from what it actually is. In this instance, the gospel has become something unrecognizable, even to some Christians, because it has been redefined, rebranded, and revamped so many times that the original intent can be hidden behind a variety of different façades. It can also be twisted to conform to the theology of an individual, a movement, or an entire worldview as is the case with the rival worldviews discussed in this book. So, what is the gospel *not*?

First off, the gospel is not primarily bad news. This is something I think many Christians struggle with. The gospel shouldn't start and end with "you're a sinner." That's what the law is for (the Ten Commandments, parts of Exodus, the entirety of Leviticus, etc.). It is a mirror to reflect our inadequacy in living up to God's standards. The law was never intended to be followed perfectly for salvation because that would be impossible. Only one man has ever lived a flawless life by the law, and that was Jesus. (In fact, this makes the gospel all about Jesus and not the individual precisely because he is the originator and model gospel deliverer.) If the law points out our inadequacy to fulfill God's standards of perfection, it then logical deems that we are somehow broken, corrupted, or fallen.

Most people recognize that the world is fallen. They will at least consent that "to err is human," and by that logic we are error prone. But how did we get this way? The simple answer is sin. We are sinful creatures. More so we are sinful by birth as will be demonstrated later in the chapter. The important thing to know now is that people usually have some idea that they are fallen, missing the mark, or sinful. Generally speaking, they do not need to be reminded of their sin, especially when being convicted by the Holy Spirit during evangelism.

The gospel mentions the fact that we are fallen but also declares that we don't have to remain fallen forever. When sewing salvation into the fabric of the human soul, the truth that we are sinners is the needle while the gospel acts as the thread.[563] The truth must first pierce our heart, but the gospel must immediately follow in order to fill the hole. This is why the gospel is called good news, and not bad news, even though the bad news precedes the good. We can't simply pierce the heart and leave the hole. We must also thread the gospel through the heart in order to bolster an individual's hope and joy in the salvation offered by God through Jesus.

With that said, some people don't realize they are fallen and have a sin issue. This requires a whole different set of conversations. Since some people

---

[563] C. H. Spurgeon, "Sin and Grace" (sermon, Metropolitan Tabernacle, Newington, November 1, 1874).

don't believe they have a sin problem, why should they care that Jesus can take away their sin? Sharing the gospel with people who don't believe they need saving may seem fruitless, but this is a whole different topic to explore. When we evangelize to members of rival worldviews, they generally believe that they are flawed and in need of salvation.

Secondly, the gospel is not primarily a call to missions or works. These aspects of the Christian life come after conversion and are a result of someone fully understanding and accepting the gospel. Jesus didn't come to earth to preach a message of caring for the poor, seeking after social justice, and watching after orphans; although, his message most certainly included such challenges. Good works are important, but they're not the point. Good works are the fruit the gospel tree bears. Without planting the gospel tree first, the fruit may never come along; if it does, it won't be rooted in anything.

Does this mean the gospel should not call Christians to declare sin when seen, work when a need arises, or generally promote a better society? Of course not. The Christian church should be inundated with missions to be salt and light in this fallen world; however, this is not the primary purpose of the gospel. The gospel changes people's lives to be open to the challenges Jesus calls us to. Without the gospel, our works are near meaningless. Of course, they'll mean something to someone, but on the grand scale of things no one ever became a Christian simply because they received a cup of soup at a homeless shelter. They became a Christian by the power of the Holy Spirit,[564] the election and drawing of God the Father,[565] and hearing the gospel of Jesus.[566]

Missions work (showing people God's love and grace) in addition to hearing the gospel (evangelism) is the formula through which the Holy Spirit convicts and converts. Remember, it isn't our job to bring people to Jesus – that's entirely the Holy Spirit's responsibility. Our job is to ensure the gospel is being preached clearly, articulately, and accurately. If this means showing people love through works in order to be heard, then we should jump on missions opportunities. Nevertheless, works do not make Christians – hearing the gospel preached does.

---

[564] Titus 3:5–7
[565] John 6:44; 14:6

So, to summarize;

The gospel is not:

- About the individual
- Bound by a brick-and-mortar institution
- Something performed or acted out
- A message spread from a soapbox
- A primarily negative message of sinfulness

The gospel is:

- All about Jesus
- Carried all over the world through spirit–filled Christians
- Something which produces good works and actions
- A message spread through relationships (family, friends, community)
- A primarily positive message of redemption

WHAT THE GOSPEL IS

This leaves us with the question of what the gospel *is*. The word 'gospel' comes from the old English *gōd-spell*, which literally means *good news*. This was, in turn, derived from the Greek *euangelion* (*eu-* "good", -*angelion* "message"). Paul uses this term to describe Jesus' message of salvation in 1 Corinthians 15:1; "Now I would remind you, brothers, of the gospel (*euangelion*) I preached to you, which you received, in which you stand."

The gospel is a message, the good news that Jesus came to live the life we could not live, die the death we should have died, and impart that life to us.[567] We need this because as members of humanity we are by nature children in rebellion from God.[568] We all deserve our due penalty for our sin, but God has graciously and mercifully provided the way for reconciliation for all of

---

[566] John 3:16–18
[567] Gal. 4:4–5; Matt. 5:17; John 10:10; Rom. 5:17; 8:3–4
[568] Rom. 3:9–12; Eph. 2:5

humanity.[569] The result is an eternity in perfect community with God, which begins the moment we have faith in this message by his grace.[570]

This reconciliation was accomplished through the second person of the Trinity, Jesus.[571] He took upon himself the nature of humanity so that he could be charged with the penalty of humanity's sin.[572] By living a perfect and blameless life, he satisfied the need for the law and divine justice of God to be met in our penalty for us.[573] Now, as our head prophet, priest (mediator), and king, Jesus freely offers to all of humanity atonement and justification before God for reconciliation and restored, eternal community with him through adoption into his family.[574] For those who receive Jesus' gracious gift, they will be resurrected in body and soul when he returns, in order that they may live in perfect, sustained, and eternal community with God.[575]

The gospel is a message, not an action. We cannot live the gospel, but we can live in a way that reflects the gospel. It is a life–giving decree given to humanity by God's grace and was first given through Jesus. It is now spread through his messenger people who, at some point in their life, received that exact same message. Ultimately, the gospel is a message of grace given to us by the savior Jesus, and is rooted in his person and work.

WHO IS SAVIOR JESUS?

I've frequently referred to the "person and work" of Jesus throughout this entire book but have intentionally waited until the last chapter to define what I mean. This is because studying the Jesuses of rival worldviews gives us caricatures of Jesus so that we may compare each of them to the real, savior Jesus. The *person* of Jesus is defined in his character – the second person of the Trinity,[576] loving,[577] serving,[578] strong,[579] mediating,[580] forgiving,[581] etc.

---

[569] Rom. 6:23; Heb. 4:16
[570] John 3:16
[571] Eph. 2:16; Col. 1:20–22
[572] Isa 53:4–5; Rom. 5:19; Phil. 2:5–8
[573] Rom. 3:23–26; 2 Cor. 5:21
[574] Mark 6:4; John 18:37; 1 Tim. 2:5; Heb. 4:14–16; 2 Pet. 1:11; Rev. 1:5
[575] 1 Cor. 15:21–22
[576] John 1:1,14; 8:58–59
[577] John 15:13; Eph. 5:2
[578] John 13:5

The *work* of Jesus is defined in what he has done, is doing, and will do – mediator,[582] prophet,[583] priest,[584] king,[585] creator,[586] rabbi,[587] blameless god–man,[588] sacrifice,[589] preeminent in the resurrection,[590] revenger,[591] justifier,[592] judge,[593] etc. This Jesus gives, serves, and loves freely without expecting any work on our part. He demands our devotion but only after accepting his person and his work first (although, every person will accept his leadership eventually). The Jesuses of rival worldviews do not fit the description of any of these character attributes or works, but they all have one thing in common – these Jesuses demand something in exchange for his love, affection, and devotion. Unlike savior Jesus, the Jesuses of rival worldviews demand works in exchange for salvation.

Big Brother Jesus of Mormonism demands the work of obedience to the Mormon ordinances. Archangel Jesus of the Jehovah's Witnesses demands a ridged lifestyle of denying social life and the work of door-to-door evangelism. Silver Medal Jesus of Islam demands strict adherence to the Qu'rān and the Five Pillars of Islam for just a *chance* at being with God one day. Robot Jesus of Scientology demands that we climb a never–ending ladder of esoteric knowledge causing tremendous financial and social strain.

Works. Every Jesus of every rival worldview in existence demands works. In fact, the four rival worldviews presented in this book have more in common with each other than they do with orthodox Christianity. This makes orthodox Christianity the most revolutionary, mind–boggling, unique worldview and faith in existence; where every other worldview demands works and where every other Jesus requires works for his love, the Jesus of scripture requires nothing and dispenses faith and grace to the glory of God

---

[579] Rev. 19:11–16
[580] 1 Tim. 2:5; Luke 23:34
[581] Luke 7:48
[582] 1 Tim. 2:5
[583] Acts 3:22
[584] Heb. 5:5
[585] Luke 1:33
[586] John 1:2–4
[587] Mark 12:35; John 18:20
[588] Matt. 3:15; 5:17
[589] Rom. 3:25; 5:19; Eph. 5:2; Heb. 9:14
[590] Col. 1:18
[591] Matt. 13:40–43; Jude 6
[592] Rom. 3:24; 5:1

and no one else. This is the fundamental and revolutionary difference between Christianity and every other worldview – grace.

We could summarize the whole gospel in that one word. Grace. It is the ebb and flow of God's salvation narrative as seen throughout the entire Bible. God showed humanity grace in the Garden when, after we rebelled against him, he kicked us out so that we did not have access to eternal life while in our rebellious state.[594] Instead, we have access to eternal life through the redemption of Jesus on the cross. God showed Noah grace when he saved him from the impending destruction of the world – a picture of God saving his people through Jesus despite the devastation that surrounds us.[595]

God showed Abraham grace by electing him to father a nation that would span all borders and time.[596] That nation would become God's spiritual children in the faith of Jesus. God showed Moses grace when he chose him to free an entire race of people from bondage and slavery – a picture of things to come through the sacrifice of Jesus who eternally delivers us from the bondage and slavery of sin.[597] God showed David grace when he forgave his sins of selfishness, murder, and adultery – a man whose throne was established to foreshadow the coming king Jesus.[598] God showed Paul grace when he struck him blind on the road to Damascus, choosing him to be one of the most influential apostles of the church who preached Jesus every chance he had.[599] God showed grace to every Christian when, despite being rebellious and ignorant of his will and desire for our lives, Jesus died for us and provided us a way to return to God for all eternity.[600]

Grace is not *a* defining difference between Christianity and all other worldviews; it is *the* defining difference. As scripture declares, "When the goodness and loving kindness of God our Savior appeared, he saved us, not because of works done by us in righteousness, but according to his own mercy (or *grace*)."[601] There are absolutely *no* works involved for our salvation – it is

---

[593] Rom. 14:9
[594] Gen. 3:22–23
[595] Gen. 6:7–8
[596] Gen. 12:1–3
[597] Exod. 6:6
[598] Psa. 32:1–2; 51
[599] Acts 9:3–6, 20
[600] John 3:16; Rom. 6:23; Heb. 4:16
[601] Titus 3:4–5, "or *grace*" added.

entirely God's grace and mercy that saves us. This is why it is so crucial to tell members of rival worldviews about the gracious savior Jesus. Maintaining any other view of Jesus, particularly one of a works–demanding "savior," is extremely dangerous as it inevitably leads a person into one of two places – pride or despair.[602]

If people believe they must work for their salvation only to realize they can't measure up to God's standards of perfection, they will sink into a deep state of despair, morose, and melancholy. In this instance, sin wins over the despairing individual. Alternatively, if people believe they must work for their salvation and think they can actually measure up to God's standards of perfection, they will rise to an inflated state of pride, self-esteem, and religiosity. In this instance, sin wins over the prideful individual. Either way, pride or despair, sin wins. We need to be prepared to share the gospel to both those who think they can merit salvation and those who know they can't.

FOR THOSE WHO THINK THEY CAN

What do we say to those of rival worldviews who are convinced that individuals can merit their own salvation? Can someone, on their own volition and effort, be worthy of salvation? This is, after all, a fundamental difference between every rival worldview and Christianity, and it's a question that many people wrestle with both inside the church and out. At the core of the question is the worthiness of each of us. If we are worthy enough for salvation, then we could assume we are able to save ourselves by impressing God and building on our pre-existing worthiness. If we are not worthy enough for salvation on our own, then we need an external source to impart worthiness onto us. So, are we currently, or can we ever be, worthy enough for God by ourselves? This very question was addressed in the Gospel of Luke during the life of Jesus.

There was a guy who lived during Jesus' time, but we don't know his name. He was a Roman captain stationed near or in the ancient city of Capernaum, which is in modern–day Israel right on the coast of the Galilean

---

[602] Gerhard O. Forde and Martin Luther, *On Being a Theologian of the Cross: Reflections of Luther's Heidelberg Disputation 1518* (Grand Rapids, Mich.: Wm. B. Eerdmans Publishing Co., 1997), 26.

Sea. (This is also an area of Palestine that Jesus frequently visited.) The captain was well liked among the local Jewish population. This was something of a rarity since most Jews viewed the Roman occupation as hostile and contrary to God's will. However, this captain was different. He was helpful to the Jews, respected their beliefs and customs, and kept the local community safe to the best of his ability.

Unfortunately, there was distress in the captain's household. He had a sick servant on his deathbed, one whom the captain really valued and loved.[603] Having befriended the locals, some Jews approached Jesus and asked him to come heal the captain's servant. They reasoned that Jesus should heal the servant because they believed the captain was *worthy* enough for the miracle. They truly felt that this captain was worthy of something. He had been good to the local Jewish community, was an upstanding Roman citizen, and even built them a synagogue.[604] Surely, if anyone was worthy of a miracle, it was this Roman captain.

The way Luke wrote this story, he would have us believe that Jesus went along with this reason since he begins to follow them to the captain's house; it appears as if he is about to perform a miracle because the captain is worthy of it.[605] But then something happens. They are stopped halfway there by some more of the captain's friends who had a message for Jesus; the captain didn't want Jesus around because he believed he was not worthy enough for Jesus.[606]

This is a strange reaction from the captain. Just a moment ago, the Jews were singing his praises, which is a very big deal. Remember, Jews and Roman Gentiles did not get along, so the honor of a Roman captain being praised to an influential rabbi by Palestinian Jews was great. However, the captain was essentially turning down that praise. He didn't find himself worthy of Jesus' presence let alone his healing works. But why doesn't he feel worthy? What about the good things the captain did for God's people; don't his works make him worthy of Jesus like the Jews said? Is the captain worthy of Jesus' healing or not?

---

[603] Luke 7:2
[604] Luke 7:5
[605] Luke 7:6
[606] Ibid.

Jesus' reaction to these questions speaks volumes. "When Jesus heard these things, he marveled at him (the captain), and turning to the crowd that followed him, said, 'I tell you, not even in Israel have I found such faith.'"[607] This is an amazing statement considering Jesus' immediate audience. The Jews who were following Jesus and singing the praises of the captain were, in their minds, the faith bearers to the world and the very people God ordained to show the rest of the world what faith was in the first place. Yet, it was the Roman, Gentile captain who displayed true faith, not the Jews.

Prior to this comment, one could almost imagine the Jews prompting Jesus to 'go ahead and give this guy a miracle' because he had worked hard enough for it. The Jews were on the same team as Jesus. In a sense, they didn't need any miracles since they were already saved, but it's always good to reach across the aisle now and then. Why not let this man who they deemed "worthy enough" have a little taste of God's love? In their minds, the Jews had faith down pat. They felt worthy enough for God's love because of their pedigree and works. Now, it was time to reward a Gentile for displaying a Jewish–level of faith and works (or rather, a religious level of "faith"). Instead, Jesus flips the script on them. The captain was the one with the faith, whereas the Jews were the ones who didn't have a clue. Can you imagine the faces those people must have made? All the bewildered, puzzled faces? The types of faces that people make when they hear the most bizarre thing but know that it's true.

The captain was right. He's not worthy to see Jesus. No one is. The Jews thought they were, and Jesus took every opportunity to tell them they weren't. The captain's faith was in Jesus' worthiness and not in himself; this is why Jesus marveled at his faith. The Jews were the faithless ones, missing the important fact that no one is worthy but Jesus. It takes a lot of humility to reach that conclusion, but it is an important one nonetheless. Without humility, we can't look past the self to realize that the world, the universe, is much bigger than us. The things we do are not impressive to God; he loves us in spite of the things we do. This includes the good things.

Those who believe they have the ability to gain God's approval and love by their own worthiness and works interpret the gospel with the same

---

[607] Luke 7:9, (the captain) added.

perspective of the Jews in Luke's story. They already believed they were people of faith, but the reality was far from the truth. They held a false sense of security in their ethnicity and works, but this security is an illusion. As scripture declares, it is "by grace [we] have been saved through faith; and that not of [ourselves], it is the gift of God. Not by works, lest any man should boast."[608]

We can do absolutely nothing to merit our own salvation because of our fallen state in sin.[609] The only way we get back to God is through his grace, mercy, and redemption.[610] Not our redemption, but his.[611] Not our work in our lives, but his finished work on the cross.[612] Not our intercession through our own perceived righteousness, but his substitutionary atonement interceding for us.[613] We are completely powerless to restore community with God. This makes the work of the cross our only hope, so that God receives all glory for restoring us to him. No one can, on their own volition and effort, be worthy of salvation. But the good news is that God has done the work for us already. This is seen in the Roman captain who had his servant healed without meriting it. Jesus has already done the work for us. We just need to understand that we can't do the work for ourselves – an understanding that requires humility in conjunction with the conviction of the Holy Spirit.

FOR THOSE WHO KNOW THEY CAN'T

What do we say to those of rival worldviews who know they can't merit their own salvation? I think the most important thing to tell them is simple – because of savior Jesus, in faith and by his grace, their sins are already forgiven. Not later, not at death, not after a lifetime of good works, but right now. They don't have to work anymore. In fact, they can't. No human being can produce enough good works to count themselves worthy of God's salvation since it isn't our works that save us, it's the work of Jesus. This is

---

[608] Eph. 2:8–9
[609] Rom. 3:23; 8:7–8
[610] Eph. 2:4–5
[611] Eph. 2:10
[612] Col. 1:20, Rom. 3:28, Titus 3:5
[613] Rom. 3:10–11; 5:8, Isa. 53:12, 1 Tim. 2:5

because God already loves us without us working for that love. We don't need to justify ourselves before God – we just need to accept God's justification.

Nowhere in the Bible is this better articulated than Romans 8:33; "Who shall bring any charge against God's elect? It is God who justifies." It is not we who justify ourselves, but God who justifies us. This verse should bring comfort to us since it absolutely demolishes any need for works or self-attained righteousness in order to be justified before God. Christianity is not just another religion teaching humanity how to justify ourselves to get to God; rather, it is the only worldview that understands that God does all the justifying work for humanity, not the other way around.

Romans 8:33 tells us that God, through Jesus Christ, has already done everything necessary for justification in God's eyes; we can neither add nor subtract from that work. There is absolutely nothing we can do to make God love us any more or any less than he already does and will for all eternity. Think about it like this – God is often referred to as our Father (*Abba*), which is best translated as *daddy*. How awful would it be for a daddy to tell his children that his love for them depends on how well they behave or how well they do in school? Bad grades means daddy doesn't love his little boy or little girl, but good grades means daddy does. Likewise, how awful would it be for the God of the universe to refer to himself as *the* daddy, yet tell us we must achieve and sustain a certain level of morality before he'll love us?

When it comes to being justified in God's sight, "Christ reconciled us to himself," and "he who began a good work in [us] will bring it to completion at the day of Jesus Christ."[614] This means that we don't need to add any works in order to make God love us. This should lead us to a posture of humility, a spirit of thankfulness, and the love–driven work of living out the gospel in our lives through what is called *sanctification*. But all these things come separate from the finished work of Jesus on the cross, given to us as a free gift.

In fact, this is why Jesus yelled "It is finished!" on the cross, and three days later he proved it by his resurrection.[615] If we try adding works to our justification thinking that we can make God love us more, then we are essentially telling Jesus that his sacrifice on the cross was not sufficient or

---

[614] 2 Cor. 5:18; Phil. 1:6

good enough for us. We must tell people who realize they can't work their way to salvation that they must accept God's grace, rid themselves of their own works, and rest easy in his justification because it is God who justifies. (Sometimes, as Christians, we need reminding of this as well.) We are saved by faith alone through God's grace alone.

BETWEEN TWO REBELS

Painting a picture for those who know they can't merit their own salvation, I think the greatest example of faith by grace alone is displayed at the crucifixion event itself. We all know the story – Jesus was falsely accused, sentenced to death by crucifixion under Pontius Pilate, crucified between two thieves, laid to rest in a tomb, and rose three days later to conquer Satan, sin, and death. While this is all correct, there is one popular misconception about the crucifixion event; Jesus was crucified between two thieves. This isn't entirely true.

According to Roman law, stealing was not enough to warrant crucifixion. Crucifixion was such a terrible, horrendous, and atrocious penalty that it was reserved for only two types of criminals – slaves and rebels.[616] The penalty for stealing (*peculatus*) would not have been crucifixion (unless, perhaps, the thief was also a slave); in all actuality, the thief would have been subject to a combination of restitution and exile depending on the severity of the theft.[617] On the other hand, the penalty for rebellion (*vis*) was capital.[618]

With this in mind, consider the unlikely possibility of Jesus being crucified with two common thieves since Jesus was charged with "inciting rebellion."[619] In modern terms, this would be like sentencing two gas station robbers and a terrorist with the same penalty. Most English Bible translations only confuse matters more since they have traditionally chosen the word 'thieves' or 'robbers' to describe the two men on either side of Jesus, but the word (*leistai*) may also connote something more sinister. To Roman ears, this

---

[615] John 19:30
[616] Gillian Clark, *Christianity and Roman Society* (Cambridge: Cambridge University Press, 2004), 4.
[617] Andrew M. Riggsby, *Roman Law and the Legal World of the Romans* (Cambridge: Cambridge University Press: 2010), 201.
[618] Ibid.

word would have brought to mind *brigands*, *vigilantes*, or *rebels*, or to modern ears *freedom fighters* or *terrorists*.[620] In some instances, it would also have brought up images of *pirates* or *buccaneers*.[621] While it is true these people may also steal and warrant the title 'thief' or 'robber,' a *leistai* would have committed something much worse to be branded with such a name. They would have rebelled against the state.

At any rate, *leistai* was not a word one would want association with, since they were considered *freedom fighters* in the minds of their supporters and *rebels* in the minds of everyone else. If the Roman authorities executed two men for simply robbing, it would have been a very unusual occurrence. There was more to their crime than petty thievery. The two men crucified with Jesus were most likely mob bosses, influential pirates, or even leaders of rebellious gangs who desired to topple the Roman authorities.

But why was Jesus crucified with these *leistai*? Since the Jewish leadership wanted to kill Jesus but didn't want to do it themselves, they needed to convince the Roman authorities that Jesus was plotting a rebellion against the empire in order to have him crucified. They needed to convince Rome that Jesus was a vigilante rebel who was leading a cause against the Roman state. Their argument was that "everyone who makes himself a king opposes Caesar," therefore presenting Jesus as a rebel against the Roman Empire.[622] It was only after they accused him of rebellion that Pilate brought him in for questioning.[623] This is why Pilate asked Jesus about being the "King of the Jews" during his questioning and may also be why an inscription was fashioned to the cross labeling him as "King of the Jews."[624]

Fast-forward to Jesus' crucifixion. He had been found guilty of rebellion and was crucified with two other rebels. Remember, Jesus' crucifixion wasn't a random, last–minute event thrown together by Pilate; it was a deliberate crucifixion of rebel leaders with Jesus being one of them. Even one of the

---

[619] Luke 23:14, *New International Version*
[620] Mark 15:27
[621] Aaron L. Beek, "Peirates, Leistai, Boukoloi, and Hostes Gentium of the Classical World: The Portrayal of Pirates in Literature and the Reality of Contemporary Piratical Actions" (honor's thesis, Macalester College, 2006), 7.
[622] John 19:12
[623] John 19:13
[624] Mark 15:2, John 19:19–20

rebels noted the fact that they were all there under the same sentence.[625] The rebels were there for the crime of rebellion, not just stealing; the punishment for such a crime was death.

As the three were being crucified, the crowd jeered at Jesus. They made offensive comments at him, insinuating that if he was truly the Messiah and there to save the Jews then wasn't it a bit suspicious that he couldn't even save himself?[626] Initially, both of the *leistai* heckled him as well, but eventually that changed. One of the rebels repented and asked Jesus to remember him in his kingdom.[627] By faith, he asked for forgiveness, and Jesus gave it.[628] We don't know for sure which of the two men this was, but Christian tradition teaches that the repentant rebel was crucified to the right of Jesus while the other was to the left.

So why is all of this important? Why does it matter whether the two criminals were petty thieves or rebels against the Roman state? What does this have to do with salvation through faith by grace alone? The importance lies squarely in the salvation of the repentant rebel. We can all relate to him. We are all rebels at the same level as the two *leistai* crucified with Jesus. We've all rebelled against God's kingdom, just as the two *leistai* had rebelled against the Roman Empire.[629] But one was forgiven while the other was not. Why? Because of his faith in Jesus alone.

This is important to share with members of rival worldviews who believe they need to earn their salvation through works – the rebel's salvation is a prime example of how we can't. The repentant rebel was at death's door on a cross when he was forgiven. He was fashioned to thick beams of wood and could not possibly have worked towards his own salvation since he lacked both the time and the ability. It was simply by faith through God's grace alone that the rebel was saved and by nothing more.

We should tell those we are dialoguing with that we are all rebels with death sentences on either side of Christ.[630] If we believe we can work our way to salvation, then we have to get off the rebel's cross somehow in order to

---

[625] Luke 23:40
[626] Matt. 27:39–43; Mark 15:29–32; Luke 23:35–37
[627] Luke 23:42
[628] Luke 23:43
[629] Rom. 3:9–12, 23; Eph. 2:5
[630] Rom. 3:23; 5:12; 6:23

perform those works. But we can't. We're stuck there, powerless to merit anything on our own. We can only trust in Jesus for our salvation through faith alone and by God's grace alone. If it is true that God demands good works from us for salvation, then that rebel wasn't saved, and Jesus was a liar. However, if we are saved by grace alone through faith alone, then that fellow rebel is a brother in Christ for all eternity.

THE BIG DIFFERENCE

At the end of the day, the savior between those two rebels is really what it's all about. While members of rival worldviews may differ in how they view their standing before God, whether it be full of pride or despair, one thing is for sure – they all need to know the big difference between their worldview and Christianity. If you haven't guessed already, the big difference is Jesus. In all facets of any rival worldview, the major difference they have with Christianity always revolves around their understanding of the person and work of Jesus. How Jesus is understood by rival worldviews will set into motion a series of theologies, regulations, and laws that all dictate how their members must be saved. Consequently, all rival worldviews subscribe to an impotent Jesus, one who is powerless to save.

Latter-day Saints teach that we must add our own works to the cross of Christ for salvation. Jehovah's Witnesses teach that Jesus is the enabler of salvation, but we must work to sustain our faith in order to enjoy God's eternal presence. Islam teaches that Jesus was the precursor to the grandest of all prophets, who spread a message of unsustainable works to humanity in the off chance that God will save people in the afterlife. Scientology teaches that Jesus is not only completely powerless to save but that he actually hinders the salvation process. They all have one thing in common – an impotent Jesus and a powerless cross. If Jesus is powerless to save, someone must step into his place as savior.

The savior in Jesus' place throughout all rival worldviews is inevitably the individual. Jesus doesn't save us; rather, we save ourselves. This is always the case, although Jesus (or God) may be given a nod as being the enabler of our salvation. Nevertheless, we are the one who must climb the ladder of salvation by our own efforts, works, and righteousness. If we desire eternal community with God, we must ascend to his level. As far as salvation is concerned, it's all about us – not God.

This is a major distinction between Christianity and rival worldviews – all rival worldviews are about us ascending to God, whereas Christianity, because of God's grace, is all about God descending to us. They all teach the world how to get rid of sin through good works, pilgrimages, door-to-door evangelism, habitual prayer, religious attendance at church or mosque, etc., but Jesus says he will get rid of our sins for us by his own grace and power.[631] He can do this because he is the good, righteous, gracious God who wants nothing more than eternal and perfect community with us.

All members of rival worldviews must have this stressed to them; grace forgives our sins because we are powerless to contribute to our own forgiveness and salvation regardless of whether we think we can. We are the lost sheep that the good shepherd is pursuing, and like a lost sheep we cannot find our way home without the shepherd calling, pursuing, searching, and one day scooping us up in his arms to be brought back into the safety, comfort, and joy of the eternal fold.[632]

Above all else, pray for members of rival worldviews. Pray for them daily. Ask God to send his grace into their lives so that they may know him. One of the greatest aspects of prayer is its effect on us because praying for them will help us to love them more. We must pray for ourselves before dialoguing with rival worldview members.[633] We should pray for them before we meet them for coffee or dinner, pray with them if they are willing, and pray for them afterwards asking God to move in their hearts and minds. Prayer, grace, apologetics – these three are key elements that all work together in order for us to share savior Jesus with those who think they already know him. And we must never forget that it's all about Jesus.

---

[631] Matt. 28:18; Luke 7:48; Acts 2:38; Eph. 1:7
[632] Psa. 4:8; Luke 15:6; John 10:11; 15:16
[633] Eph. 6:10–18

Epilogue

"For 'everyone who calls on the name of the Lord will be saved.'
How then will they call on him in whom they have not believed?
And how are they to believe in him of whom they have never heard?
And how are they to hear without someone preaching?
And how are they to preach unless they are sent? As it is written,
'How beautiful are the feet of those who preach the good news!'"

Romans 10:13–15

What are you waiting for?
Go tell them about Savior Jesus.

Glossary of Theological Terms

Adventism – A Christian movement that began in the 19th century under the leadership of William Miller who taught the imminent return of Christ (his *advent*) and that hell was not a literal place of torture. Instead, the sinner would be annihilated upon Christ's return. The Seventh-Day Adventist Church finds its historical roots in this movement.

Agnosticism – From the Greek *a* (no) and *gnosis* (knowledge). The belief that the existence of God can neither be proven nor disproven. It is usually accompanied by no religious affiliation.

Apologetics – From the Greek *apologia*, to defend. The art of rendering the orthodox Christian faith persuasive to non-believers. *See* 2 Peter 3:15.

Apostolic Succession – A theory of ecclesiology (church government) that states the universal church should maintain a centralized office or seat of authority in succession of and from the biblical apostles.

Apotheosis (theosis) – From the Greek *to deify*. The transformation of a human being into a god upon their mortal death.

Arianism – A 4th century theological heresy taught by Arius of Alexandria who believed Christ had a complete human nature but was not coequal and coeternal with God the Father. Arius denied the divinity of Jesus Christ.

Atheism – From the Greek *a* (no) and *theos* (god). The belief that God does not exist. This belief is usually complimented with a strict, naturalistic worldview. *See also* agnosticism.

Atonement – The saving work of Christ that brings reconciliation between God and humanity. Thus, the word "at-one-ment" describes the act of peace between the holy God and sinful human.

Catechesis – From the Greek *katēchēo*, to instruct. The idea that Christians should be developed in the Christian faith through organized education prior to baptism and/or throughout their life.

Congregationalism – A form of church government that views Christ as the head (Col. 1:18) and the subsequent priesthood of all believers (1 Pet. 2:9) for all manner of decision–making. A popular form of church government in North America where democratic ideals are held high in public values.

Donatism – A belief that rose in 4th century Rome. Donatists believed that Christians who denounced their faith during persecution were ineligible to accept the sacraments, have spiritual gifts bestowed upon them, and return to the Christian faith community.

Epistemic – From the Greek *epistēmē*, knowledge or science. A form of philosophical inquiry (epistemology) into the nature of knowledge, how we acquire it, and how we can verify acquired knowledge.

Eschatology – From the Greek *escatos*, last or farthest. The study of the end times; moreover, with particular attention to biblical prophecies concerning Jesus' second coming and the events surrounding the end of the world.

Evangelism – From the Greek *euangelion*, good news. The intentional proclamation (with the anticipation of a reaction from the hearer) of the good news that God the Father had sent Jesus Christ to reconcile sinners to God through the regeneration of the Holy Spirit.

Fatalism – The philosophical idea that all actions and events occur by predefined and immutable fate.

Gnosticism – From the Greek *gnosis*, knowledge. In Christianity, this was an early cult that taught salvation through esoteric knowledge. It was often accompanied by fabricated "gospels" to support their view.

Hermeneutic – A theory and practice of biblical interpretation, which may be subject to the interpreter's presuppositions. Proper hermeneutics seeks to discount presuppositions through the use of studying context, original language, and exposition.

Manichæism – Founded by Mani in the 3rd century, it was a gnostic religion that taught a dualistic struggle of good and evil in the concept of god.

Monotheism – The belief that there exists only one god.

Moral Absolutism – An ethical view that certain actions are absolutely right or wrong, devoid of the context of the act. In light of rival worldviews, there is either truth or a lie – the gospel or a false gospel.

Original Sin – The fallen, sinful, rebellious condition humanity finds itself in even before a person is born due to the sin of humanity's federal head Adam.

Orthodoxy – From the Greek *orthos* (true) and *doxas* (belief). The standard, core beliefs Christians should adhere to.

Pelagianism – A 5th century theological heresy taught by British monk Pelagius who taught that human beings are born and live essentially good in terms of morality, a stark difference from the doctrine of total depravity.

Polytheism – The belief that there exists multiple gods.

Reincarnation – The belief that a person's essence or soul will return to a living body when the previously inhabited body dies.

Replacement Theology – Also known as supercessionism, it is the belief that God's relationship with the elect is experienced in covenants. The first covenant, that with national and ethic Israel, has been completely replaced with the new, that with Christianity and the Church.

Seminary – Graduate-level theological and ministerial training designed to prepare men and women for Christian ministry and ordination.

Subjective Absolutism – A moral theory postulating that an action is right if someone approves of it. Commonly expressed as, "what's right for me is right for me and what's right for you is right for you."

Substitutionary Atonement – The term for describing that Jesus lived the life we cannot live, he died the death we should have died, and he paid the price we should have paid.

Total Depravity – The belief that the sin of Adam has negatively affected the whole of the human race in every aspect (body, soul, and mind), thus rendering them wholly incapable of rescuing themselves from God's holy judgment.

Trinity – The orthodox Christian belief that God exists as one being in three unique persons; the Father, the Son, and the Holy Spirit. They are all co-equal and co-eternal. Also referred to as *trinitarianism*.

Quick Reference Chart

	Mormonism	Jehovah's Witness	Islam	Scientology
Founder	Joseph Smith (1805–1844)	Charles T. Russell (1852–1916)	Muhammad (570–632)	L. Ron Hubbard (1911–1986)
God	Three gods: Heavenly Father, Jesus, Holy Ghost	One god: Jehovah	One god: Allah	Exists in everyone, we must harness our godlike potential
Jesus	Created being, spiritual brother	Created being, Michael the Archangel	Second greatest prophet to Muhammad	Engram implant, root of psychological issues
Salvation	By God's grace after all we can do (works)	Jesus enables, we must finish by works	By loving Allah and good works	Works through auditing and OT levels
Scripture	Bible (JST, KJV), Book of Mormon, Pearl of Great Price, Doctrine & Covenants	Bible (NWT), Watchtower and Awake magazines	Qu'rān, Hadīths, parts of the Bible (Psalms, Gospels)	*Dianetics*, writings of L. Ron Hubbard
Resurrection of Jesus	Yes	Yes	No	No

Study Guides

Study Guide 1: What is Apologetics?

In chapter 1, read sections *Introduction – Contextualization*:

1. What does *apologetics* mean?
2. What is the prerequisite to apologetics according to Peter, and why is this so important?
3. We can win the _____, but lose the _____. How does this affect our view of apologetics?
4. What are the Three A's of Apologetics? Discuss what is meant by all three.
5. When engaging in apologetics, who is ultimately guiding the conversation? Why does this matter?
6. Why should we vet our sources of information about other worldviews? Are Christians sometimes guilty of being lazy researchers?
7. What is the main goal of apologetics?
8. What is a "rival worldview," and why use this term over "cult," "religion," or "faith group"? Do you agree/disagree with the author on the use of this term?
9. What is the one, common belief between all rival worldviews?
10. Read Romans 1:25. Why are rival worldviews not "on the same level" as Christianity?

In chapter 1, read sections *Reactive Apologetics– First Bank*:

1. Why is reactive apologetics unhelpful? If you can, discuss an example of reactive apologetics you have witnessed and its results.
2. Read Ephesians 6:12. Apologetics is not against people, (flesh and blood), but rather ideas people believe (spiritual forces). How does this affect apologetics in dialogue on the gospel?
3. What does 'Satan' mean in Hebrew? With that in mind, what does he do to God's word in order to lure people into rival worldviews?
4. What is *eisegesis*, and why is it so dangerous? Can you think of an example of *eisegesis*?
5. Many Christians believe that only educated people should engage in apologetics. Is this true? Who did Jesus choose as his disciples?
6. Whose job is it to convert people? How does this affect your view of apologetics?

In chapter 1, read sections *Politically Incorrect – Ocean in a Vase*:

1. What is the difference between child-like faith and child-like naiveté?
2. What evidence from scripture do we have that indicates that God invites us to examine him and his claims?
3. Considering political correctness, why is it difficult for those in Western society to evangelize?
4. What is the best apologetic and why?
5. What is ironic about selfishly debating the existence of a selfless God?
6. According to Augustine, why is love the greatest apologetic? Why isn't intellect greater than love?

Study Guide 2: Mormonism and Big Brother Jesus

In chapter 2, read sections *Introduction – Westward Ho!*:

1. Is it possible to evangelize to Mormons without knowing something about Joseph Smith? Why or why not?

2. According to Smith's account of his First Vision, does he ever identify God the Father and Jesus by name? Why is this an important detail?

3. How should we discuss Joseph Smith's First Vision with Latter-day Saints? What distinction should we make about their faith and the vision?

4. If Smith's death arises in a conversation with a Mormon, how should it be discussed? Who's death should we compare Smith's to and why?

In chapter 2, read sections *Mormon: The Bible – Jesus had a Smart Phone*:

1. Why do Mormons reject all English translations of the Bible with the exception of the KJV and JST?

2. Why do Latter-day Saints perform proxy baptism? How can we explain why this is wrong?

3. What will most of your conversation with Latter-day Saints concerning the Book of Mormon be about – its origin or its content? Why is this important?

4. Does the Book of Mormon complete or compliment the Bible in Mormon thought? Why is this an important distinction?

5. Discuss: If the Book of Mormon could be proven to be historically false, why should Latter-day Saints trust its theological aspects?

6. As far as archeological evidence is concerned, what are the differences between the Book of Mormon and the Bible?

In chapter 2, read sections *Book of Mormon – Eternal Progression*:

1. How is Satan viewed in Mormonism given his work in "freeing" humanity? Why is this dangerous to believe?

2. Read 2 Nephi 25:23; "For we know that it is by grace that we are saved, after all we can do." What does this Book of Mormon verse teach about salvation? Does the Bible agree or disagree?

3. How does the Book of Mormon contradict Mormonism? How can we use this in evangelism?

4. According to Mormonism, is God the Father (or Heavenly Father) a fixed or progressing being? What are the implications of this belief?

5. What is the difference between becoming godlike and becoming gods?

6. Why is the Hebrew word for God, *elohim*, in plural form?

7. Should we immediately reject Mormon authority (e.g., writings from Joseph Smith or Brigham Young) when dialoging with Latter-day Saints or should we use it? Why or why not?

In chapter 2, read sections *Big Brother Jesus – The Gospel*:

1. According to Mormon president Brigham Young, how was Jesus conceived? What are the implications of this belief?
2. What is the purpose of the cross in Mormonism? What are the implications of this belief?
3. What does the Jesus of Mormonism require from us that the Jesus of Christianity does not? Discuss the implications of this major difference between the two Jesuses.
4. How do Latter-day Saints view salvation? Why?
5. Can people finish or earn their own salvation if the cross begins or enables it? Why or why not?
6. Why does 1 Corinthians 15:40–41 not support the Mormon view of heaven?
7. What reasons make it difficult for Mormons to leave Mormonism?
8. What is the best tool at our disposal during evangelism to Mormons?

Study Guide 3: Jehovah's Witnesses and Archangel Jesus

In chapter 3, read sections *Introduction – A Cross By Any Other Shape*:

1. Why did Charles T. Russell decide to start the Watchtower Society? Is this a valid reason? Why or why not?
2. Even though the Watchtower Society has predicted the end of the world many times, the organization continues to grow. Why is this?
3. When did Jehovah's Witnesses develop door-to-door evangelism? Do you believe this is an effective method?
4. According to Watchtower Society theology, who is Jesus? What are the implications of this?
5. How do Jehovah's Witnesses view the cross? Why is this important?

In chapter 3, read sections *Annihilationism – New World Translation*:

1. What is the consequence of believing in annihilationism?
2. What is the relevance of 144,000 to a Jehovah's Witness? How does this differ from what the Bible actually teaches?
3. What is Arianism? Does this idea agree with scripture? Why or why not?
4. How does the NWT translation of John 1:1 intentionally alter its meaning?
5. Should we bring out the Greek NT the moment a Jehovah's Witness comes to our home? Why or why not?

In chapter 3, read sections *The Trinity – The Gospel*:

1. Why is the argument from ignorance not persuasive against the Trinity?
2. What extra–biblical evidence suggests that Christians believed the Trinity as far back as 100CE? How could you use this with Jehovah's Witnesses?
3. Before someone can understand the work of Jesus, they must understand the person of Jesus. Why is this so important?
4. What are the consequences of a Jehovah's Witness leaving the Watchtower Society? How can we take this into consideration when sharing the gospel with them?
5. Watchtower Society view of salvation is a hybrid of grace and works. With this in mind, discuss how you would present the gospel to a Jehovah's Witnesses.

Study Guide 4: Islam and Silver Medal Jesus

In chapter 4, read sections *Introduction – Houris*:

1. What is the difference between the terms *Muslim* and *Islam*?
2. What are the Five Pillars of Islam? Why are these so important to Muslims?
3. Why did Muhammad's relationship with Jews, Christians, and pagans change during his time in Medina? What was the result of Muhammad's change of heart towards them?
4. Why do Muslims only accept certain aspects of the Bible, and what are the accepted portions? How does this affect evangelism?

5. Is Islamic religious garb for women a misogynistic requirement, a cultural preference, or both? How should Christians treat this issue?

6. What is the main difference between what martyred Muslim males and females receive as a reward in the afterlife?

In chapter 4, read sections *Greater Jihad – The Crucifixion*:

1. What is the difference between the greater jihad and the lesser jihad?

2. If a Muslim points out the violence in Christianity's history, what should our response be?

3. Should we argue over whether or not Islam is a religion of peace? If so, why? If not, what should our focus be considering Islam's violent founder and past?

4. Can a Muslim ever be completely sure they have salvation?

5. Read Sūra 'Āli 'Imrān 3:31 (on page 177), then read Ephesians 2:4–5. What is the prerequisite of love from Allah? What is the prerequisite of love from God? Discuss the implications.

6. Given the Islamic understanding of sin and the individual, why do Muslims desire to see all of culture under the auspices of Islam?

7. What is the problem with believing that humans are born in a morally neutral condition?

8. Why is it important to discuss the concept of original sin with Muslims?

9. Why do Muslims deny the crucifixion? How can we convince them otherwise?

In chapter 4, read sections *Arabic Heritage – The Abrahams*:

1. Why is it so important to Arabic Muslims that Muhammad's lineage be traced back to Ishmael and Abraham?

2. What are the political and spiritual consequences for Muslims if Isaac is the child of promise and not Ishmael?

3. What is the inheritance given through the promise of Abraham?

4. Some Christians believe this promise includes the divine right to the physical land of Israel. Do you agree or disagree? Why or why not?

5. Are Christianity, Judaism, and Islam simply three expressions of one Abrahamic faith? Why or why not?

6. Why do people believe that Christianity, Judaism, and Islam are all different faiths that worship the same god?

In chapter 4, read sections *Jesus & Muhammad – Sharing the Gospel*:

1. Do Muslims consider Muhammad their savior?
2. What is the greatest difference between Jesus and Muhammad? What are the implications for Muslims of this difference?
3. Do you believe prejudice exists among North American Christians concerning Muslims? If so, does this hinder evangelism? If not, why not?
4. Do you agree or disagree with the author that Christians should describe Jesus as "the beloved son who originates from the Father" rather than "Son of God" when initially dialoguing with Muslims about the gospel?
5. Since Muslims are steeped in a works-based theology, the concept of God's grace in Jesus will most likely be radically life changing for them. How would you share God's grace with a Muslim?

Study Guide 5: Scientology and Robot Jesus

In chapter 5, read sections *Introduction – What Do Scientologists?*:

1. In Hubbard's mind, why did *Dianetics* fail the first time? What allowed it to come back in popularity? Does this reveal Hubbard's true motives in starting the Church of Scientology?
2. What is an E-meter? Why is this device important to the Church of Scientology, especially with regard to new or potential members?
3. What major P.R. event occurred at Saint Hill Manor in England, which altered Scientology's course forever? Discuss why you believe Hubbard reacted the way he did.
4. What is Operation: Snow White? Why is it revealing of Hubbard's character?
5. Why is it impossible to pinpoint the beliefs of Scientology? Why is this important to remember when sharing the gospel with Scientologists?
6. Which two men influenced Hubbard the most as evidenced by unique ideas in Scientology? Why does this matter?

7. What is the core of Scientology's worldview? Discuss what this means.

In chapter 5, read sections *Ideas Unique – Adventures*:

1. Scientology borrows heavily from the Eastern belief of reincarnation. How would you discuss reincarnation with a Scientologist in light of scripture?
2. How does a Scientologist progress to become a "Cleared Theta Clear," the highest OT level? Do you believe this is works-based salvation? Why or why not?
3. Why is esoteric knowledge so dangerous? Are there any aspects of the gospel or Jesus that are esoteric? Why or why not?
4. What is OT III? If you can answer this question, congratulations.
5. What do you make of OT III as a "creation narrative" (an explanation for how humans were created and why we exist)? Is there any merit or redeeming factors to this story that we can relate to the gospel?

In chapter 5, read sections *Dangerous Appeal – Gospel*:

1. What is the appeal of gossip, and how does this relate to esoteric knowledge?
2. What was the tempting promise for Adam and Eve's rebellion? How is this repeated in Scientology?
3. Is our salvation accomplished through something we know or something God (Jesus) did? Why is this an important distinction to make with Scientologists?
4. What is the dual–aspect approach of Scientology's appeal? How would you respond to this?
5. All sin issues are actually what kind of issues? Why is this important to understand?
6. Given Scientology's small membership, why does it wield so much influence?
7. How can we better evangelize to Scientologists (hint: vocabulary)? What are the potential benefits and difficulties of this?
8. Was Hubbard correct when he said, "[Mankind's] ethical and moral standards are high, his ability to seek and experience

pleasure is great. His personality is heightened and he is creative and constructive"?[634] Why or why not?

Study Guide 6: Savior Jesus

In chapter 6, read sections *Introduction – Who Is Savior Jesus?*:

1. What do you think of when you hear the word *gospel*?
2. Why are there so many interpretations of the *gospel*? Have you encountered the different interpretations of the gospel mentioned in the beginning of the chapter?
3. What is the gospel primarily *not*? Is there any bad news in the good news?
4. During evangelism, when is it appropriate to explain to people that they have a sin issue? When is it not? Give and discuss examples.
5. Do you agree or disagree with the author that the gospel is not primarily a call to missions or works?
6. What does it mean that "Jesus came to live the life we could not live, die the death we should have died, and imparts that life to us?"
7. Do you agree that the gospel is a message and not an action? Or, in other words, can we "*be* the gospel?" Why or why not?
8. What do all the Jesuses of rival worldviews demand that savior Jesus does not? How do they (the other Jesuses) demand it?
9. For those who believe they must merit their salvation by works, which two places do they inevitably fall to? Have you experienced either (or both) of these places?
10. What is *the* defining difference between Christianity and all other worldviews? How should this affect our evangelism?

In chapter 6, read sections *For Those Who – The Big Difference*:

1. Can someone, on their own volition and abilities, earn their salvation? Why or why not?
2. Why is worthiness at the core of whether or not we can earn our own salvation?
3. According to the Gospel of Luke, the local Jewish population believed the Roman captain was worthy enough for Jesus, but the

---

[634] L. Ron Hubbard, *Dianetics: The Modern Science of Mental Health* (Los Angeles: Bridge Publications, Inc., 2007), 208.

Roman captain did not. Why did Jesus attribute this as "faith"? (*See Luke 7:9*)

4. What is required to realize that we are not worthy of salvation in conjunction with the conviction of the Holy Spirit? Why is this important?

5. How should we approach evangelism with those who think they can earn their salvation? Discuss practical ways.

6. What is the most important thing to tell people who know they cannot earn their own salvation?

7. What is unique to Christianity compared to all other worldviews about our justification?

8. What is the big difference between orthodox Christianity and all rival worldviews? How is this related to grace?

9. Discuss what you think the author means by, "all rival worldviews are about us ascending to God, whereas Christianity, because of God's grace, is all about God descending to us."

10. Above all else, what should we do for members of rival worldviews? Why is this important?

Bibliography

Abanes, Richard. *Inside Today's Mormonism: Understanding Latter-day Saints in Light of Biblical Truth.* Eugene, Oreg.: Harvest House Publishers, 2004.

'Abd al-'Ati, Hammudah. *Islam in Focus.* 4th ed. trans. Al-Falah. Cairo: Al-Falah Foundation for Translation, Publication & Distribution.

Abd-Allah, Umar F. "Theological dimensions of Islamic Law." *The Cambridge Companion to Classical Islamic Theology.* ed. Tim Winter. Cambridge: Cambridge University Press, 2008.

Abdul-Rahman, Muhammad Saed. *The Meaning and Explanation of the Glorious Qur'an.* Vol. 10. 2nd ed. London: MSA Publications, Ltd., 2009.

Akhtar, Shabbir. *A faith for all seasons: Islam and the challenge of the modern world.* Lanham, Mary.: Ivan R. Dee Publisher, 1991.

Allen, Joseph L. and Blake J. Allen. *Exploring the Lands of the Book of Mormon.* Revised ed. American Fork, Utah: Covenant Communications, Inc. 2011.

Andrew, Laurel B. *Early Temples of the Mormons: The Architecture of the Millennial Kingdom in the American West.* Albany, NY: State University of New York Press, 1978s.

Ankerberg, John, John Weldon, and Dillon Burroughs. *The Facts on Jehovah's Witnesses.* Eugene, Oreg.: Harvest House Publishers, 2008.

Arrington, Leonard J. and Davis Bitton. *The Mormon Experience: A History of the Latter-Day Saints.* New York: Alfred A. Knopf, Inc., 1992.

Arweck, Elisabeth. "Hubbard, L. Ron (b. *1911; d. 1986*)." *Encyclopedia of New Religious Movements*. ed. Peter B. Clarke. Oxon, United Kingdom: Routledge, 2006.

Atack, Jon. *A Piece of Blue Sky: Scientology, Dianetics, and L. Ron Hubbard Exposed*. New York: Kensington Publishing Corporation, 1990.

Aziz, Zahid. *Islam, Peace and Tolerance*. Wembley, United Kingdom: Ahmadiyya Anjuman Lahore Publications, U.K., 2007.

Balch, David L. and Carolyn Osiek. *Early Christian Families in Context: An Interdisciplinary Dialogue*. Grand Rapids, Mich.: Wm. B. Eerdmans Publishing, 2003.

Bashir, Shahzad. "Muhammad in Sufi eyes: prophetic legitimacy in medieval Iran and Central Asia" *The Cambridge Companion to Muhammad*, ed. Jonathan E. Brockopp. Cambridge: Cambridge University Press, 2010.

Beek, Aaron L. "Peirates, Leistai, Boukoloi, and Hostes Gentium of the Classical World: The Portrayal of Pirates in Literature and the Reality of Contemporary Piratical Actions." Honor's thesis, Macalester College, 2006.

Berkey, Jonathan P. *The Formation of Islam: Religion and Society in the Near East, 600-1800*. Cambridge: Cambridge University Press, 2004.

Berko, Anat. *The Path to Paradise*. Westport, Conn.: Greenwood Publishing Group, Inc., 2007.

Bernstein, Fred A. "In Pasadena, a Model for Scientology's Growth Plan." *The New York Times*. http://www.nytimes.com/2010/11/10/business/10scientology.html (accessed October 30, 2011).

Bowker, John. *What Muslims Believe*. Oxford: Oneworld, 1995.

Bowman, Robert M. *Jehovah's Witnesses*. Grand Rapids, Mich.: Zondervan Publishing House, 1995.

Brockopp, Jonathan E. *The Cambridge Companion to Muhammad*. Cambridge: Cambridge University Press, 2010.

Brodie, Fawn M. *No Man Knows My History: The Life of Joseph Smith*. New York: Vintage Books, 1995.

Browne, Michael. "Should Germany Stop Worrying and Love the Octopus? Freedom of Religion and the Church of Scientology in Germany and the United States." *Indiana International & Comparative Law Review*. Indiana University: Trustees of Indiana University. 9 Ind. Int'l & Comp. L. Rev. 155, 1998.

Burton, Rulon T. *We Believe: Doctrines and Principles of the Church of Jesus Christ of Latter-day Saints.* Draper, Utah: Tabernacle Books, 1994.

Chapman, David W. *Ancient Jewish and Christian Perceptions of Crucifixion.* Tübingen, Germany: Mohr Siebeck, 2008.

Chryssides, George D. *Historical Dictionary of Jehovah's Witnesses.* Lanham, Mary.: Scarecrow Press, Inc., 2008.

Church of Jesus Christ of Latter-day Saints, The. "Church Grows Rapidly," http://www.lds.org/library/display/0,4945,40-1-3474-2,00.html (accessed January 8, 2012).

Teachings of Presidents of the Church: Brigham Young. Salt Lake City, Utah: Church of Jesus Christ of Latter-day Saints.

Clark, Gillian. *Christianity and Roman Society.* Cambridge: Cambridge University Press, 2004.

Corydon, Bent. *L. Ron Hubbard: Messiah or Madman?* New York: Barricade Books, 1992.

Crowley, Aleister. *The Book of the Law.* reissue ed. Newburyport, Mass.: Samuel Weiser, 1987.

Crumley, Bruce. "France Moves Closer to Banning Burqa." *TIME Magazine.* http://www.time.com/time/world/article/0,8599,1983871,00.html (accessed January 9, 2012).

Davies, Douglas J. *An Introduction to Mormonism.* Cambridge: Cambridge University Press, 2003.

Deng, Yinke. *Ancient Chinese Inventions.* Cambridge: Cambridge University Press, 2011.

Djupe, Paul A. and Laura R. Olson, *Encyclopedia of American Religion and Politics.* New York: Facts on File, Inc., 2003.

Donner, Fred M. "The Historical Context" *The Cambridge Companion to the Qur'ān.* ed. Jane Dammen McAuliffe. Cambridge: Cambridge University Press, 2006.

Dreher, Rod. "Islam According to Oprah: Is Oprah Winfrey a threat to national security?" *New York Post.* October 8, 2001.

Driscoll, Mark and Gerry Breshears. *Doctrine: What Christians Should Believe.* (Wheaton, Illi.: Crossway Books, 2010.

Eaton, Eric R. and Kenn Kaufman. *Kaufman Field Guide to Insects in North America.* New York: Houghton Mifflin Company, 2007.

Erickson, Millard J. *Christian Theology*. 2nd ed. Grand Rapids, Mich.: Baker Books, 1998.

Executive Committee of the Southern Baptist Convention. *Annual of the 2007 Southern Baptist Convention: 150th Session, 162nd Year*. San Antonio, Texas: 2007.

Farmer, Brian R. *Understanding Radical Islam: Medieval Ideology in the Twenty-First Century*. New York: Peter Lang Publishing, 2008.

Firestone, Reuven. "Jihad," *Medieval Islamic Civilization: An Encyclopedia*, Vol. 1. ed. Josef W. Meri. New York: Taylor & Francis Group, LLC., 2006.

Forde Gerhard O. and Martin Luther. *On Being a Theologian of the Cross: Reflections of Luther's Heidelberg Disputation 1518*. Grand Rapids, Mich.: Wm. B. Eerdmans Publishing Co., 1997.

Fowler, Andrew. *The Most Dangerous Man in the World*. Carlton, Australia: Melbourne University Press, 2011.

Fudge, Edward and Robert A. Peterson, *Two Views of Hell: A Biblical & Theological Dialogue*. Downers Grove, Illi.: InterVarsity Press, 2000.

Gallagher, Eugene, V. and W. Michael Ashcroft, *Introduction to New and Alternative Religions in America*. Westport, Conn.: Greenwood Press, 2006.

Geisler, Norman L. and Abdul Saleeb, *Answering Islam: The Crescent in Light of the Cross,* 2nd ed. Grand Rapids, Mich.: Baker Books, 2002.

Geisler Norman L. and William E. Nix. *A General Introduction to the Bible*. Chicago: Moody Press, 1986.

Givens, Terryl. *By the Hand of Mormon: The American Scripture that Launched a New World Religion*. Oxford: Oxford University Press, 2002.

Cyril, Glassé and Huston Smith. *The New Encyclopedia of Islam*. reprinted ed. Walnut Creek, Cali.: AltaMira Press, 2001.

Goetz, Philip W. and Margaret Sutton, *The New Encyclopedia Britannica: Volume 1*. Chicago: Encyclopædia Inc, 1983.

Grabbe, Lester L. "Joseph Smith and the *Gestalt* of the Israelite Prophet." *Ancient Israel: The Old Testament in Its Social Context*. Minneapolis, Minn.: Augsburg Fortress, 2006.

Greggs, Tom. *New Perspectives for Evangelical Theology: Engaging with God, Scripture and the World*. Oxon, United Kingdom: Routledge, 2010.

Grossman, Cathy Lynn. "Is Barack Obama's mother a Mormon in heaven now?" USA Today, *Faith & Reason,* http://content.usatoday.com/ communities/religion/post/2009/05/66469311/1 (accessed January 9, 2012).

Grundy, Paul. "Jehovah's Witness Statistics." J.W. Facts, http://www.jwfacts.com/watchtower/statistics.php (accessed January 9, 2012).

Grunebaum, Gustave Edmund and Gustave Edmund Von Grunebaum, *Medieval Islam: A Study in Cultural Orientation.* 2nd ed. Chicago: University of Chicago Press.

Gruss, Edmond C. *Jehovah's Witnesses: Their Claims, Doctrinal Changes and Prophetic Speculation.* 2nd ed. Maitland, Flor.: Xulon Press Inc., 2007.

Gruss, Edmond C. and Lane A. Thuet. *What Every Mormon (and non Mormon) Should Know: Examining Mormon History, Doctrine and Claims.* Maitland, Flor.: Xulon Press, Inc., 2006.

Hall, Timothy L. *American Religious Leaders.* New York: Facts on File, Inc., 2003.

Hexham, I. "Jehovah's Witnesses." *Evangelical Dictionary of Theology,* 2nd ed., Walter A. Elwell, ed. Grand Rapids, Mich.: Baker Academic, 2001.

Hinkley, Gordon B. 2004. "Four Cornerstones of Faith." *Ensign* 34, no. 2 (February): 2-7.

Hubbard, L. Ron. *Dianetics: The Modern Science of Mental Health.* Los Angeles: Bridge Publications, Inc., 2007.

_____. *Scientology 8-8008: How to Increase Your Spiritual Ability from Zero to Infinity.* Los Angeles: Bridge Publications, 2007.

Khan, M. A. Muqtedar. *Jihad for Jerusalem: Identity and Strategy in International Relations.* Westport, Conn.: Greenwood Publishing Group, Inc., 2004.

Kinsella, Kevin and Cynthia A. Taeuber. *An Aging World II.* Darby, Penn.: Diana Publishing Co., 1993.

Knox, Zoe. "The Watch Tower Society and the End of the Cold War: Interpretations of the End-Times, Superpower Conflict, and the Changing Geo-Political Order." *Journal of American Academy of Religion.* December 2011, Vol. 79, No. 4, pp. 1018—1049.

Kotar, S. L. and J. E. Gessler, *The Rise of the American Circus, 1716-1899.* Jefferson, NC: McFarland & Company, Inc., Publishers, 2011.

Jaffer, Abbas and Masuma Jaffer. *An Introduction to Qur'anic Sciences.* London: ICAS Press, 2009.

Johansen, Jerald Ray. *A Commentary on the Pearl of Great Price: A Jewel Among the Scriptures.* Bountiful, Utah: Horizon Publishers & Distributors Inc., 1985.

Lanning, Michael Lee. *The Battle 100: The Stories Behind History's Most Influential Battles* (Naperville, Illi.: Sourcebooks, Inc., 2005.

Leonard, Glen M. *Nauvoo: A Place of Peace, A People of* Promise. Salt Lake City: Deseret Book Co., 2002.

Madigan, Daniel A. "Themes and topics." *The Cambridge Companion to the Qur'ān.* ed. Jane Dammen McAuliffe. Cambridge: Cambridge University, Press 2006.

Marquardt, H. Michael. 'Joseph Smith's Egyptian Papers: A History.' *The Joseph Smith Egyptian Papyri: A Complete Edition.* ed. Robert K. Ritner. Salt Lake City, Utah: Signature Books Publishing, LLC.: 2011.

McKeever, Bill and Eric Johnson. *Mormonism 101: Examining the Religion of the Latter-day Saints.* Grand Rapids, Mich.: Baker Publishing Group, 2000.

Methvin, Eugene H. "Scientology: Anatomy of a Frightening Cult." *Reader's Digest,* May 1980.

Millet, Robert L. *A Different Jesus: The Christ of the Latter-day Saints.* Grand Rapids, Mich.: Wm. B. Eerdmans Publishing Co., 2005.

Miller, Russell. *Bare-faced Messiah: The True Story of L. Ron Hubbard.* Toronto: Key Porter Books, 1987.

Miller, William. *A Christian's Response to Islam.* Nutley, NJ: Presbyterian & Reformed, 1977.

Milisauskas, Sarunas. *European Prehistory: A Survey.* New York: Kluwer Academic, 2002.

Mormonism Research Ministry, The. "Prominent People Mormons Have Baptized by Proxy," http://www.mrm.org/prominent-people-baptized-by-proxy (accessed January 9, 2012).

Motzki, Harald. "Alternative accounts of the Qur'āns formation." *The Cambridge Companion to the Qur'ān*, ed. Jane Dammen McAuliffe. Cambridge: Cambridge University Press, 2006.

Natan, Yoel. *Moon-o-theism: Religion of a War and Moon God Prophet*. Vol. I. Morrisville, NC: Lulu Enterprises, Inc., 2006.

Navas, Patrick. *Divine Truth Or Human Tradition? A Reconsideration of the Roman Catholic- Protestant Doctrine of the trinity in Light of the Hebrew and Christian Scriptures*. Bloomington, Indi.: ArthurHouse, 2006.

Noah, Mordecai Manuel. *Discourse on the Evidences of the American Indians Being the Descendants of the Lost Tribes of Israel*. (New York: James Van Norden, 1837.

Oppenheimer, Mark. "In the Clear: On Scientology." *The* Nation. http://www.thenation.com/article/164059/clear-scientology (accessed November 5, 2011).

Packer, Cameron J. "Cumorah's Cave." *Journal of Book of Mormon Studies*. 2004, Vol. 13, No. 1, pp. 50—57.

Penton, M. James. *Apocalypse Delayed: The Story of Jehovah's Witnesses*. 2nd ed. Toronto: University of Toronto Press, 1997.

Peters, Francis E. *Muhammad and the Origins of Islam*. Albany, NY: State University of New York Press, 1994.

Peterson, Eugene H. *The Message Remix: The Bible in Contemporary Language*. Colorado Springs, Colo.: NavPress, 2006.

Phelan, James. "Have You Ever Been a Boo-Hoo?" *The Saturday Evening Post*. March 21, 1964.

Pratt, Orson. *Divine Authenticity of the Book of Mormon*. Liverpool: 1850.

Public Broadcasting Station (PBS), "Myths & Realities," http://www.pbs.org/independentlens/knocking/myths.html (accessed January 9, 2012).

Qualls, Corethia. "Boats of Mesopotamia before 2000 B.C." PhD diss., Columbia University, 1981.

Raine, Susan. "Surveillance in New Religious Movements: Scientology as a Case Study." *Religious Studies and Theology*. Vol 28. No 1. London: Equinox Publishing, 2009.

Reitman, Janet. *Inside Scientology: The Story of America's Most Secretive Religion*. New York: Houghton Mifflin Harcourt Publishing Company, 2011.

Rhodes, Ron. *Reasoning from the Scriptures with Muslims*. Eugene, Oreg.: Harvest House Publishers, 2002.

Rhodes, Ron and Marian Bodine. *Reasoning from the Scriptures with Mormons*. Eugene, Oreg.: Harvest House Publishers, 1995.

Riggsby, Andrew M. *Roman Law and the Legal World of the Romans*. Cambridge: Cambridge University Press: 2010.

Roberts, R. Phillip. *Mormonism Unmasked*. Nashville, Tenn.: B&H Publishing Group, 1998.

Rubin, Uri. "Muhammad's Message in Mecca: Warnings, Signs, and Miracles." *The Cambridge Companion to Muhammad*. ed. Jonathan E. Brockopp. Cambridge: Cambridge University Press, 2010.

Russell, Charles T. *Studies in the Scriptures*. Vols. 1-6. London: International Bible Students Association, 1916.

_____. *The Time Is at Hand*. Brooklyn, NY: Charles T. Russell, 1916.

Saleh, Walid A. "The Arabian Context of Muhammad's Life." *The Cambridge Companion to Muhammad*, ed. Jonathan E. Brockopp. Cambridge: Cambridge University Press, 2010.

Selverstone, Harriet S. *Encouraging and Supporting Student Inquiry: Researching Controversial Issues*. Westport, Conn.: Greenwood Publishing Group, Inc., 2007.

Shirazi, Faegheh. *Muslim Women in War and Crisis: Representation and Reality*. Austin, Tex.: University of Texas Press, 2010.

Shoemaker, Stephen J. *The Death of a Prophet: The End of Muhammad's Life and the Beginnings of Islam*. Philadelphia: University of Pennsylvania Press, 2012.

Shook, Charles A. *The True Origin of the Book of Mormon*. Cincinnati, Ohio: Standard Publishing Co., 1914.

Smart, Ninian. *The World's Religions*. 2d ed. Cambridge: Cambridge University Press, 1998.

Smith Jr., Joseph. *History of the Church of Jesus Christ of Latter-day Saints*. Vols. 1-6, 2nd ed. Salt Lake City: The Deseret Book Company, 1973.

Smith, Joseph Fielding. "The King Follett Discourse" *Teachings of the Prophet Joseph Smith: Taken from His Sermons and Writings as they are Found in the Documentary History and Other Publications of the Church and Written or Published in the Day's of the Prophet's Ministry.* Salt Lake City: Deseret Books, 1984.

Smith, Lucy Mack. *Biographical Sketches of Joseph Smith, the Prophet, and His Progenitors for Many Generations.* (Liverpool: S. W. Richards, ltd., 1853.

Sorenson, John L. "The Years of the Jaredites." Neal A. Maxwell Institute, http://maxwellinstitute.byu.edu/publications/transcripts/?id=28 (accessed January 9, 2012).

Spurgeon, Charles H. *The Soul Winner.* Grand Rapids, Mich.: Wm. B. Eerdmans Publishing Co., 1963.

Stanley, Paul. "Albert Mohler Suggests Mormonism is a 'Rival Worldview.'" *The Christian Post.* http://www.christianpost.com/news/albert-mohler-suggests-mormonism-is-a-rival-worldview-57753/ (accessed January 24, 2012).

Szulc, Tad. "Journey of Faith." *National Geographic Magazine.* December 21, 2001.

Talmage, James E. *The Articles of Faith.* Salt Lake City: The Deseret News, 1919.

Top, Brent L. *LDS Beliefs: A Doctrinal Reference.* eds. Robert L. Millet, et. al. Salt Lake City: Deseret Book Co., 2011.

Trible, Phyllis and Letty M. Russell. "Unto the Thousandth Generation," *Hagar, Sarah, and their Children: Jewish, Christian, and Muslim Perspectives.* eds. Phyllis Trible and Letty M. Russell (Louisville, Kent.: Westminster John Knox Press, 2006.

Tucker, Ruth A. *Another Gospel: Cults, Alternative Religions, and the New Age Movement.* Grand Rapids, Mich.: Zondervan, 1989.

Tuckett, Christopher M. "Sources and methods." *The Cambridge Companion to Jesus.* ed. Markus Bockmuehl. Cambridge: Cambridge University Press, 2001.

Turner, Anthony John. *Early Scientific Instruments: Europe, 1400-1800.* London: Philip Wilson Publishers, 1987.

Upton, Charles. *Legends of the End: Prophecies of the End Times, Antichrist, Apocalypse, and Messiah from Eight Religious Traditions.* Hillsdale, NY: Sophia Perennis, 2004.

Urban, Hugh B. "Fair Game: Secrecy, Security, and the Church of Scientology in Cold War America." *Journal of the American Academy of Religion.* June 2006.

_____. *The Church of Scientology: A History of a New Religion.*
Princeton: Princeton University Press, 2011.

Vogel, Dan. *Joseph Smith: The Making of a Prophet.* Salt Lake City:
Signature Books, 2004.

_____. *Early Mormon Documents,* Vol. 5 (Salt Lake City: Signature
Books, 2003), 21.

Watt, W. Montgomery. *Muhammad: Prophet and Statesman.* Oxford: Oxford
University Press, 1961.

Whitney, Orson F. *Life of Heber C. Kimball.* Salt Lake City: Juvenile
Instructor Office, 1888.

Widtsoe, Osborne J. P. and Joseph F. Smith. *The Restoration of the Gospel: A
Mormon Perspective.* Salt Lake City: Deseret Book Co., 1925.

Wills, Tony. *A People for His Name: A History of Jehovah's Witnesses and an
Evaluation* 2nd ed. Morrisville, NC: Lulu Enterprises, Inc., 2006.

Wordsworth, Christopher. *The New Testament of our Lord and Saviour Jesus
Christ: In the Original Greek with Introductions and Notes.* Vol. 4. London:
Rivingtons, 1862.

Wright, Melanie J. "Latter-Day Saints," *A Dictionary of Jewish-Christian
Relations,* eds. Edward Kessler and Neil Wenborn. Cambridge: Cambridge
University Press, 2005.

Young, Brigham. *Journal of Discourses.* 26 vols. Liverpool: The Church of
Jesus Christ of Latter-day Saints.

Zeitling, Irving M. *The Historical Muhammad.* Cambridge: Polity Press, 2007.

Mormonism & Big Brother Jesus, page 59, footnote #110:

[1] Utah State Historical Society, *State of Deseret* Vol. VIII (Salt Lake City,
1940), 156–157.
[2] Ibid., 216.
[3] Ibid., 217.
[4] Todd Compton, *In Sacred Loneliness: The Plural Wives of Joseph Smith*
(Salt Lake City: Signature Books, 1997), 10.
[5] Ibid., 464.
[6] Jeffrey Odgen Johnson, "Determining and Defining 'Wife' — The
Brigham Young Households", *Dialogue: A Journal of Mormon Thought,* vol.
20, no. 3 (Fall 1987) pp. 57–70.

[7] Eric Alden Eliason, *Mormons and Mormonism: An Introduction to an American World Religion* (Champaign, IL: University of Illinois Press, 2001), 70.

[8] 2 Nephi 26:33

[9] Will Bagley, *Blood of the Prophets: Brigham Young and the Massacre at Mountain Meadows* (Norman, Oklahoma: University of Oklahoma Press, 2002).

CPSIA information can be obtained at www.ICGtesting.com
Printed in the USA
LVOW07s1111131115

462443LV00002B/30/P